Foucault
The Birth of Power

Foucault

The Birth of Power

Stuart Elden

polity

First published in 2017 by Polity Press

Polity Press
65 Bridge Street
Cambridge CB2 1UR, UK

Polity Press
350 Main Street
Malden, MA 02148, USA

ISBN-13: 978-1-5095-0725-2 (hardback)
ISBN-13: 978-1-5095-0726-9 (paperback)

A catalogue record for this book is available from the British Library.

Library of Congress Cataloging-in-Publication Data

Names: Elden, Stuart, 1971-
Title: Foucault : the birth of power / Stuart Elden.
Description: Malden, MA : Polity Press, 2017. | Includes bibliographical references and index.
Identifiers: LCCN 2016025050 (print) | LCCN 2016038644 (ebook) | ISBN 9781509507252 (hardback) | ISBN 9781509507269 (pbk.) | ISBN 9781509507283 (Mobi) | ISBN 9781509507290 (Epub)
Subjects: LCSH: Foucault, Michel, 1926–1984. | Power (Philosophy)–History.
Classification: LCC B2430.F724 E425 2017 (print) | LCC B2430.F724 (ebook) | DDC 194–dc23
LC record available at https://lccn.loc.gov/2016025050

Typeset in 10.5 on 12 pt Sabon
by Toppan Best-set Premedia Limited
Printed and bound in Great Britain by CPI Group (UK) Ltd, Croydon

For further information on Polity, visit our website: politybooks.com

Contents

Acknowledgements

This book developed out of the research for *Foucault's Last Decade* (Polity, 2016), to which it forms a prequel. As such, many of the debts incurred in the writing of that previous book are shared with this one.

Stephen Legg and Eduardo Mendieta both generously read the entire manuscript and made several useful suggestions. I also want to thank Andrew Barry, Natalie Bouchard, Cecile Brich, Sebastian Budgen, Neil Brenner, Graham Burchell, Jeremy Crampton, Michael Dillon, Sophie Fuggle, Colin Gordon, Peter Gratton, Bernard Harcourt, Laurence Paul Hemming, Marcelo Hoffman, Morris Kaplan, Mark Kelly, Léopold Lambert, Murray Low, Steven Maynard, Felix de Montety, Adam David Morton, Clare O'Farrell, Stephen Shapiro, Kevin Thompson, Alex Vasudevan, Nick Vaughan-Williams, and Perry Zurn. I am again grateful to Daniel Defert, and thank Foucault's nephew Henri-Paul Fruchaud for a very helpful conversation at the Bibliothèque Nationale. I wrote reviews of each of Foucault's first three Collège de France courses for *Berfrois* journal (www.berfrois.com), and thank Russell Bennetts and the team for their interest. I also thank the readers of my Progressive Geographies blog who followed this project through its development. Some resources produced during this work are available at www.progressivegeographies.com/resources/foucault-resources.

Work in this book was presented to audiences in Australia (University of Melbourne; Monash University); Canada (Memorial University, Newfoundland); Italy (University of Palermo); Sweden (University of Stockholm); United Kingdom (University of Lancaster; University of East London; The Galleries of Justice, Nottingham; the Historical

Materialism conference at the School of Oriental and African Studies; the London School of Economics; University College London; Institute of Historical Research); and the United States of America (Purchase College, State University of New York). The final stages of writing were conducted while a visiting senior research fellow at the Institute of Advanced Studies, University College London. I thank Tamar Garb, Catherine Stokes and their colleagues for the welcome.

For access to archival material I am grateful again to the staff at the Bibliothèque Nationale de France (BNF) Richelieu, especially Marie Odile Germain and Laurence Le Bras, and the Institut Mémoires de l'édition contemporaine (IMEC) in Caen. I have also used the British Library Rare Books room and Newsroom, BNF François-Mitterrand, Senate House library, the State Library of Victoria, and the libraries of the University of Warwick, Monash University, University of Melbourne, London School of Economics and New York University. The University of Warwick supported archive visits. At Polity Press I am grateful to John Thompson and Pascal Porcheron, and the two anonymous readers of the original manuscript. Neil de Cort saw the book through production, Susan Beer copy-edited the text and Lisa Scholey compiled the index.

An earlier version of Chapter 3 was published as 'A More Marxist Foucault? Reading *La société punitive*', *Historical Materialism*, vol. 23 no. 4, 2015, pp. 149–68; and parts of Chapter 4 as 'Discipline, Health and Madness: Foucault's *Le pouvoir psychiatrique*', *History of the Human Sciences*, vol. 19 no. 1, February 2006, pp. 39–66. Parts are used with permission of Brill and Sage respectively.

Above all I thank Susan for her love and support in my life outside the archive.

Abbreviations

To ease reference, key texts are referred to by abbreviations. For texts where one book is translated in a single book, such as the lecture courses, the French page number is given first, followed by the English after a slash. So PP 105/103 would refer to the lecture course *Le pouvoir psychiatrique*, p. 105 in the French text, and p. 103 in the English translation *Psychiatric Power*. I have frequently modified existing translations.[1]

Throughout this book, English titles are used for books available in translation; French for untranslated works or unpublished manuscripts, though an English translation of the title is provided the first time they are used.

Texts by Foucault and others

A   *Les Anormaux: Cours au Collège de France (1974–5)*, eds. Valerio Marchetti and Antonella Salomani, Paris: Seuil/Gallimard, 1999; trans. Graham Burchell as *Abnormal: Lectures at the Collège de France 1974–5*, London: Verso, 2003. This course is referred to as 'The Abnormals'.

AK   *L'Archéologie du savoir*, Paris: Gallimard/Tel, 1969; trans. Alan Sheridan as *The Archaeology of Knowledge*, New York: Barnes & Noble, 1972.

AL   Groupe d'information sur les prisons, *Archives d'une lutte 1970–1972*, eds. Philippe Artières, Laurent Quéro and Michelle Zancarini-Fournel, Paris: Édition de l'IMEC, 2003.

C   Daniel Defert, 'Chronologie', DE I, 13–64; trans. Timothy
           O'Leary in Christopher Falzon, Timothy O'Leary and Jana
           Sawicki (eds.) *A Companion to Foucault*, Oxford: Black-
           well, 2013, pp. 11–83.

CMCA   Michel Foucault, 'The Crisis of Medicine or the Crisis of
           Antimedicine?' trans. Edgar C. Knowlton, Jr, William J.
           King and Clare O'Farrell, *Foucault Studies*, no. 1, 2004,
           pp. 5–19.

CT   *Le courage de la vérité: Le gouvernement des soi et des autres
           II: Cours au Collège de France*, eds. Frédéric Gros, Paris:
           Gallimard/Seuil; trans. Graham Burchell as *The Courage
           of Truth (The Government of the Self and Others II): Lec-
           tures at the Collège de France 1983–4*, London: Palgrave,
           2011.

DE   *Dits et écrits 1954–88*, eds. Daniel Defert and François
           Ewald, Paris: Gallimard, 4 vols., 1994 – with reference to
           volume number, and also includes text number for ease of
           reference to the two editions of this text and to bibliog-
           raphies of English translations.[2] Thus 'DE#81 II, 99–104'
           means text 81, in Volume II, pages 99–104.

DP   *Surveiller et punir – Naissance de la prison*, Paris: Gallimard/
           Tel, 1975; trans. Alan Sheridan as *Discipline and Punish –
           The Birth of the Prison*, London: Penguin, 1976.

E   Roger-Pol Droit, *Michel Foucault, Entretiens*, Odile Jacob,
           Paris, 2004.

EP   François Fourquet and Lion Murard, *Les équipements du
           pouvoir: Villes, territoires et équipements collectifs*, Paris:
           Union Générale d'Éditions, 1976 [1973].

EW   *Essential Works*, eds. Paul Rabinow and James Faubion,
           trans. Robert Hurley and others, London: Allen Lane, 3
           vols., 1997–2000.

FL   *Foucault Live: Interviews 1961–1984*, ed. Sylvère Lotringer,
           New York: Semiotext[e], 1996.

GEN   *Généalogie des équipements de normalisation: Les équipe-
           ments sanitaires*, ed. Michel Foucault, Fontenay-sous-Bois:
           CERFI, 1976.

HFA   'Histoire de la folie et antipsychiatrie', in Philippe Artières,
           Jean-François Bert, Frédéric Gros and Judith Revel (eds.),
           Cahier de L'Herne 95: Michel Foucault, Paris: L'Herne,
           2011, pp. 95–102.

HM   *Histoire de la folie à l'âge classique*, Paris: Gallimard, 1972
           [1961]; trans. Jonathan Murphy and Jean Khalfa as *History
           of Madness*, London: Routledge, 2006.

HSu   *L'Herméneutique du sujet: Cours au Collège de France (1981–82)*, eds. Frédéric Gros, Paris: Gallimard/Seuil, 2001; trans. Graham Burchell as *The Hermeneutics of the Subject: Lectures at the Collège de France*, London: Palgrave, 2005.

IN   Groupe d'information sur les prisons, *Intolérable*, ed. Philippe Artières, Paris: Éditions Verticales, 2013.

LCP   *Language, Counter-Memory, Practice: Selected Essays and Interviews*, ed. Donald F. Bouchard, Ithaca: Cornell University Press, 1977.

LWK   *Leçons sur la volonté de savoir: Cours au Collège de France, 1970–1971*, suivi de *Le savoir d'Œdipe*, ed. Daniel Defert, Paris: Gallimard/Seuil, 2011; trans. Graham Burchell as *Lectures on the Will to Know: Lectures at the Collège de France 1970–71*, London: Palgrave Macmillan, 2013.

MD   Groupe Information Santé, *La médecine désordonnée: D'une pratique de l'avortement à la lutte pour la santé*, Paris: GIS, 1974.

MG1   Michel Foucault, Blandine Barrett Kriegel, Anne Thalamy, François Beguin and Bruno Fortier, *Les machines à guérir (aux origines de l'hôpital moderne)*, Paris: Institut de l'environnement, 1976.

MG2   Michel Foucault, Blandine Barrett Kriegel, Anne Thalamy, François Beguin and Bruno Fortier, *Les machines à guérir (aux origines de l'hôpital moderne)*, Brussels: Pierre Mardaga, revised edn 1979.

MLC   Michel Foucault et le membres du GIS, 'Médecine et luttes des classes', *Vers une antimédecine? Le médecine, la malade et la société*, special issue of *La Nef*, no. 49, 1972, pp. 67–73.

OD   *L'ordre du discours*, Paris: Gallimard, 1970; trans. Ian McLeod as "The Order of Discourse", in Robert Young (ed.), *Untying the Text: A Post-Structuralist Reader*, London: Routledge, 1981, pp. 48–78.

Œ   *Œuvres*, Bibliothèque de la Pléiade, ed. Frédéric Gros, Paris: Gallimard, 2 vols., 2015.

ONA   Groupe Information Santé, *Oui, nous avortons!* Paris: Éditions Gît-le-Cœur, 1973.

PH   *Politiques de l'habitat (1800–1850)*, ed. Michel Foucault, Paris: CORDA, 1977.

P/K   *Power/Knowledge: Selected Interviews and Other Writings 1972–7*, ed. Colin Gordon, Brighton: Harvester, 1980.

PP   *Le pouvoir psychiatrique: Cours au Collège de France (1973–4)*, ed. Jacques Lagrange, Paris: Seuil/Gallimard,

2003; trans. Graham Burchell as *Psychiatric Power: Lectures at the Collège de France 1973–4*, London: Palgrave, 2006.

PR *Moi, Pierre Rivière, ayant égorgé ma mère, ma sœur et mon frère: Un cas de parricide au XIXe siècle*, presented by Michel Foucault, Paris: Gallimard/Juilliard, 1973; trans. Frank Jellinek as *I, Pierre Rivière, Having Slaughtered my Mother, my Sister, and my Brother: A Case of Parricide in the Nineteenth Century*, Lincoln: University of Nebraska Press, 1982.

PS *La société punitive: Cours au Collège de France (1972–3)*, ed. Bernard E. Harcourt, Paris: Gallimard/Seuil, 2013; trans. Graham Burchell as *The Punitive Society: Lectures at the Collège de France 1972–3*, London: Palgrave, 2015.

SKP *Space, Knowledge and Power: Foucault and Geography*, eds. Jeremy W. Crampton and Stuart Elden, Aldershot: Ashgate, 2007.

SMBD *'Il faut défendre la société': Cours au Collège de France (1975–6)*, eds. Mauro Bertani and Alessandro Fontana, Paris: Seuil/Gallimard, 1997; trans. David Macey as *'Society Must Be Defended'*, London: Allen Lane, 2003.

TIP *Théories et institutions pénales: Cours au Collège de France (1971–1972)*, ed. Bernard E. Harcourt, Paris: Gallimard/Seuil, 2015.

Archival material

BNF Archives et Manuscrits, Bibliothèque Nationale de France, Paris

IMEC Fonds Michel Foucault and Fonds Groupe d'Information sur les prisons, l'Institut Mémoires de l'édition contemporaine, l'abbaye d'Ardenne, Caen, http://www.imec-archives.com/

IMEC's catalogue codes have changed over time as material is reorganized. References are correct at the time materials were consulted.

Classical texts are referred to by the usual conventions. I have generally used the bi-lingual editions in the Loeb library.

Introduction: Out of the 1960s

On 8 August 1970 Foucault wrote in a letter to his partner Daniel Defert that he 'had promised an afterword for the re-publication of *Les mots et les choses*, but now these things are of no interest to me' (C 36/44). Four months later, on 2 December 1970, Foucault gave his inaugural lecture at the prestigious Collège de France. There he outlined his new research agenda, which would lead him from the political stakes of knowledge to the workings of power, taking in analysis of prisons, hospitals and mental health and, in time, would lead to his last great project on sexuality. By the time *Surveiller et punir*, which we know in English as *Discipline and Punish*, appeared in February 1975 a much more explicitly political Foucault was clearly evident.

Les mots et les choses was published in 1966 and translated as *The Order of Things*. It is a book which shares much with his earlier works *History of Madness* from 1961 and *Birth of the Clinic* from 1963. It was followed by *The Archaeology of Knowledge* in 1969, which is often seen as the theoretical culmination of the work Foucault conducted in the 1960s. The roots can be traced back further, of course, with the research for the *History of Madness* begun in the mid-1950s.[1] *History of Madness* was initially presented as Foucault's primary thesis, with the secondary thesis a translation of Kant's *Anthropology*, along with notes and a substantial introduction.[2] Foucault had lectured on anthropology from Kant to Dilthey at the École Normale Supérieure and Lille in the 1950s.[3] Some of the themes in the Kant introduction were developed in *The Order of Things*. With the advent of the new decade though, it appears that Foucault wanted to move in another direction.

In 1969 Foucault had returned to France after several years in Tunisia, first to the experimental University of Vincennes, and then, following his election, to a chair at the Collège de France. Foucault claimed that Tunisia was a political awakening for him, and the events of May 1968 meant that France was much changed from the place he had left behind. On his return Foucault quickly became involved in activist work, particularly concerning prisons but also around health issues such as abortion rights. His active involvement in a number of political campaigns in this period was often around the same issues as his academic work. In addition, in his seminars and elsewhere Foucault built research teams to conduct collaborative work, often around issues related to his lectures and activism.

If *The Archaeology of Knowledge* was a methodological treatise, *Discipline and Punish* was a call to arms. What had happened to Foucault such that the research he had conducted on previous topics – work that had occupied him for so much of the 1960s – was something he wanted to move beyond? What was the nature of this transformation, and how did this transition in his thought and action take place? *Foucault: The Birth of Power* offers an answer.

Approach and Sources

Through a careful reconstruction of Foucault's work and preoccupations this book therefore provides a detailed intellectual history of Foucault in this period as writer, researcher, lecturer and activist. Our ability to trace Foucault's preoccupations is considerably enhanced by a range of newly available materials, both published texts as well as archival documents. Like the account offered in my previous book *Foucault's Last Decade*,[4] this book makes extensive use of all this material. Its sources include his first courses at the Collège de France, multiple shorter pieces and interviews, boxes of manuscripts available at the Bibliothèque Nationale de France (BNF), as well as material relating to his activism and collaborative research archived at the Institut Mémoires de l'édition contemporaine (IMEC). Because of the dates of their collection I have not, for this book, used the archive at the Bancroft Library in Berkeley.

Foremost among the new publications are his annual research courses at the Collège de France, which comprise lectures delivered from late 1970 until 1984. The requirement of professors there is to report on their ongoing projects, rather than teach. As such, the lectures give a fascinating insight into the development of ideas and the germination of projects. The first three courses include a wide range of analyses of ancient Greece, the Dark Ages, the Middle Ages, early modern France and Europe through to the nineteenth century. In these courses and the next, in publications, and in collaborative work within and beyond the Collège, Foucault would turn his attention to detailed examinations of asylums, hospitals and public health, and, of course, the prison. It is now clear that *Discipline and Punish*, though the principal output from that work, was by no means the only one. It was grounded upon a much wider range of concerns and projects. By the time that book appeared in early 1975 Foucault had already begun to prepare materials for his last major project on sexuality and government of the self and others, which would occupy him until his untimely death in 1984. That project is the focus of *Foucault's Last Decade*.

Foucault: The Birth of Power has a focus on the years immediately preceding that decade, on 1969–74, the period between the publication of *The Archaeology of Knowledge* and the completion of *Discipline and Punish*. It therefore acts as prequel to the treatment of the subsequent and final phase of his work in *Foucault's Last Decade*. Noting the gap between *The Archaeology of Knowledge* and *Discipline and Punish*, David Macey suggests 'the period 1971–3 was the most intensely political in Foucault's life and the multiple activities in which he was involved left little time for writing'.[5] While undoubtedly correct about the political activism, and that most of Foucault's publications from this time take the form of transcripts of spoken material – lectures, interviews, media events or other talks – there was much going on below the surface, which is only slowly coming to light.

One of the first tasks undertaken was to build a detailed timeline, drawing extensively on Defert's work for *Dits et écrits*, but also adding dates of lectures, interviews, press conferences and other activism. This was based on various sources including the Eribon and Macey biographies, Foucault's friend Claude Mauriac's journals, notes in texts, and newspapers. This allowed material to be worked through in a roughly chronological order. Seeing the interconnection of lectures, conversations, publications and working notes helped enormously in understanding what Foucault was trying to do, and how he was trying to do it. The account offered here tries to do justice to that. It is not a biography, but rather an exercise in the history of thought or intellectual history. It is, in a sense, a genealogy of the emergence of questions of power and, indeed, the notion of genealogy, in Foucault's work. It attempts to situate works in contexts, to draw connections, and to integrate a study of Foucault's political activism and collaborative research work within a study of his better-known writings and his lectures. Secondary literature has been referenced when useful, though as yet there is limited material on the early courses. In going beyond Foucault's own texts the general principle has been not to discuss people who have read Foucault, but rather to discuss what Foucault read.

Lecture Courses

The Collège de France lecture courses are an especially useful resource, with their editorial apparatus of notes, variant readings and contextual material. The early courses were among the last to appear, in part because of the difficulty in establishing the texts. While for most of the courses tape recordings were extant, and could be transcribed, with the first three courses the editors had to use other sources. For 1970–1's *Lectures on the Will to Know*, Defert edited the course on the basis of the manuscript used for its delivery; a procedure followed by Bernard Harcourt for 1971–2's *Théories et institutions pénales* [Penal Theories and Institutions]. While Foucault prepared his courses in extensive detail, he did not write them out in fully formed sentences to be read word-for-word. The manuscript pages give a sense of how he wrote his lectures and how he elaborated them in spoken performance – some passages are written out, others are more note-like. Contrary to a journalist's report included in the preface to all volumes of this series (e.g. LWK viii/x), there was improvisation and extrapolation around planned themes.[6] It can be hard to tell the difference between his point and those he is discussing or arguing against (primary authorities or other historians). The manuscripts alone can be difficult to follow, and the editors have reconstructed what is there, with scrupulous textual fidelity, rather than extrapolated from it to what might have been said. Notes specify where material was crossed out, pages inserted, or where Foucault reorganized the running order. Readers are forced to do some of the interpretative work themselves.

With 1972–3's *The Punitive Society* a transcript was made shortly after the course's delivery, from tapes which are now lost: one archival copy has the 1973–4 course recorded over the top. Foucault reviewed and corrected the transcript, which was used as the basis for the course by Harcourt, along with comparison to the manuscript. From 1973–4's *Psychiatric Power* onwards, all the courses are based on tape recordings, with supplements from course manuscripts and related materials. These later volumes used the manuscript to supplement the spoken record, but for the first two courses there is only one of the two sources to draw upon. There are a few exceptions, notably the 'annex' appended to the final lecture of the first course (LWK 189–92/195–9); and at times Defert is able to draw on the notes made by a member of Foucault's audience, Hélène Politis, though he respects Foucault's reluctance to publish the notes of an audience member.[7] Likewise, François Ewald and Harcourt note that the manuscript of the second course accords well with what was actually delivered, but the auditors who confirmed this are not generally used to provide further detail.[8] In both courses there are pages of manuscript missing in part or whole, and these have generally had to be left absent from the printed text.

Between 21 and 25 May 1973 Foucault delivered a series of lectures given at the Pontifical Catholic University of Rio de Janeiro, under the title of 'Truth and Juridical Forms'. These five lectures used and developed material from the first three Collège de France courses. Foucault finished teaching in Paris around March each year, and then frequently took the lectures on the road with him. These lectures were published in Portuguese in 1974, in French in 1994; and in English in 2000 (without the 23-page round-table discussion that followed the fifth lecture).[9] The first two lectures, on Nietzsche and Oedipus, respectively, develop arguments made in *Lectures on the Will to Know*. *Théories et institutions pénales* only provides the material for a single lecture, on feudal law and the Carolingian Empire. The fourth and fifth lectures develop *The Punitive Society*, especially around panopticism and institutions. As the transcript is based on a recording, it helps to fill in detail about the first and second course, for which only Foucault's manuscripts survive from Paris. The Rio lectures demonstrate what Foucault did with this material when he took it on the road, and how he elaborated from these fragmented notes. They are a tantalizing glimpse of what might have been done with the material in Paris. However, the Rio lectures developed themes from the courses rather than just replicated them, and drew on some of the manuscript materials Foucault had prepared for, but not delivered in, Paris.

The Rio lectures are also important because they provide a strong link between the first three Paris courses, and show how their concerns are related, especially through the explicit focus on three concepts: measure, inquiry and examination. Measure was a fundamental theme of *Lectures on the Will to Know*; inquiry emerges in the study of the transition from Germanic law to the Middle Ages in *Théories et institutions pénales*, and examination is a key focus of *The Punitive Society*. Foucault suggests that 'what is called the *inquiry* – the inquiry as practised by philosophers of the fifteenth to the eighteenth century, and also by scientists, whether they were geographers, botanists, zoologists, or economists – is a rather characteristic form of truth in our societies'. In time, though it would be replaced with the examination (DE#139 II, 541; EW III, 4–5). 'This examination was the basis of the power, the form of knowledge-power, that was to give rise not, as in the case of the inquiry, to the great sciences of observation, but to what we call the "human sciences" – psychiatry, psychology, sociology' (DE#139 II, 595; EW III, 59). Taken together, these three courses form a powerful initial triptych, developing conceptual terminology for the analysis of a wide range of phenomena.

Other Materials

Other materials utilized in this study include the interviews and other short pieces that appeared during this period. In the posthumous collection *Dits et écrits*, which collected almost all the authorized pieces published in Foucault's lifetime, the original edition was in four volumes. Volume I covered 1954–69; Volume II 1970–5; Volume III 1976–9; and Volume IV 1980–8 – the last extended to include a few pieces authorized before Foucault's death but which appeared later due to publishing delays. The shorter periods of later volumes are not simply because Foucault published more conventional pieces, but because many more of his lectures, especially those given outside France, were published, and because he took part in an increasing number of interviews, round-tables and press-conferences. As Foucault's friend and sometime research collaborator Gilles Deleuze noted: 'If Foucault's interviews form an integral part of his work, it is because they extend the historical problematization of each of his books into the construction of the present problem, be it madness, punishment or sexuality'.[10] This is certainly true, but even more so in terms of the record of his political activities.

We have a still incomplete sense of Foucault's activism, which dramatically increased in the period in question in this book. As Deleuze and others have long recognized, Foucault's political work is crucial in understanding the transition from *The Archaeology of Knowledge* to *Discipline and Punish*.[11] While most of the documents of the Groupe d'Information sur les prisons (GIP) have been published in French, with an English selection forthcoming, little is said about his involvement with other groups, including parallel ones on health and asylums. Much of the material relating to the GIP and the health group is archived at IMEC, and I have made extensive use of their collection. The material there extends to cover other collaborative

work, including with the Centre d'Études, de Recherche et de Formation Institutionnelle (CERFI). This was a group founded in 1967 by
Félix Guattari, developing from the earlier Fédération des Groupes
d'Études de Recherches Institutionnelles (FGERI). Foucault's research
with this group and researchers he met through it ran in parallel to his
major works until at least the mid-1970s, and he later made attempts
to constitute other collaborative ventures as a visitor in Louvain,
Vermont and, especially, Berkeley.[12]

The archive of Foucault's personal papers has also become partly
available in the last few years. In 2012, Defert sold 37,000 pages of
material to the BNF, after this resource had been declared a 'national
treasure' by the government to prevent it leaving France. Loosely cat-
egorized into 110 boxes, at the time of writing about forty are available to researchers. Tantalizing indications of what are in the other
seventy boxes can be found throughout the editorial apparatus of the
recent *Œuvres* – a collection of Foucault's major works in the prestigious Bibliothèque de la Pléiade series with Gallimard. As yet, the
available archive material largely comprises Foucault's reading notes,
both for his books and lecture courses. These notes help enormously
in contextualizing Foucault's work, and editors of his courses have
used these extensively in their editorial apparatus. Unfortunately the
notes are undated, and Foucault filed them thematically. He would
add notes from a much later date to earlier folders, or move earlier
notes into new folders, which can make their use difficult. At the
moment, the only course whose manuscript is listed in the catalogue
is *Théories et institutions pénales*. There are also five boxes of material that have been available for many years, comprising an early draft
of *The Archaeology of Knowledge* and preparatory drafts of what
became the second and third volumes of the *History of Sexuality*.
The latter were discussed in *Foucault's Last Decade*. As yet, pre-
Collège de France courses at Vincennes, Tunis and elsewhere are not
available, nor are the manuscripts of unpublished works, including,
most notably, the fourth volume of the *History of Sexuality*. There
are plans to publish much of this.[13] What is available, though, does
give a very interesting insight into Foucault's working practices and
I have tried to use these in the account offered here.

From Tunisia and Vincennes to the Collège de France

While the courses have not yet been published, we do know something of Foucault's teaching in Tunisia and Vincennes. Foucault
moved to Tunisia in September 1966, on a three-year secondment

from the University of Clermont-Ferrand. There, for the first time since the mid-1950s, he taught philosophy. Defert describes his course on 'Philosophical Discourse' as developing themes from *The Order of Things*, alongside a public course 'on Western culture' (C 29/34). There were also courses on Descartes (which seems to have owed much to Edmund Husserl), Nietzsche, painting from the Renaissance to Édouard Manet, and psychology.[14] Some of Foucault's individual lectures from this time have been published, but only one on Manet – intended to be the basis of a book with Minuit – in a critical edition.[15] Foucault was therefore outside France during the events of May 1968, but the events coincided with his own political re-awakening, born out of student struggles against the Habib Bourguiba dictatorship. 'In Tunisia I was led to help students...I was forced to enter the political arena. It was not May '68 in France, but March '68, in a third world country' (DE#281 IV, 79; EW III, 279–80; see DE#160 II, 774; E 119–20).[16]

The Archaeology of Knowledge was published while Foucault was in Tunisia, on 13 March 1969. Given the date of its publication it seems a curiously apolitical book. Defert recalls that 'the dry descriptions of things he had said in previous works, and his way of differentiating himself from structuralism all frustrate expectations' (C 34/42). This was due, in part, to the complicated gestation of the book. Foucault had finished writing *The Order of Things* on 4 April 1965 (C 27/31), and it was published the next year. He moved to Tunisia shortly afterwards, but had already begun writing the manuscript that was to become *The Archaeology of Knowledge*, confessing in a letter of 12 November 1966 to Defert that 'the theory of discourse is still a shambles, 396 pages to re-do' (C 29/34). Nine months later, in August 1967, he finished writing the manuscript, but left it until November 1968 before he gave Alain Badiou the task of reducing and editing it for publication (C 31/37, 33/40).

Unusually for Foucault's books, a complete early draft dating from 1965–6 survives.[17] It had been given by Foucault to Defert to read, and while Foucault often discarded his early draft materials when books were complete, Defert kept this copy, and it is available at the Bibliothèque Nationale.[18] It can perhaps best be described as a different book on the same topic. There are more references to literary works than in the published book, including Honoré de Balzac, Marcel Proust, James Joyce, Alain Robbe-Grillet and Shakespeare's *Henry V*. There is some expanded discussion of Foucault's relation to the history of ideas tradition, including a few remarks on Georges Dumézil, Ernst Cassirer, Wilhelm Dilthey and Arthur O. Lovejoy, alongside Georges Canguilhem. There are some mentions of analytic philosophy including Ludwig Wittgenstein and Hilary Putnam as well as German thought – G. W. F. Hegel and Johann Gottlieb Fichte. Key terms in the published book like the historical *a priori* are absent; others are given much more extensive discussion. The way the book links to Foucault's earlier historical studies is very clear, but there is also a clear relation to the parallel work he did on literature in the 1960s. Foucault suggests the book is a challenge to the anthropology of the past 150 years,[19] and that the project is orientated towards 'the diagnostic of what is "today"', a notion which perhaps anticipates *Discipline and Punish*'s notion of a 'history of the present'.[20] Fragments of a later draft version also survive.[21]

In the published book, especially in Part II, Chapter 3, Foucault gives some indications of future projects, including the question of knowing 'how criminality could become an object of medical expertise, or sexual deviation a possible object of psychiatric discourse' (AK 70/48). In the concluding chapter of Part IV in a section entitled 'Other Archaeologies' he outlines a much fuller research agenda of possible work, noting that he is not far along the path with any, but including the idea of a project on sexuality. This could be, of course, an archaeological analysis, 'orientated towards the *episteme*', and looking at the establishment of scientific knowledge in biology and psychology, along with Freud's rupture.

But I can also see another direction for analysis: instead of studying the sexual behaviour of men at a given period [*époque*] (by seeking its law in a social structure, in a collective unconscious, or in a certain moral attitude), instead of describing what men thought of sexuality (what religious interpretation they gave it, to what extent they approved or disapproved of it, what conflicts of opinion or morality it gave rise to), one would ask oneself whether, in this behaviour, as in these representations, a whole discursive practice is not at work; whether sexuality, quite apart from any orientation towards a scientific discourse, is not a group of objects that can be talked about (or that is forbidden to talk about), a field of possible enunciations (whether in lyrical or legal language), a group of concepts (which can no doubt be presented in the elementary form of notions or themes), a set of choices (which may appear in the coherence of behaviour [*conduites*] or in systems of prescription). Such an archaeology would show, if it succeeded in its task, how the prohibitions [*interdits*], exclusions, limitations, values, freedoms, and transgressions of sexuality, all its manifestations, verbal or otherwise, are linked to a particular discursive practice. It would reveal, not of course as the ultimate truth of sexuality, but as one of the dimensions in accordance with which one can describe it, a certain 'way of speaking'; and one would show how this way of speaking is invested not in scientific discourses, but in a system of prohibitions and values. (AK 261–2/192–3)

Foucault adds that this would be an analysis not of the *episteme* – that is an examination of knowledge alone – but 'of which we might call the ethical' (AK 262/193). An early indication of the project he would begin in earnest in 1974, this is already an outline of some important methodological developments.

On leaving Tunisia Foucault did not return to Clermont-Ferrand, but instead taught at the new and experimental University of Vincennes (now Paris-VIII) from 1969–70.[22] His courses there included ones on 'Sexuality and Individuality' and 'Nietzsche and Genealogy' (C 34/41).[23] Defert suggests that he first develops the promises of *The Archaeology of Knowledge*, and provides a 'history of heredity and of racial hygiene' (C 34/41). Heredity was a recurrent theme in Foucault's work. Foucault discussed the question of heredity in relation to mental illness as far back as 1953, when he taught in Lille and at the École Normale Supérieure, in material which was related to his first book, *Maladie mentale et personnalité*.[24] That book was published in 1954, and then in a substantially revised edition as *Maladie mentale et psychologie* in 1962.[25] The work on these themes also informs the preparatory work for the introduction to Kant's *Anthropology*, translated and edited as his secondary thesis. The theme of heredity continues in Foucault's 1970s work. It comes up briefly in his television debate with Noam Chomsky (DE#132 II, 473–4), and is a key focus of his later work on race, where he discusses 'the technology of eugenics with the problem of heredity, racial purification, and the correction of the human instinctual system by purification of the race' (A 124/133; SMBD 53/61, 225/252).[26] It also appears in his interest in the question of degeneration discussed in the 1974–5 course *The Abnormals* (A 124/133) and his wider work on sexuality. Nietzsche is a focus of the first Collège de France course and a lecture at McGill in 1971, and then again in Rio in 1973. Genealogy is of course the topic of his short essay 'Nietzsche, Genealogy, History', published in 1971. With this essay's stress on emergence, provenance, lineage and birth (DE#84, II, 137; EW II, 370), it is clear that Foucault did not just envisage heredity as a topic of study, but as providing a model for the kind of work he wanted to undertake (see Chapter 1). His time at Vincennes was also important for political activism, leading to occupations, conflict with the police, arrest and interventions to protest the exclusion of students.[27]

Foucault had not been at Vincennes long before his next move was planned. On 30 November 1969 a chair in the 'history of systems of thought' was created at the Collège de France and while this was clearly intended for Foucault, he was not formally elected to it until 12 April 1970.[28] For his election, Foucault had outlined much of the work he intended to do over the coming years, which set out an agenda for his early lecture courses. When Jules Vuillemin proposed the chair he commented that 'the history of systems of thought is not therefore the history of man or of men who think', it should 'eliminate the subject but preserve the thought, and attempt to construct a history without human nature'.[29] When he came to propose Foucault for this chair, outlining Foucault's work to date and his future plans, he suggested that 'a history of thought, thus conceived, has for its principal material archives more than texts, institutions and techniques more than theories. As a consequence thought is discovered in collective forms, stripped of individual variants. In this perspective, slow transformations tend to detach themselves from original inventions and the play of economic, political and social determinations matters more than logical coherence'.[30] In Foucault's own presentation of his previous work and future plans, 'Titres et travaux', he expressed his approach in these terms:

> So an object took shape for me: the knowledge [*savoir*] invested in complex institutional systems. And a method asserted itself: instead of only running through the library of scientific literature, as one was apt to do, I would need to examine a collection of archives comprising official orders, statutes, hospital or prison records, court proceedings, and so on. It was at the Arsenal and the Archives Nationales that I undertook the analysis of a knowledge whose visible body is not theoretical or scientific discourse, nor literature either, but a regulated, everyday practice. (DE#71 I, 842–3; EW I, 5–6)

Foucault also notes that for *The Order of Things* he tried a different approach, which was to 'neutralize the whole practical and institutional side but without giving up the idea of going back to it one day' (DE#7 I, 843; EW I, 6). This meant that that study was focused entirely on 'domains of knowledge', to undertake an archaeology of them. To elaborate this question he wrote the 'clarification' which was *The Archaeology of Knowledge*. But now, in late 1969, he is at pains to stress that 'this knowledge is embodied not only in theoretical texts or empirical instruments but also in a whole set [*ensemble*] of practices and institutions' (DE#71 I, 844; EW I, 7).

Following *History of Madness*, Foucault's work from the mid-late 1960s is sometimes seen as comprising two main strands – archaeology and literature. The first strand, on what might be said to be on the limits of language, and which is usually understood under the rubric of 'archaeology', was developed and taken to a conclusion of sorts in *The Order of Things* and *The Archaeology of Knowledge*. The second comprised literary work including a book on Raymond Roussel,[31] and shorter pieces on the likes of Gustave Flaubert, the Marquis de Sade, Jules Verne, Georges Bataille, Pierre Klossowski, André Breton, Alain Robbe-Grillet, Maurice Blanchot and others – published in journals like *Tel Quel* and *Critique*. These ran in parallel with the other work: *Raymond Roussel* was published almost simultaneously with *Birth of the Clinic*. In a 1975 interview Roger-Pol Droit suggests that if the shorter pieces were brought together as a book this would give an unusual view of Foucault's work (E 86). In English, the *Language, Counter-Memory, Practice* volume from 1977 did collect many such pieces. Some of that work blurs with what might be thought of as another element – the work on theorists like Deleuze and, partly with Deleuze, on Nietzsche. The book on the painter René Magritte and the abandoned one on Manet come from this time period as well.[32] Together these demonstrate a concern with art and a generalized concern with madness or thought at the limit.[33] In March 1970 Foucault gave a number of lectures at SUNY Buffalo, including one on 'the search for the absolute in [Flaubert's] *Bouvard et Pécuchet*' (C 35/43), on the Marquis de Sade, on Nietzsche, and a version of 'What is an Author?' But with some exceptions, these would be some of the last texts he would devote to these themes.[34] His candidacy presentation is revealing in that he does not mention this more literary output.

If archaeology and literature form two themes of the 1960s, there is another strand to Foucault's work in this period, which is more explicitly political. This is the continuation of work on questions of madness and medicine, and which partly anticipates later work on sexuality. One of the earliest of texts was entitled 'Religious Deviations and Medical Knowledge', originally delivered at a colloquium on heresy organized by the well-known medieval historian, Jacques le Goff in 1962 and finally published in 1968.[35] In this piece, and the ensuing discussion, Foucault is interested in the way witchcraft and religious heresy were closely interconnected. But something else happens in the discussion which points the way to future investigations. Armand Abel, a Belgian medieval Islamic scholar, suggests that there is a relation between heresy and the 'sinner with terrible morals (sexual anomalies, communities of women, etc.)' (DE#52 I, 633). In his response to the questions, Foucault makes a series of points.

> We all agree on the progressive hereticisation [*hérétisation*] of witchcraft in the 16th and 17th centuries, or at least that the heretic and

the witch are treated in the same way. And I would agree with Canon Delaruelle on the anticipation of certain natural concepts by theology before their use by medicine: at the end of the 17th century it is the Church itself which convenes doctors in relation to Jansenists and the Cévennes Protestants. Fléchier asks doctors to testify that this is merely pathological phenomena, visions, hallucinations: religious conscience was more 'progressive' than medical conscience in this series of events. I also agree with Professor Abel that that is an association [*appartenance*] of madness to a number of phenomena of religious irredentism and it would need a structural study of the whole, a synchronic study, as the system is clearly different in each epoch. (DE#52 I, 635)

There are some compressed ideas floated here, and Foucault's point is not always clear. The historical points can be elaborated, but 'religious irrendentism' is a striking yet ambiguous phrase. Irredentism is a political movement seeking to incorporate territories outside the existing boundaries of a state on the grounds of national or ethnic affinity. The term is most associated with Italian claims in the late nineteenth century. Does Foucault mean it to imply that the Catholic Church is trying to reincorporate breakaway elements? Carrette translates the phrase as 'religious territoriality' in a note following the translation of the lecture.[36] Foucault's last point is redolent of the structuralist language he was using around this time, such as in the first edition of *Birth of the Clinic*, removed for the second edition of 1972.[37]

Other key pieces in this occasional series would include 'L'eau et la folie' (1963); 'Madness, the Absence of Work' (1964); 'Message ou bruit' (1966); and 'Médecins, juges et sorciers au XVIIe siècle' (1969).[38] The last of these is especially interesting, and its date is striking. It is closer to the work of the *History of Madness* and, in parts, to *Birth of the Clinic*, than other work of the 1960s, though it comes out several years later. It shares some interests with work of the early 1970s, particularly the likely content of *Théories et institutions pénales* and other lectures from that time, but also as far forward as *The Abnormals*. It is of course conceivable that Foucault wrote it much earlier than its publication, perhaps for a lecture, though there are no indications in either its original publication or in *Dits et écrits* that suggest this.

Foucault returned to these questions, among many others, in *The Abnormals* course in 1975, but Colin Gordon suggests it might have been something more. Gordon notes that the 'Religious Deviations' and 'Médecins, juges et sorciers' pieces are the fullest treatment we have of a book Foucault promised in *History of Madness*.[39]

A later study will show how experience of the demonic and its waning between the sixteenth and eighteenth centuries should not be understood as a victory of humanitarian or medical theory over the old, wild [*sauvage*] universe of superstition, but as a taking up again [*reprise*], within a critical experience, of the forms that had previously borne the threat of a tear in the fabric of the world [*du déchirement du monde*]. (HM 39 n. 1/597 n. 83)

Foucault regularly promised books that he did not write. In his candidacy presentation he proposes a detailed study of the knowledge [*savoir*] of heredity.[40]

It developed throughout the nineteenth century, starting from breeding techniques, on through attempts to improve species, experiments with intensive cultivation, efforts to combat animal and plant epidemics, and culminating in the establishment of a genetics whose birth date can be placed at the beginning of the twentieth century. On the one hand, this knowledge responded to quite particular economic needs and historical conditions. Changes in the dimensions and forms of cultivation of rural properties, in the equilibrium of markets, in the required standards of profitability, and in the system of colonial agriculture deeply transformed this knowledge; they altered not only the nature of its information but also its quantity and scale. On the other hand, this knowledge was receptive to new developments in sciences such as chemistry or plant and animal physiology. (Witness the use of nitrate fertilizer or the technique of hybridization, which had been made possible by the theory of plant fertilization, defined in the eighteenth century.) But this dual dependence does not deprive it of its characteristics and its internal regulation. It gave rise both to adapted techniques (such as those of Vilmorin for species improvement) and epistemologically productive concepts (such as that of hereditary trait, explained in detail if not defined by Naudin). Darwin was not mistaken when he found in this human practice the model enabling him to understand the natural evolution of species. (DE#71 I, 844–5; EW I, 7–8)

What is interesting, as Foucault's reading notes attest, is that heredity is a theme that links madness, medicine, crime and sexuality, as well as the specialized knowledge of biology.[41] That would encompass aspects of all of his major works, from the early 1960s to the 1980s. But it is quickly surplanted as his focus. As early as the autumn of 1970, on a visit to Japan, he told Moriake Watanabe he had 'the intention of writing a book on systems of punishment and on the definition of crime in Europe' (DE#82 II, 115). That aspiration becomes, four years later, the manuscript of *Discipline and Punish*.

The Order of Discourse

Crime and punishment, heredity and racial hygiene, Nietzsche and genealogy, sexuality and individuality; the Vincennes years provide an outline for the work to come. Indeed, his inaugural lecture, 'The Order of Discourse', brings together many of these concerns. It was published as a short book in 1971. As Foucault notes, 'due to limitations of time, certain passages were shortened or changed in the lecture. They are restored here' (OD 6; see C 37/46). Unfortunately these passages are not marked, and in the absence of a recording of the lecture – none of the archives has a copy – it is not possible to distinguish between what was said, what was written, and what may have been changed after the event in the editing process.[42]

The lecture is, at least in its written form, a beautifully crafted piece, in which Foucault begins with modest and playful allusions to a wish to be anonymous in the face of language, using Samuel Beckett to question the idea of beginning (OD 8/51).[43] He closes by acknowledging his debts to Georges Dumézil and Georges Canguilhem, but with deference to his predecessor in this chair, suggests that his 'greatest debt is to Jean Hyppolite'. In doing so he makes some of his most intriguing references to the spectre of Hegel in his thought (OD 74–9/73–5). In a well-structured lecture, Foucault returns to his initial reticence to speak at the close, and suggests that it was because he was following in the footsteps of Hyppolite, and that the choice of the Collège in giving him this chair was 'in large part paying homage to him'. And it is Hyppolite's absence that Foucault feels, the absence of a voice, a void he must himself fill, 'doing so in this place where I once listened to him, and where he is no longer here to hear me' (OD 81–2/76).

In the lecture Foucault proposes a hypothesis in relation to the 'site [*lieu*] or perhaps the very provisional theatre' in which his work sits (OD 10/52). The choice of a geographical and performative space is illuminating, given Foucault's interest in both. The hypothesis is 'that in every society the production of discourse is at once controlled, selected, organized and redistributed by a certain number of procedures whose role is to ward off its powers and dangers, to gain mastery over its chance [*aléatoire*] events, to evade its ponderous, formidable materiality' (OD 10–11/52).

In this, and other passages, Foucault signals a shift in emphasis from the work of *The Archaeology of Knowledge*, where he had largely analysed discourse on its own terms, without the political context, without attention to power relations (though see AK 222/162–3).

But this is not in itself a new focus, as it returns to themes and questions he had treated extensively in the *History of Madness* and *Birth of the Clinic*. In this inaugural lecture, prohibition is one of the key things Foucault seeks to analyse, with sexuality and politics two of the places where these prohibitions are found most strikingly, 'as if discourse, far from being that transparent or neutral element in which sexuality is disarmed and politics pacified, is in fact one of the places where sexuality and politics exercise in a privileged way some of their most formidable forces [*puissances*]' (OD 11–12/52).

Foucault then turns to how some of these questions relate to his previous concerns of the divide between reason and madness (OD 12/53). He wonders if, alongside that divide, and the previous one of prohibition, there might be a third, that between true and false (OD 15/54). While he offers some cautions, he does note that 'there is no doubt that this division is historically constituted' (OD 16/54). To illustrate this claim, he provides a number of instances from ancient Greece of Hesiod to Plato, through to the sixteenth century and the nineteenth century (OD 17–19/54–6). The question of the 'will to truth' is explored in the course that followed this inaugural lecture, to be analysed in Chapter 1 below. He immediately notes that these three divides within discourse are external, and there are also internal procedures including commentary, and its relation to what is commented upon (OD 23–8/56–8); the question of the author (OD 28–31/58–9); and the establishment of disciplines (OD 31–6/59–61). Foucault's examples of disciplines, tellingly, are medicine and botany (OD 33–8/60–61) – one pointing backward to his work in *Birth of the Clinic*, and the other forward towards a potential project on heredity.

Along with the external and internal procedures, Foucault notes the importance of the question of 'the condition of their application, of imposing a certain number of rules on the individuals who hold them, and thus of not permitting everyone to have access to them' (OD 38/61). While the question of power relations was hardly absent from the previous procedures, here it comes very clearly to the fore. And yet, surprisingly, the language is still largely absent. Foucault instead wonders about how 'a certain number of themes in philosophy...correspond to these activities of limitation and exclusion, and perhaps also to reinforce them' (OD 47/64). While ours is, he suggests, a society in which discourse is valued, there are at the same time 'prohibitions, barriers, thresholds and limits', instituted in order to master its proliferation, remove its dangers, and 'in order to organize its disorder according to figures which dodge what is most uncontrollable about it' (OD 52/66). Logophilia, he suggests, paired with logophobia. This fear should not be effaced, but instead we should aim to 'analyse it in its conditions, its play and effects' (OD 53/66). This historical examination of its condition of possibility is as good an outline of Foucault's work – early through to late – as any other (see E 125).[44] He outlines three decisions we must take to undertake this work: 'we must call into question our will to truth, restore to discourse its character as an event, and finally throw off the sovereignty of the signifier' (OD 53/66).

All of these preliminary sketches are to indicate some of the themes he aspires to pursue over the coming years. In order to approach these topics he proposes 'certain methodological requirements...a principle of reversal...a principle of discontinuity...a principle of specificity...a rule...of exteriority'. The last is perhaps the most interesting, because he suggests that rather than digging into the interior of discourse, we must instead look outwards, 'towards its external conditions of possibility, towards what gives rise to the aleatory series of these events, and fixes its limits' (OD 53–5/67).

> Four notions, then, must serve as the regulating principle of the analysis: the event, the series, the regularity, the condition of possibility. Term for term we find the notion of event opposed to that of creation, series to unity, regularity to originality, and conditions of possibility opposed to signification. (OD 55–6/67)

Those other four notions – creation, unity, originality and signification – have for Foucault, preoccupied much work in the history of ideas. He acknowledges the work of the *Annales* school, and their focus on the *longue durée*, but suggests that in some sense their work should not be seen as a challenge to the 'mapping of the event', but rather as a stretching of it, 'discovering new strata' (OD 57/68). Foucault wants to build on the 'effective work of historians', and instead of reliance on 'consciousness and continuity', or 'sign and structure', he want to focus on the notions of 'the event and the series, along with the play of the notions which are linked to them: regularity, chance [*aléa*], discontinuity, dependence, transformation' (OD 58–9/68). One challenge Foucault identifies is that while 'the event is not of the order of bodies...yet it is not something immaterial either'. Searching for a term, he proposes the 'at first sight paradoxical direction of a materialism of the incorporeal' (OD 59/69).

By introducing three aspects in this work, that of 'chance [*hasard*], the discontinuous, and materiality', he suggests he has found a way to 'connect the history of systems of thought to the practice of historians' (OD 61–2/69). Foucault's development of these ideas in his potential future practice is revealing. He suggests that the analyses will fall into two groups: critical and genealogical. The first bear some comparison to his archaeological works, because they aim 'to grasp the forms of exclusion, of limitation, of appropriation...showing how they have been modified and displaced, what constraint they have effectively exerted, to what extent they have been evaded'. This is what he calls the analysis of the 'principle of reversal' (OD 62/70). The other aspect, the genealogical, is a development of this: not entirely distinct, but the addition of another perspective. It is, he suggests, a way of examining the other three principles: 'how did series of discourses come to be formed, across the grain of, in spite of, or with the aid of these systems of constraints: what was the specific norm of each one, and what were their conditions of appearance, growth, variation' (OD 62–3/70).

Foucault outlines many potential projects to follow, and it is hard to believe he, or anyone, could have accomplished them all. They range from the definite to the very provisional. Some are retrospective – the question of madness, or the history of medicine – or relate to previous courses on the question of heredity. Foucault suggests a project on this topic would look at discourses up to the start of the twentieth century and how these were reconfigured in modern genetics. Foucault did extensive reading on this topic, but did not deliver on this promise.[45] But this lecture also shows why he did not pursue this in earnest: he remarks that 'this is the work that has just been done by François Jacob with a brilliance and an erudition which could not be equalled' (OD 71/73). Indeed, his review of Jacob's book *La logique du vivant: Une histoire de l'hérédité* [*The Logic of Life: A History of Heredity*] was published in November 1970 in *Le Monde*, days before the inaugural lecture (DE#81, II, 99–104).[46] There he describes it as too modest in its subtitle, and as the 'most remarkable history of biology ever written' (DE#81, II, 102, 104).

Under the critical rubric Foucault also provides a summary outline of the course he is about to begin the following week: *Lectures on the Will to Know* (OD 64–5/70–1). Some of the other projects outlined are developed in his seminars, such as the question of 'psychiatric expertise and its role in penal practices' (OD 65/71), and work on medicine was also pursued in collaborative work. Others seem a throwback to work he had outlined in the 1960s, such as a study of 'the way in which literary criticism and literary history in the eighteenth and nineteenth centuries constituted the person of the author and the figure of the oeuvre' (OD 66/71). His literary work and especially the lecture 'What is an Author?' had been concerned with just such questions. Another project, for which some notes remain in the archive, concerns 'the role played by Freud in psychoanalytic knowledge' (OD 67/71).[47]

Foucault stresses that the critical and genealogical are tasks which 'are never completely separable' (OD 67/71). They must 'alternate, and complement each other, each supporting the other by turns' (OD 71/73). Indeed, one project, which he outlines at some length, appears both in the critical and genealogical parts. In the first, he suggests:

> I might try to analyse a system of prohibition of language, the one concerning sexuality from the sixteenth to the nineteenth century. The aim would be to see not how this interdiction has been progressively and fortunately effaced, but how it has been displaced and re-articulated from a practice of confession in which the forbidden behaviour was named, classified, hierarchized in the most explicit way, up to the appearance, at first very timid and belated, of sexual thematics in nineteenth-century medicine and psychiatry...(OD 63/70).

Later in the lecture, now in the outline of genealogical work, he adds:

> Earlier on I mentioned one possible study, that of the prohibitions which affect the discourse of sexuality. It would be difficult, and in any case abstract, to carry out this study without analysing at the same time the sets of discourses – literary, religious or ethical, biological and medical, juridical too – where sexuality is discussed, and where it is named, described, metaphorized, explained, judged. We are very far from having constituted a unitary and regular discourse of sexuality; perhaps we never will, and perhaps it is not in this direction that we are going. No matter. The prohibitions do not have the same form and do not function in the same way in literary discourse and in medical discourse, in that of psychiatry or in that of the direction of conscience. Conversely, these different discursive regularities do not have the same way of reinforcing, evading, or displacing the prohibitions. So the study can be done only according to pluralities of series in which there are prohibitions at work which are at least partly different in each. (OD 69–70/72)

Given the focus that this study of sexuality, and the one on systems of punishment and discipline, would eventually take, it is remarkable that one word is almost entirely absent from the discussion. That word, of course, is 'power', *pouvoir*. But it does appear in one key passage, where Foucault is contrasting the two approaches, and suggests that genealogy examines 'the series where discourse is effectively formed: it tries to grasp it in its power of affirmation, by which I mean not so much a power which would be opposed to that of denying, but rather the power to constitute domains of objects, in

respect of which one can affirm or deny true or false propositions'
(OD 71–2/73).

The final section is the tribute to Dumézil, Canguilhem and Hyppolite, and the retreat back into reticence and ambivalence about the
task allotted to him. But the body of the lecture has been anything
but modest in its ambitions. And, stingingly, having outlined these
projects and elaborated the approaches he intends to employ, he signs
off the penultimate part of the lecture with this rebuke: 'Let those
with gaps in their vocabulary say – if they find this term more con-
venient than meaningful – that all this is structuralism' (OD 72/73).

In this inaugural lecture Foucault has outlined in summary form a
significant development in his thought, but rather than a repudiation
of work that went before, it is a supplement, a modification, a new
stress or emphasis. In the project outline of sexuality he has set out
one of the key concerns that would occupy him until his death in
1984, though he does not turn to it in detail until 1974. That project
is the focus of *Foucault's Last Decade*. But in this lecture he has
also given multiple indications of what will be pursued in lectures,
seminars and collaboration in the intervening years. The early 1970s,
from the streets to the archive, from the classroom to the desk, are
productive and prolific years in Foucault's career. He delves deep into
history, relates those concerns to the present, develops theoretical
tools and rethinks earlier positions, and produces one major book,
collaborative volumes, anonymous and co-signed texts, and enables
other voices. His interests return to madness and medicine, while
focusing on the prison and other closed institutions, yet also developing themes of habitat and social medicine. He outlines and develops
Nietzsche's work in great detail, while also engaging with a range of
Marxist thinkers and concepts. These topics and questions are the
focus of this book.

1

Measure: Greece, Nietzsche, Oedipus

Truth and the Will to Know

Foucault's inaugural lecture was delivered on 2 December 1970. Exactly one week later, he began his first course, *La volonté de savoir* – the will to know, or will to knowledge. The publication of the course was under the title *Leçons sur la volonté de savoir, Lectures on the Will to Know*, in order to avoid confusion with the first volume of the *History of Sexuality*, when Foucault reused the title. As the introduction indicated, there are textual issues to contend with in this course, which does not exist in recordings, and its manuscript is sometimes fragmented and disjointed. A lecture on Nietzsche from after the course finished is included in place of missing material, and it also includes a manuscript entitled *Le savoir d'Œdipe* [The Knowledge of Oedipus or Oedipal Knowledge], which develops themes from the course and was used as the basis for lectures elsewhere. Nietzsche and Oedipus are two crucial themes of the course, framed by a wider reading of Greece in which Foucault notes how particular forms of knowledge are linked to political power. It is clear from this course that Foucault's knowledge of Greek thought is extensive. Unlike his 1980s courses, where sometimes text is transliterated, the Greek words and quotations in the manuscript remain in Greek characters, and are presented as such in the French volume, though not in the English translation.[1]

If we follow the standard story, Foucault has a concern with knowledge as a problem and archaeology as an approach in the late 1960s; which was replaced by a focus on power and the genealogical methodology in the first part of the 1970s; a turn to governmentality in the latter part of the 1970s; and a concern with ethics, truth and practices of the self, especially in Greek thought, in the 1980s until the end of his life. Several key works of secondary literature, notably Alan Sheridan's 1980 *The Will to Truth* with its two parts on 'The Archaeology of Knowledge and 'The Genealogy of Power' and the influential Dreyfus and Rabinow volume *Michel Foucault: Beyond Structuralism and Hermeneutics*, have proposed that chronology and many others have solidified this orthodoxy.[2] There is, for example, a large literature on the 'late' or 'last' Foucault.[3] The thematic arrangement of the English *Essential Works* – Ethics, Aesthetics, Power – has reinforced this view; which is especially unfortunate given that the chronological arrangement of the French *Dits et écrits* had already shown this was considerably more complicated. This course fundamentally undermines that chronology, showing the relation of concerns from the early 1970s to the final courses and books. Suggestions that Foucault turns to the Greeks only late in his life, or that issues around truth and subjectivity only emerge in his final writings are no longer, if they ever were, tenable. As well as being his first Collège de France course, it is therefore a good place to begin in reassessing all his mid-late period work.

As well as showing the initiation and continuation of key themes, this course is also important because it links the question of knowledge much more explicitly to work on power. In developing these themes of power and their relation to knowledge it does not just propose a genealogy of power. Instead it proposes a genealogy of *knowledge* alongside an archaeology of knowledge. Thus instead of replacing one approach with the other it complicates any simplistic understanding of a shift *from* archaeology *to* genealogy.[4] As Defert puts it, 'archaeology as method and *The Order of Things* are clearly propaedeutics to genealogy. Genealogy, as Foucault presents it, is not the crisis of archaeology: they are mutually supportive'.[5] The course also proposes a genealogy of an ethic of truth, and spends considerable time discussing the relation of truth to subjectivity, particularly in the work on Oedipus. So, as well as anticipating Foucault's work up to the mid-1970s – *Discipline and Punish* and the first volume of *The History of Sexuality* – as might have been expected from a course that initiates a sequence of courses on penal institutions and theories, the punitive society, psychiatric power and the abnormals – this course opens up themes that would occupy Foucault for the rest of his life. The power-knowledge relation, anticipated in the 'The Order of Discourse' inaugural lecture, is developed here, albeit without the precision of terminology that would later be employed. Like the next two lecture courses, *Lectures on the Will to Know* makes possible *Discipline and Punish*, but here there is no overlap of material, just of problematic. In its focus on the Greeks it shares a subject matter with the 1980s; but in its concern with money, agriculture and juridical and political practice it also links to the late 1970s work on governmentality. So, while there are certainly very many developments in Foucault's work; there are not the radical breaks that are sometimes suggested. This course, along with others at the Collège and many other recently available materials, is therefore invaluable in better understanding his intellectual chronology.

In the very first minutes of the first lecture of this course, Foucault notes that the theme of 'the will to know' could 'also be given to most of the historical analyses that I have carried out up until now' (LWK 3/1). It certainly pertains to what he intends to do, and 'all these analyses – past or still to come' can effectively be understood as 'fragments for a morphology of the will to know' (LWK 3/1; 217/224). The phrase invokes Nietzsche, and his 'will to power', *der Wille zur Macht*, and the relation between Foucault and Nietzsche is greatly clarified by the materials in this volume. In that opening lecture Foucault notes how there is an issue of the semantic order relation between *volonté*, will, and *désir*, desire. (We know from later discussions how he resisted Deleuze's stress on desire for his own interest in pleasure.)[6] Foucault asks us what relation there is between his phrase ' "*volonté de savoir*" and the more familiar "*désir de connaître*" ' (LWK 4–5/3). The latter, which might be glossed as the desire to know or to understand, he will trace to Aristotle (LWK 7/5). But this contrast or relation links to a further complication: *savoir* is similarly a verb and a noun. *Le savoir* is knowledge, distinguished by Foucault from *la connaissance* in *The Archaeology of Knowledge*.[7] In this course, he bemoans the 'inadequacy of the instruments of historical analysis provided by epistemology', and asks: what are the 'relations between the will to *savoir* and forms of *connaissance*, on the theoretical level, and on the historical level' (LWK 5/3). The French title of that earlier book is *L'archéologie de savoir*, which would not be translated as 'the archaeology to know'. But *Le volonté de savoir* could be either 'the will to know' or 'the will to knowledge', and at times Foucault clearly intends both.

Foucault covers a great deal of material in this course and in related materials, including the first two lectures of his 'Truth and Juridical Forms' course in Rio in 1973. Initially the discussion in Paris is based around Aristotle, especially the first book of the *Metaphysics*, with allusions to Greek tragedy. He sets up a contract between Aristotle and those who came after him, including Spinoza, Kant and, especially, Nietzsche. There is an extended discussion of the Sophists, and the challenge made to them by Plato and Aristotle, particularly in the latter's *Sophistical Refutations*, the *Analytics* and the *Metaphysics*. Foucault suggests that Sophism functions as the exclusion that makes philosophy possible; and spends some time discussing Sophism as a technique of thought and argument. He suggests that Sophism requires us to take seriously the materiality of enunciations and propositions. One definition is especially striking:'Sophism: a perverse manipulation tending to establish a relation of domination. Polemical anagram or rearrangement [*anagramme*]. Such a cruel discourse. Games of desire and power' (LWK 63/64). This last quotation is a good indication of the sometimes note-form of these lectures.

Much of the rest of the course looks at the Greeks with discussions of judicial and poetic discourse, especially drawing on juridical texts from the founding of Greek colonies in Egypt, especially Alexandria (LWK 69/72), Homer's *Iliad*, and Hesiod, especially around themes of justice, truth and power. Foucault tells the story from the *Iliad* of a dispute in a chariot race, where Menelaus accuses Antilochus of committing a foul. Rather than turn to a witness, Antilochus is asked to swear an oath by Zeus that he did not commit a foul. It is when he fails to do this verbal test that the foul is acknowledged. Foucault sees this as an indication of a different way of producing the truth, of test rather than testimony. It is one he locates in ancient Greece and will find again in the Middle Ages (LWK 72/74–5; DE#139 II, 556; EW III, 18).[8]

Greek ritual ordeals [*rituel ordalique*] are examples of the test procedure. These can be the well-known ordeal where a physical or verbal action had to be undertaken to resolve a situation. These were frequently used when there was an imbalance between the two adversaries and an oath by one was not acceptable. Women, slaves and children, as well as lower rank men might be subject to an ordeal. The only example here is the ordeal by rock [*l'épreuve du rocher*], where a supposedly guilty woman jumped off a cliff into the sea. He notes that 'a whole history could be written of the relationship between truth and torture [*le supplice*]' (LWK 83/85), which is a theme that is elaborated in the course from 1971–2, and various traces elsewhere. His brief examples here are the Inquisition and Masochism (LWK 83–4/85–6), but subsequent lecture courses from Rio in 1973, Montreal in 1974 and Louvain in 1981 and naturally the opening scenes of *Discipline and Punish* suggest a number of other examples. It seems that, even here, the question of confession is key in his mind, with its complicated interrelations between the exercise of power, the construction of knowledge, and the constitution of truth.

Indeed, he suggests that with the Inquisition 'the test [*l'épreuve*] of truth is complicated by the Christian behaviour of confession [*l'aveu*]. But the Inquisition is not purely and simply a matter of techniques for getting the confession' (LWK 83/85–6). This is a theme he will elaborate in much more detail in *Théories et institutions pénales*.

The key concern in this course is then not knowledge so much as truth, but in a contested, political sense, rather than a detailed 'objective' manner. Indeed, Foucault quickly moves from a focus on knowledge to use the phrase 'the will to truth [*vérité*]' (LWK 4/2). The key themes of the course will, he suggests, revolve around 'the play [*le jeu*] between these three notions: *savoir, vérité, connaissance*' (LWK 4/3). He outlines a number of themes that he suggests will be discussed over future courses, including the knowledge of economic processes between the sixteenth and eighteenth centuries; and how knowledge of sexuality is organized and arranged between the seventeenth and nineteenth centuries. These are not fulfilled immediately, though we might see them as anticipating work done later in the 1970s. He also outlines how his seminar will begin to examine penal codes and systems in the nineteenth century, especially in relation to the 'insertion of a discourse claiming scientific status (medicine, psychiatry, psychopathology, sociology)' within penal matters (LWK 3–4/1–2; see Chapter 4). He asks 'if, finally, we can articulate this will to know, which has taken the form of a will to truth, not on a subject or an anonymous force but on real systems of domination' (LWK 6/4). The resistance to a subject is clear (LWK 5/3), and truth is a continual theme, with Foucault suggesting it should rather be described as 'the system of truth and falsehood' (LWK 6/4).

Out of this range of themes three will be treated here in some detail: the relation of truth, knowledge and power in Greek juridical and political practice; the engagement with Nietzsche in this course and related materials; and the reading of Oedipus Foucault develops in the early 1970s.

Greek Juridical and Political Practice

In ancient Greece Foucault suggests that truth is linked to the exercise of sovereignty. This differs under different systems: in the Homeric, it is with the sovereignty of Zeus, which declares the definition of the truth. In the system of classical law, 'it is within a pre-constituted space of sovereignty that the truth is called for, formulated, proven' (LWK 75/78). Foucault suggests that 'between these two truths, the whole system of power is modified' (LWK 75/78). This then becomes one of the key themes of the course, a project of analysing 'the transformation of the truth system – judicial decision – political sovereignty' in these two systems (LWK 75/78). Foucault's contrast is between the archaic period (800 BCE – 480 BCE) and the more familiar classical period. In the former he suggests that knowledge is 'linked to political power and the State apparatus in these two ways, knowledge is quite naturally located in the hands of functionaries: knowledge is a State service and a political instrument. Hence its character is necessarily secret. It does not have to circulate or be widespread. It is linked directly to the possession of power' (LWK 113/119). In the later system there is a fundamental transformation:'Knowledge will be separated from the State apparatus and the direct exercise of power; it will be detached from political sovereignty in its immediate application and become the correlate of justice, of the *dikaion* as a natural, divine and human order' (LWK 114/119).

> The knowledge that was the secret of efficient power is going to become the order of the manifest, measured world, effectuated daily and for all men in its truth...two correlated transformations therefore: one revealing truth as knowledge of things, time and order; and the other shifting knowledge from the domain of power to the region of justice. (LWK 114/119)

Of course, Foucault does not see this as a simple set of changes. He suggests that 'the justice-truth linkage and the knowledge-power break will never be definitively established; they will constantly be called into question' (LWK 115/120).

In order to interrogate this, the lectures provide a number of examples of juridical and political practices. These include justice and injustice in Greek thought and practice; agrarian crises and the role of politics and the army; the institution of money; law (*nomos*), economy and politics; the emergence of the *polis* (city-state);[9] the pure and the impure, and the relation of this archaic rite to other oppositions; *nomos*, money and new religious practices; criminality and the will to know. Foucault discusses the management of agrarian crises between the seventh and sixth centuries, in particular in terms of fragmented lands and the legacy of colonization (LWK 115–17/121–3); advances in the army, especially in terms of the developments of mining techniques and the use of iron, and the new types of inter-city and intra-city warfare (LWK 117–19/123–4); the emergence of a new class of artisans [*l'artisanat*] (LWK 119–20/124–6); and wider political transformations including slavery, the development of urban civilization, changes in production, etc. (LWK 120–3/126–9).

Foucault highlights three key developments: money, the law, and justice. Money is 'not just a measure of exchange, but is instituted mainly as an instrument of distribution, division [*repartition*], and social correction' (LWK 123/129–30). The law, *nomos*, is written law, in distinction to an oral tradition of *thesmos*, or non-written rules (LWK 143–5/149–52), and is not 'simply political constitution but the very discourse of social order'. Justice is a term that relates to 'a religious model' (LWK 123/129–30). These terms are not distinct, and Foucault particularly stresses the relation between money and the law – *nomisma* and *nomos* – and law and justice obviously relate. *Nomos* has four underpinnings [*points d'appui*]: 'writing, discourse, pedagogy, nature' (LWK 147/153).[10] As has long been known, from Hannah Arendt and Carl Schmitt among others, *nomos* is division as well as law; and Foucault relates '*nomos* and *nomisma*' to 'division and measure' (LWK 158/165).[11] In the course summary he notes that the 'search for a *nomos*' is a quest for 'a just law of distribution ensuring the order of the city by installing a reigning order in the city that is the order of the world' (LWK 220/228). Foucault wrote these summaries at the end of each course for the *Annuaire du Collège de France*, usually around June. In the course as delivered he specifies that the invention of money enables the maintenance of indebtedness and inequalities alongside 'a division of lands [*un partage des terres*]', with political power concentrated in the wealthy (LWK 143/149).

In later lectures Foucault looks at rituals around the pure and the impure, and the relation of this archaic rite to two other oppositions: criminality/innocence and ignorance/knowledge [*savoir*] (LWK 161/167, 172/179). He suggests that 'purity is the required condition to tell of and see the *nomos* as the manifestation of order' (LWK 181/188). The purity/impurity relation is linked to *nomos* in a number of ways, but for Foucault it helps to explain why impurity must be expelled from 'the space of the *nomos*', through mechanisms such as 'division, separation, non-mixing...the law that says one must exclude' (LWK 181–2/188). We can see here the influence his work would have on Giorgio Agamben, the continuation of Foucault's interest in the spatial partitions of the mad and the sick, familiar from his work of the 1960s, and also an anticipation of his claim that 'discipline is above all an analysis of space' (DE#229, III, 516; SKP 147).

Crucial to all these concerns is the notion of measure. Measure is a means of creating knowledge, but it is also a means of exercising power. Foucault had suggested that measure was one of the kinds of knowledge that Greek and then Western thought had inherited from Eastern models of knowledge.

1. knowledge of the origin, of the genesis and of succession; cosmological, philosophical, historical knowledge;
2. knowledge of quantities, accounts and measures: mathematical knowledge; physical knowledge;
3. knowledge of the event, occasion, moment: technical knowledge of agronomy [science of agriculture], medicine; magical knowledge
   NB: The first two knowledges ultimately organized Western science: origin and measure, succession and quantity; temporal and numerical order' (LWK 107–8/112–13).

The last has a rather different trajectory, which Foucault very briefly sketches. 'Knowledge [*savoir*] of the moment is gradually marginalized: Stoic logic, magical knowledge [*connaissance*]; the medical tradition which leads to clinical medicine, which substitutes for the *connaissance* of the moment, the medical occasion, the spatialization of pathogenic sites [*foyers pathogens*]' (LWK 108/113). It is in 'military, political and revolutionary strategy, that the knowledge of the event, moment and opportunity is developed anew' (LWK 108/113).

As Foucault clarifies, measure can be both calculation and norm (LWK 127/133). Norm, as we know from Foucault and Canguilhem's work, is both a statistical derivation and a standard to which people are subjected. This can be found in a range of political systems. Here in Greece Foucault suggests that it can apply to both 'tyrant or legislator', where 'the person holding power is the city quantity surveyor: the measurer of lands, things, wealth, rights, powers, and men' (LWK 127/134). All kinds of things and relations fall under this relation:

> We should not forget that before being inscribed in Western consciousness as the principle of quantification, harmony, and classical non-excess, Greek measurement was an immense social and polymorphous practice of assessment, quantification, establishing equivalences, and the search for appropriate proportions and distributions.
>
> We can see how introducing measure is linked to a whole problem of peasant indebtedness, the transfer of agricultural properties, the settlement of debts, equivalence between foodstuff or manufactured objects, urbanization, and the establishment of a state form.
>
> At the heart of this practice of measurement the institution of money appears. (LWK 128/134)

Foucault notes that money is *metron*, 'an instrument of measure' (LWK 136/142), but he means this in the dual sense of *la mesure*, which can mean 'moderation, limit' as well as measure.[12] Money can be used to address extreme wealth through taxation and extreme poverty through redistribution.

In general terms Foucault traces a fundamental transition here, which has structural similarities with some of his later work on a quite different historical period. He says that 'in the archaic system, wealth and power were shared out by the same distribution'. But with the reforms of Solon in the sixth century BCE, known as the *eunomia*, there are two principles:

- If someone takes too much power, they are punished by the city
- If someone seizes too much wealth, they must expect the punishment of Zeus. (LWK 152/158)[13]

As Foucault later notes, the status of rich or poor is outside the *eunomia* of Solon; 'it is luck [*hasard*], it is chance [*chance*] or fate, it is the will of the Gods' (LWK 154/160). In a sense it is external to politics. So there are 'new and complex relations between economics and politics' after Solon and his *eunomia*; it is no longer simply that riches give power (LWK 153–4/159–60).

Out of these changes appears 'an absolutely new notion: the city-state, the *polis*, as a set of citizens insofar as they are possessors of a share of power [*détenteurs d'une partie du pouvoir*] and that power as a whole is exercised through them all' (LWK 153/160). Foucault therefore contrasts an earlier form of sovereign power with the power of the *nomos*, 'as a principle of distribution, value and wisdom, the origin on which it is founded, and the order whose reign it establishes not only over men, but over the stars, the seas, animals and plants' (LWK 156/163).

> It is there that can be mapped the place of a knowing and neutral [*connaissant et neutre*] subject, the form of an unveiled [*dévoilée*] truth and the content of a knowledge [*savoir*] no longer magically linked to the repetition of an event but to the discovery and maintenance of an order.
>
> It is there, in that zone, that the figure appears of someone who, behind a truth, without wealth or power, will reveal the law of things to give strength and vigour to a human law which is at the same time incomprehension [*méconnaissance*]. (LWK 157/163)

That passage clearly links concerns throughout Foucault's entire career, from the idea of order to the subject, and the relation of truth and knowledge. But it is also a transformation of power. In this model law, power is no longer:

- what is exclusively held by a few;
- that to which others are unilaterally subject [*subi*];

— what is exercised from time to time and instantaneously in actions, words, commands or ritualized levies [*Ce qui s'exerce ponctuellement et instantanément dans les gestes, dans des paroles, dans des commandements ou des prélèvements ritualisés*]

Power is what is exercised permanently through all the citizens. The totality of a social body begins to appear as the site where power is applied to itself [*s'applique à lui-même*]. Power arises from a body on which it is exercised. (LWK 153–4/160)

The power that Foucault sees here is not a top-down model of domination, concentrated in a single source and exercised over those who do not have it; and it is not focused in spectacular bursts or displays. Rather it operates through what he would later call a micro-physics of small actions and continual operations. Power operates within society, from within a network of relations.

There is also the notion of 'popular power', the negative figure of which is in Plato, Aristotle, and legislators. This power is the opposite of the *nomos*, because it is changeable, likely to be swayed by 'speech [*discours*], discussion, the vote and changeable will [*volonté mobile*]'. 'It is excluded from *savoir* (political knowledge [*savoir*] and knowledge [*savoir*] of things)' (LWK 183/190). 'Popular power only listens to its interests and its desires. It is violent: it imposes its will on everyone. It is murderous.' Foucault notes that this is especially in relation to the wise man [*le sage*], and in the course as actually delivered, rather than the manuscript, makes the explicit reference to Socrates (LWK 183/190 and n).

Popular power is criminal in its essence…criminal in its relation to the *nomos*, to law as the foundation of the city's existence. Popular power is a crime against the very nature of the city. (LWK 183/190)

We can see here, as elsewhere, the contemporary political resonances of this course. The course was delivered at the same time as the inception of the GIP, with their manifesto read by Foucault on 8 February 1971, two days before the seventh lecture of the course. The work of that group will be discussed in Chapter 5, but it is striking that this course too could be read as a history of the present, perhaps no more so than in his understanding of the impact of Solon. In terms of the power shift in ancient Greece, Foucault would later make almost the same contrast between quite different historical periods, outlining his theory of power as a contrast to sovereign models of practice and theories that seek to make sense of quite different operations with an out-dated model. What is striking here is that Foucault's analysis of power is developed out of his reading of the Greeks and as a means of understanding this contrast between the archaic and the classical periods.

Nietzsche and Invention

Foucault's discussion of power therefore develops, in part, from his reading of ancient Greece. Yet his discussion of Nietzsche at this time indicates that this engagement also helped to shape his view of this question. Unfortunately, a detailed discussion of Nietzsche, given as the last part of the 16 December lecture and as the whole of the 23 December 1970 lecture has not been preserved, probably because it was removed to serve as the basis for a presentation elsewhere.[14] This volume therefore includes a lecture on Nietzsche given at McGill in April 1971 as an effective replacement for the missing material from the course. We also have other resources to draw upon, including the well-known essay 'Nietzsche, Genealogy, History' from 1971, and some indications of Foucault's previous work on Nietzsche. Defert notes that Foucault had lectured on Nietzsche at the University of Vincennes in the winter of 1969–70; then at SUNY Buffalo in March 1970, followed by this Collège de France course, and then at McGill in April 1971.[15] Defert himself notes elsewhere that a Vincennes course on Nietzsche was given in February 1969 (C 34/41), so it is unclear if the course was repeated in Winter 1969–70, or whether there were two separate courses. While there have been discussions of publishing the Vincennes lectures, to date nothing has appeared and the papers archived at the BNF from this period are not yet available for consultation. Foucault's reading notes on Nietzsche are however available at the BNF.[16]

As Defert recounts, Foucault wrote him a letter in July 1967 saying he had realized why Nietzsche had long held a fascination: 'A morphology of the will to know in European civilization, which has been neglected in favour of an analysis of the will to power' (C 31/37; compare LWK 3/1; 217/224). Such a project is developed in the 1970–71 course, and shapes some of the work of the next two courses. In the Vincennes lectures, Defert notes, Foucault makes it clear that while genealogy is not clearly defined before *On the Genealogy of Morality*, from as early as *The Birth of Tragedy* Nietzsche had identified something that can be translated as 'the will to know', *Wissengier*; a lust for knowledge or science, which is elsewhere described in similar terms as an *entfesselten Wissentrieb* or *Erkenntnistrieb*, an unfettered drive for science or knowledge.[17]

Defert suggests that this means there is a 'genealogy of knowledge [*connaissance*]' proposed in his work, and this precedes the *Genealogy*'s analysis of 'the question of the value of values'.[18] Paralleling this, Foucault's initial proposal with Nietzsche is a genealogy of knowledge, which stands in contrast to one of power. For Defert, 'Foucault identified a will to know [*savoir*] which cannot be assimilated to knowledge [*connaissance*] or will to truth that Heidegger, following Nietzsche in this, assimilates to the will to power [*puissance*]'.[19] The development of the early 1970s is that the two become combined. It is notable here that Foucault offers the French phrase *le volonté de puissance*, the standard French translation, to translate Nietzsche's *der Wille zur Macht*. But elsewhere he understands Nietzsche's *Macht* as *pouvoir*, not *puissance*; *pouvoir* having a more creative sense because of its relation to capacity, *pouvoir* being a verb 'to be able' as well as a substantive. In that more developed conceptualization, Foucault seems to parallel the distinction in German between *Kraft* and *Gewalt* – force and violence – and *Macht* – power. Nietzsche largely analyses *Macht*; Foucault *pouvoir*. Foucault would continue his work on power throughout the 1970s, developing through *Discipline and Punish* and his lecture courses.[20]

As Defert stresses, the 1976 book that reuses this course's title, the first volume of *The History of Sexuality*, 'is as much a genealogy of the constitutive *savoir* of the *dispositif* of sexuality, as a genealogy of modern morals'.[21] Defert suggests that it was *The Birth of Tragedy*, rather than *On the Genealogy of Morality*, which was the key text,[22] but Foucault also references many of Nietzsche's other works in this course, including *The Gay Science* [Le gai savoir] (LWK 219/227). The BNF archive shows that Foucault's notes on Nietzsche were extensive, and indicate a careful reading of the entire corpus. The notes are grouped together thematically, and include materials from as early as the 1950s alongside notes clearly destined for the 'Nietzsche, Genealogy, History' essay in the late 1960s or early 1970s. It is not possible definitively to disentangle the material, but it is clear that Foucault had a very detailed knowledge of the entirety of Nietzsche's texts, and that he returned to them throughout his career.

Because of the missing material in the course manuscript we only have fragments of what Foucault said on Nietzsche in Paris. Foucault suggests that 'until Nietzsche, desire and will were never able to rid themselves of their subordination to knowledge [*connaissance*], [and] if the desire to know was always doubled by the precondition of knowledge [*connaissance*], the reason is this fundamental relationship to truth' (LWK 24–5/24). The presentation is orientated around

Nietzsche's relation to the tradition before him, notably Spinoza and Kant: 'Kant is the danger, the tiny daily peril, the network of traps; Spinoza is the great other, the sole [*unique*] adversary' (LWK 28/27). Foucault puts Nietzsche to work as 'an attempt to free the desire to know [*connaître*] from the form and law of knowledge [*connaissance*]' (LWK 25/25). Foucault finds in Nietzsche an 'analysis of the desire, instinct, and will to know [*connaître*]', which is 'irreducible to knowledge [*connaissance*] itself' (LWK 27/26). There are, though, tensions in Nietzsche's thought, not least his employment of 'huge doses of knowledge borrowed from the sciences: biology, history, philology' (LWK 27/27). For Foucault this positivism is there in Nietzsche and cannot simply be evaded; rather it is the core of his attempt to break with traditional philosophical structures of knowledge. It is Spinoza's linkage of truth and knowledge that makes someone like Kant possible, so 'to avoid the trap of Kant one has to kill Spinoza... Spinoza is the condition of Kant' (LWK 28/27–8). The manuscript breaks off at this point, with a suggestion that it is naïve to think turning to Spinoza could be a break from 'the idealism of philosophical discourse' (LWK 28/28), a suggestion Defert notes may be directed at Louis Althusser.[23]

The McGill lecture treats the question of how we can use Nietzsche to trace the history of truth. Foucault begins the lecture with a famous passage from Nietzsche's early essay 'On Truth and Lie in an Extra-Moral Sense'. This is the story of the 'invention of knowledge [*connaissance*]' by the intelligent animals whose actions are described as 'the moment of the greatest lie and the most supreme arrogance of universal history' (LWK 195/202–3).[24] Invention, *Erfindung*, *invention*, Foucault notes, is opposed to origin, and is 'not a synonym for beginning [*commencement*]' (LWK 195/203).[25] In this light Foucault suggests that *connaissance* does not have an origin but it does have a history, and that this means it is not innate in human nature. He takes this to mean that 'behind knowledge is something altogether different, something foreign, opaque, and irreducible to it', but this is not the perception of empiricism (LWK 196/203). Knowledge is 'allied first with malice – mockery, contempt, hatred' (LWK 197/204). This is the contrast. For Aristotle the will to know [*savoir*] is curiosity, a quest for *connaissance*, marked in relation to sensation and inherently linked to life. For Nietzsche, 'the will to know refers not to knowledge but something altogether different, that behind the will to know there is not a sort of pre-existing knowledge that is something like sensation, but 'instinct, struggle, the will to power' (LWK 190/197). As he later explains in more detail, 'instinct, interest, play and struggle' are not some kind of origin of knowledge, which it breaks from at a later point, but rather 'its permanent, perpetual, inevitable, necessary support' (LWK 198/206).

Knowledge was invented, and truth is also an invention but of even later date (LWK 199/206). Nietzsche unravels the idea that knowledge is a quest for truth, suggesting that truth is something imposed later, and that what precedes it is not even the 'non-true', but something which 'is prior to the division specific to truth' (LWK 200/207–8). This might be a desire for knowledge of a different kind: 'a primary and corporeal knowledge prior to any truth and governed entirely by need…life, struggle, the hunt, food, rivalry' (LWK 201/209). The elaboration of these themes is not solely concerned with knowledge and truth. Knowledge is always perspective, incomplete, but neither in a Husserlian sense that phenomena are all we can address, or in a Kantian claim that the thing-in-itself remains fundamentally unknowable. Nietzsche's argument is that knowledge is grounded on the very thing that prevents us from knowing, 'its force and not its form', that is 'instinct, malice, greed for knowledge, desire' (LWK 198–9/206). From this reading of Nietzsche, Foucault establishes that the exercise of knowledge is linked to the exercise of power:

> Knowledge [*connaissance*] is based on a network of relations:
> – different in their form; it may involve destruction, appropriation, punishment, domination;
> – different in their points of support [*points d'appui*] and the terms between which they establish relations; body to body, group to group, individual to a thing, animal or god.
> The basis of knowledge [*connaissance*] is thus this play of differences. (LWK 202/210)

The contrast then is not only between Nietzsche and Aristotle, but Nietzsche opposed to many elements within the history of philosophy. He challenges a view of philosophy close to Husserlian phenomenology: 'Against the warm softness of a phenomenon, we must set the murderous tenacity of knowledge' (LWK 198/206). He also shifts into a semi-Heideggerian register: 'Freedom is the being of truth; and it is the duty of the will. An ontology (freedom of the truth will be God or nature); an ethics (the will's duty will be prohibition, renunciation, passage to the universal). This fundamental liberty is the mutual articulation of will and truth', and can be found in various forms in Plato, Kant and Heidegger. But Foucault suggests that 'for Nietzsche, the will-truth relation is quite different. Truth is only an element in the will on the basis of its singular characteristics and its most precise determinations, and in the form of constraint and domination. Their mutual articulation is not freedom, but violence' (LWK 206/215). This has profound implications for knowledge, which Foucault claims which have not yet been fully understood. It 'makes an "ideology" of knowledge [*savoir*] as an effect of freedom and reward [*récompense*] of virtue impossible' and allows us to rethink 'the history of knowledge [*connaissance*] and science; the status we give to their universality; and the connection of science to certain forms of society or civilization' (LWK 207/215).

What Foucault finds in Nietzsche is invaluable, and he suggests that the analysis allows an analysis

- to speak of sign and interpretation, of their inseparability, without reference to a phenomenology;
- to speak of signs without reference to any 'structuralism';
- to speak of interpretation without reference to an original subject;
- to connect up analyses of systems of signs with the analysis of forms of violence and domination;
- to think of knowledge as an historical process before any problematic of the truth, and more fundamentally than in the subject–object relation. Knowledge [*connaissance*] freed from the subject–object relation is knowledge [*savoir*]. (LWK 205/213–14)

We can see here a range of things Foucault has been developing in his work of the 1960s with the resistance to phenomenology and structuralism, though with an interest in signs; his concern of the 1970s with the relation of knowledge to forms of power; the problem of the subject which he will eventually work through by writing its genealogy; and the question of the relation between truth and subjectivity. Whether all of this is genuinely derived from this reading of Nietzsche alone is questionable; but the suggestion undoubtedly highlights a number of his central concerns. It allows him to make the fundamental claim that the subject–object relation is a product of *connaissance* rather than its foundation; and illusion, error and lie [*mensonge*] operate as categories of the distribution of non-true truth (see LWK 209/216–17). In Foucault's reading, Nietzsche thus functions, in contrast to Aristotle (LWK 209/218), as one of 'two paradigms of the will to know'.[26]

Defert's editorial material for this course puts Foucault in relation to Heidegger and Deleuze, in what is a barely acknowledged but lively 'subterranean dialogue'.[27] Defert notes, for example, at least one unmistakable echo of Heidegger's *Nietzsche*.[28] That book, based on lectures in the late 1930s and texts from the 1940s was first published in 1961 and translated by Pierre Klossowski in 1971.[29] Foucault took very detailed notes on Heidegger in the 1950s,[30] reading most texts in German and ranging from *Being and Time* to essays, including 'Who is Nietzsche's Zarathustra?' and 'Nietzsche's Word: God is Dead'.[31] He had access to some at-the-time unpublished manuscripts, including the 1929/30 course *Die Grundbegriffe de Metaphysik*,[32] and was at least aware of Heidegger's *Nietzsche* in 1966 (DE#41 I, 566). Defert underlines that Foucault's contrast of Nietzsche to Aristotle is opposed to Heidegger's inscription of Nietzsche within the metaphysical tradition, as an inversion of Plato.[33] While Heidegger had, for Foucault, rescued Nietzsche from 'literary or psychologistic interpretations', and situated him within the philosophical tradition, Defert suggests that he wants to go in a different direction. Defert notes that the translation of the 'On Truth and Lie' piece by Angèle Kremer-Marietti in *Le livre du philosophe* was one spur to this reading; others came from Deleuze's *Difference and Repetition* and, presumably his earlier book on Nietzsche; and Marcel Detienne's *The Masters of Truth*.[34] Even deeper, perhaps, is the link Defert makes between Foucault and Eugen Fink, especially *Spiel als Weltsymbol*.[35] Fink's reading of Nietzsche, and his interest in the 'game' or 'play', is undoubtedly fascinating. But Fink is barely referenced by Foucault,[36] and too much of a dialogue seems unfortunately unlikely. If there is another key figure in Foucault's dialogue with Nietzsche interpretations, beyond Heidegger, Deleuze and Klossowski, it is Karl Jaspers, whose work is extensively quoted in Foucault's reading notes.[37] Defert also notes that the teaching on Nietzsche led to the 'Nietzsche, Genealogy, History' essay, first published in the *Hommage à Jean Hyppolite* volume in January 1971.[38]

Yet *Hommage à Jean Hyppolite* predates the 1971 McGill lecture, and must have been in press by the time Foucault began his Paris course in December 1970. The themes of the essay actually go in a quite different direction. The volume developed from a tribute session to Hyppolite held at the École Normale Supérieure on 19 January 1969. Foucault's contribution to that event was a different piece, published in June in *Revue de métaphysique et de morale* (DE#67 I, 779–85). That piece is much more explicitly tied to Hyppolite's own work, and especially his debt to and development of Hegel. In the essay there is, of course, discussion of truth, knowledge and error, but the explicit focus is rather different. The links may be more explicit to the Vincennes course on Nietzsche, but also demonstrate the interest in questions of heredity. The Nietzsche essay is part of a collection that contributes to the aim of providing essays that address the 'different domains' of Hyppolite's work, in areas such as 'history of thought, philosophy of science, epistemology, psychoanalysis'.[39]

The essay has been extensively discussed before, but a few points are worth stressing.

The essay, in distinction to the *Lectures on the Will to Know*, proposes a mode of reading and historical analysis, rather than a topic of inquiry. Foucault calls this 'genealogy'. Now while Nietzsche had used that term, notably in *On the Genealogy of Morality*, it is not immediately obvious that he means this as a description of his approach. Most of Nietzsche's references are critical – it is in some sense an interrogation of those who propose genealogies of morality, not a description of the interrogation itself.

The key part of Foucault's essay is devoted to a close textual analysis of Nietzsche's use of what might appear to be related words around the ideas of origin: *Ursprung, Entstehung, Herkunft, Abkunft, Geburt, Anfang, Erbschaft, Erfindung.* These would be loosely translated as origin, emergence, provenance, lineation, birth, beginning, inheritance, invention. Only the last really relates to the McGill lecture. The rest are carefully distinguished by Foucault from 'origin' words, stressing that 'the genealogist needs history to expose [*conjurer*] the chimera of the origin' (DE#84 II, 140; EW II, 373). *Herkunft* is stock or descent [*provenance*], yet genealogy 'does not resemble the evolution of a species and does not map the destiny of a people' (DE#84 II, 141; EW II, 374); *Enstehung* is 'emergence, the moment of arising…always produced in a particular state of forces' (DE#84 II, 143; EW II, 375). It is clear that here the old project on heredity becomes to some degree, and with these qualifications, a means of conducting research rather than a topic of it. Later in the essay he notes how Nietzsche 'associates the terms *Herkunft* and *Erbschaft* [inheritance]' (DE#84, II, 141; EW II, 374). But, he cautions,'we should not be deceived into thinking that this heritage is an acquisition, a possession that accumulates and solidifies; rather, it is an unstable assemblage of faults, fissures, and heterogeneous layers that threaten the fragile inheritor from within or from underneath' (DE#84, II, 141–2; EW II, 374).

Foucault distinguishes this approach from 'history in the traditional sense', linking back to Nietzsche's early text on history as the second *Untimely Meditation* (DE#84 II, 146; EW II, 379). The dual operations of parody and disruption are central to the approach: 'Genealogy is history in the form of a concerted carnival…the systematic dissociation of our identity' (DE#84 II, 153–4; EW II, 386). He also stresses the relation of the body and history in several places (i.e. DE#84 II, 142–3; EW II, 375–6). In the final part of the essay there is a sense of how this approach is able to intersect with the topics proposed in the first Collège de France course. Here Foucault highlights some shifts from how Nietzsche discussed this in the second *Untimely Meditation*. Now it 'it is no longer a question of judging the past in the name of a truth that only we can possess in the present, but of risking the destruction of the subject of knowledge [*connaissance*], in the endless deployment of the will to knowledge [*savoir*]' (DE#84 II, 156; EW II, 388–9). In the final lines of the 'Nietzsche, Genealogy, History' essay, Foucault notes that Nietzsche's three modes of history in the *Untimely Meditations* are transformed in genealogy:

> In a sense, genealogy returns to the three modalities of history that Nietzsche recognized in 1874. It returns to them despite the objections that he raised in the name of life and its power to affirm and create. But they are metamorphosed in the return: the veneration of monuments becomes parody; the respect for ancient continuities becomes systematic dissociation; the critique of past injustices by the truth held by man today becomes the destruction of the subject of knowledge [*connaissance*] by the injustice appropriate to the will to know [*volonté de savoir*]. (DE#84 II, 156; EW II, 389)

In the original manuscript of this essay this last term is actually 'the will to truth [*volonté de vérité*].'[40]

In May 1973 Foucault returned to Nietzsche as the theoretical framing of his 'Truth and Juridical Forms' lectures, which was apparently the last detailed analysis of Nietzsche he made. He suggested that:

> In Nietzsche, one finds a type of discourse that undertakes a historical analysis of the formation of the subject itself, a historical analysis of the birth of a certain type of knowledge [*savoir*] – without ever granting the preexistence of a subject of knowledge [*connaissance*]. (DE#139 II, 542; EW III, 5–6)

Foucault then adds an interesting gloss to his recounting of Nietzsche's story. He suggests that the comment that 'knowledge was invented on a star at a particular moment' is given in an 'insolent and cavalier manner'. This was 1873, the period of neo-Kantianism, two years after Hermann Cohen's *Kants Theorie der Erfahrung* [Kant's Theory of Experience],[41] and here Foucault suggests that Nietzsche's claim is that 'time and space are not forms of knowledge [*connaissance*], but more like primitive rocks onto which knowledge [*connaissance*] attaches itself' (DE#139 II, 543; EW III, 6). Foucault draws a sharp contrast between *Erfindung* as invention and *Ursprung* as origin – a contrast made in the 1971 lecture, but even sharper in the etymological work of 'Nietzsche, Genealogy, History'. In 1973 he contrasts

Nietzsche's account of the invention of religion to Schopenhauer's search for the origin of religion; or the invention rather than the origin of poetry, or, more familiarly, with that of moral ideals (DE#139 II, 543–4; EW III, 6–7). The point here though, concerns knowledge, which is not 'man's oldest instinct', but 'simply the outcome of the interplay, the encounter [*affrontement*], the junction, the struggle, and the compromise between the instincts' (DE#139 II, 545; EW III, 8). Foucault contrasts Nietzsche sharply with Kant on these questions: 'the conditions of experience and the conditions of the object of experience are completely heterogeneous'. For Kant 'the conditions of the experience and those of the object of experience were identical', whereas for Nietzsche 'between knowledge [*connaissance*] and the world to be known there is as much difference as between knowledge and human nature' (DE#139 II, 546; EW III, 9). He also, drawing on *The Gay Science* §333, contrasts Nietzsche with Spinoza (DE#139 II, 548; EW III, 11). Instead of the philosophical tradition's sense that knowledge is 'congruence, bliss and unity', Nietzsche suggests that the 'root of knowledge' is 'hatred, struggle, power relations' (DE#139 II, 549; EW III, 12). From that, and Foucault recognizes there are conflicting accounts in Nietzsche, he derives the idea of a 'political history of knowledge…a historical analysis of what I call the politics of truth' (DE#139 II, 550; EW III, 13).

This is why Foucault suggests that his work should be situated rather differently from much work in the 'history of ideas, of knowledge, or simply history', and in opposition to 'a certain university or academic tradition of Marxism' which takes the 'subject of knowledge' or 'the traditional philosophical conception of the subject' as an unproblematic starting point. Rather, he suggests that work should be initated from a distinct place: an inquiry which would 'show the historical construction of a subject through a discourse understood as consisting of a set of strategies which are part of social practices' (DE#139 II, 540; EW III, 3–4). Of these, he suggests that 'juridical practices' are the most important of the 'social practices whose historical analysis enables one to locate the emergence of new forms of subjectivity' (DE#139 II, 540; EW III, 4). In distinction to the Marxist account Foucault therefore suggests 'the political and economic conditions of existence are not a veil or an obstacle for the subject of knowledge [*connaissance*] but the means by which subjects of knowledge are formed, and hence relations of truth. There cannot be particular types of subjects of knowledge, orders of truth, or domains of knowledge [*savoir*] except on the basis of political conditions that are the very ground on which the subject, the domains of knowledge, and the relations of truth are formed' (DE#139 II, 552–3;

EW III, 15). Foucault's central analysis of power develops out of his work on knowledge; is born out of his reading of the Greeks; and is theoretically enriched by his engagement with Nietzsche.[42]

Oedipus, Knowledge and Political Power

The final lecture of *Lectures on the Will to Know* looks at the relation between crime, purity and truth, principally through a reading of Sophocles' tragedy *Oedipus Tyrannus*, which is developed in the supplementary manuscript 'The Knowledge of Oedipus'.[43] Defert notes that the manuscript was used as the basis for a lecture given at State University of New York, Buffalo in March 1972; at Cornell University in October 1972 and in Rio in 1973. Defert adds that there are six or seven variant forms of this lecture in Foucault's papers, and that its argument is anticipated in an early text on Deleuze, 'Ariane s'est pendue' (DE#64 I, 767–71).[44] In Buffalo the lecture was part of a seminar entitled 'The Will to Truth in Ancient Greece', with a focus on Hesiod, Homer, Sophocles and Euripides' *Bacchae*, and he also gave a lecture on the history of money which used and elaborated material from this course (C 41/51; see LWK 151–2/158, 157–9/163–5). The Rio lecture was the second of the 'Truth and Juridical Forms' series. Foucault would continually return to Oedipus after this time. A decade later, for instance, he devoted several lectures of *On the Government of the Living* and part of the *Wrong-Doing, Truth-Telling* course to a re-reading of the story.[45]

In the early 1970s Foucault is concerned with questions that occupy him in the course as a whole. Indeed Defert insightfully suggests that this reading sits in relation to the rest of the course rather as the discussion of Velázquez's *Las Meninas* does to *The Order of Things*, because 'it identifies and pieces together all the constitutive elements of the transformation of the juridical-religious truth-test in archaic Greece into the political-juridical truth-report of classical Greece'. It is a crucial dramatization of this stage in 'the history of the production of truth'.[46] This focus means that Foucault takes a distance from other readings. Freud's reading of the story has obviously taken centre-stage, but in 1972 Foucault's friends and colleagues Deleuze and Guattari published the book *Anti-Oedipus*.[47] The Paris lectures precede the book, but in Rio in 1973 Foucault explicitly allies himself to it, and then two years later, at the beginning of *Discipline and Punish*, stresses how much he owes to their work (DP 32 n. 1/309 n. 2).[48] In a discussion in Rio in May 1973 Foucault is accused by Hélio Pellegrino of having an 'extremely curious' position in relation to Oedipus (DE#139 II, 624). Foucault responds by suggesting that 'Oedipus' does not exist for him, and that he is interested in the figure mobilized in the texts *Oedipus Rex* and *Oedipus at Colonnus* by Sophocles, along with other classical Greek sources. Foucault suggests that many analyses of Oedipus – it seems clear he is including Pellegrino – are pre-Deleuzian, though post-Freudian (DE#139 II, 625). Foucault denies the idea that Pellegrino proposes, that Oedipus uncovers 'a fundamental structure of human existence'. Instead, for Foucault, following Deleuze, it is 'a certain kind of constraint, a certain relation of power that society, the family, political power etc. establishes over individuals' (DE#139 II, 625–6).

Freud saw the story of Oedipus in terms of truth and desire, in a universal form, whereas Foucault suggests that it is rather about 'the historical constraints of our system of truth', one to which Freud himself belonged (LWK 185/192; see 189/196). So while Freud concentrates on the sexual aspects, Foucault is more interested in how Oedipus is searching for the truth, and how the play dramatizes the relation between truth, power and right or law [*le droit*]. As Foucault puts it in Rio, rather than Freud's vision of the Oedipus story as 'the oldest fable of our desire and our unconscious...an atemporal truth or a deeply historical truth of our desire...a truth of nature', Foucault follows the Deleuze/Guattari suggestion that it is 'a certain way of containing desire...an instrument of limitation and constraint...an instrument of power, a certain manner by which medical and psychoanalytic power is brought to bear on desire and the unconscious' (DE#139 II, 553–4; EW III, 16).

Foucault is concerned with Oedipus as he is presented in Sophocles' play, rather than the tradition of myth that Sophocles drew upon. He wants to show how the tragedy is

Representative and in a sense the founding instance of a definite type of power and knowledge [*savoir*], between political power and knowledge [*connaissance*], from which our civilization is not yet emancipated. It seems to me that there really is an Oedipus complex in our civilization. But it does not involve our unconsciousness and our desire, nor the relations between desire and the unconscious. If there is an Oedipus complex, it operates not at the individual level but at the collective level; not in connection with desire and the unconscious but in connection with power and knowledge. That is the 'complex' I want to analyse. (DE#139 II, 554–5; EW III, 17)

He continually stresses how 'the power of Oedipus is linked to a knowledge [*savoir*]' and asks 'what is this knowledge linked to the conquest and exercise of power?' (LWK 239/244; see 243/249).

> In Sophocles' play Oedipus basically represents a certain type of what I would call knowledge-and-power, power-and-knowledge. It is because he exercises a certain tyrannical and solitary power, aloof from both the oracle of the gods – which he does not want to hear – and what the people say and want, that, in his craving to govern by discovering for himself, he finds, in the last instance, the evidence of those who have seen... (DE#139 II, 567; EW III, 30)

In *Oedipus*, he suggests, we can find a 'struggle of knowledges and powers [*de savoirs et de pouvoirs*], a struggle between forms of power-knowledge [*pouvoir-savoir*]' (LWK 250/256). As Foucault states, anticipating much later concerns: 'The problem of political knowledge – what one must know to govern and regulate [*redresser*] the city – a problem which is so important in the second half of the fifth century is without doubt born of the final erasure [*l'effacement définitif*] of this ancient figure' (LWK 251/256). There are elements of the test or challenge as a means of generating truth, but also of the witness or testimony (DE#139 II, 557; EW III, 19–20). On these terms, Foucault suggests the play 'is a way of shifting the enunciation of the truth from a prophetic and prescriptive type of discourse to a retrospective one that is no longer characterized by prophecy but, rather, by testimony' (DE#139 II, 561; EW III, 23); it is a form of *enquête*, an inquiry (LWK 230/235, 232/237), what the medieval period will call an *enquête du pays*, an administrative inquiry (LWK 245/250 & n. *).

Outside the main focus on truth, power and knowledge, perhaps the key to Foucault's reading is the analysis of Oedipus as king, as political leader. Foucault stresses the importance of the title of the play – *Oedipus Tyrannus*. As he notes, it is difficult to translate *Tyrannus* (DE#139 II, 562; EW III, 24–5). *Oedipus Rex* or *Oedipus the King* is too neutral; *Oedipus the Tyrant* is overly pejorative.

> Oedipus is the man of power, the man who exercises a certain power. And it is characteristic that the title of Sophocles' play is not *Oedipus the Incestuous*, or *Oedipus the Killer of his Father*, but *Oedipus the King*. What does the kingship of Oedipus mean?
>
> We may note the importance of the thematic of power throughout the play. What is always in question, essentially, is the power of Oedipus, and that is why he feels threatened. (DE#139 II, 562; EW III, 25)

As Foucault insistently stresses, Oedipus does not protest his innocence, or claim that he acted unawares. Rather, 'his only problem is power – can he stay in power? It is this power that is at stake from the beginning of the play to the end'. This is the way Oedipus challenges Tiresias, the blind prophet, and the way he challenges Creon (DE#139 II, 562–3; EW III, 25). When Oedipus is told that he is not the son of Polybus, he worries whether his uncertain birth will deprive him of the power of being king. When his actions are revealed, the people of Thebes say to him 'we were calling you our king'.[49] Foucault notes the imperfect tense 'were calling', and says that this demonstrates that the power he had has been stripped from him (DE#139 II, 563–4; EW III, 26).

In an important analysis of the closing lines of the play, Foucault notes that Creon's final words to Oedipus are 'do not try to be master [*kratein*] anymore' (1522–3). In other words, do not exercise power [*kratos*], the power you had, but have no longer [*akratēsas*], which Foucault says means both 'you who rose to the top and who no longer have that power'. Foucault notes how the final words of the people to Oedipus are 'you who were *kratistos*'.[50] Their opening greeting had been '*o kratunon Oidipous*'.[51] From the present tense of 'Oedipus the all-powerful' to the past of 'you who were at the zenith of power', Foucault argues that 'the entire tragedy has unfolded between these two greetings. It is the tragedy of political power and power-holding' (DE#139 II, 564; EW III, 26). What is interesting is that although Oedipus obviously gained this power over time, the play begins with him in the seat of power, even if most of it retrospectively looks backwards at what has been done.

To describe Oedipus as a *tyrannus* should not be understood strictly as 'tyrant', because Polybus and Laius are also *tyrannus*. However, according to Foucault, Oedipus shows some of the important characteristics of this kind of power. His changing fate, from abandoned child to powerful king is 'characteristic of the figure of the tyrant'. His healing of the city from the Sphinx is described as '*orthosan*, 'to raise up', *anorthōsan polin*; 'to raise up the city". The same expression is used to describe Solon, and also used to describe other tyrants in the seventh and sixth centuries (DE#139 II, 564–5; EW III, 27). To these two positive characteristics – the rise from obscurity, and the benefit to the city – are added negative ones – assuming the city belongs to them alone, and autocratic rule, without regard for custom and *dike*, justice (DE#139 II, 565–6; EW III, 28). Foucault adds that the tyrant is not just characterized by power, but also by knowledge. Oedipus, of course, took power because he was able to solve the riddle of the Sphinx: he demonstrated *sophos*, wisdom. Oedipus is the one who has found, *ēurēka*; but to save Thebes again he will have to find, *euriskein*, again. This is a solitary kind of finding, a finding that needs to see with its own eyes, a continual search for knowledge (DE#139 II, 566; EW III, 28–9).

> Oedipal knowledge, the excess of power and the excess of knowledge were such that he became unnecessary: the circle closed on him or, rather, the two fragments of the tessera were fit together – and Oedipus, in his solitary power, became unnecessary. Once the two fragments were conjoined, the image of Oedipus became monstrous. With his tyrannical power, Oedipus could do too much; with his solitary knowledge, he knew too much. In that state of excess, he was also his mother's husband and his sons' brother. Oedipus is the man of excess, the man who had too much of everything – in his power, his knowledge, his family, his sexuality. (DE#139 II, 567–8; EW III, 30)

There are a number of crucial things we could take from Foucault's reading. The notion of the tyrant, *tyrannus*, and how there is simultaneously a positive and a negative way of reading this is perhaps the most central. It is positive as a rise from ignoble origins, and as someone allowing the *polis* to rise up; it is negative because of the tendency to focus power on the single individual, and the refusal to be bound by custom and justice. This is a play, Foucault claims, about power. But it is also a play about knowledge. And it is when this excess of power, and this excess of knowledge come together that 'the image of Oedipus became monstrous'. We find this in the play, when the messenger is reporting Jocasta's death: 'oh how she wept, mourning the marriage-bed where she let loose that double brood – monsters – husband by her husband, children by her child'.[52]

The use of the terminology of monstrosity to understand political leadership is touched upon here (LWK 231/236), a theme that would be considerably developed in the *Abnormal* lectures. Perhaps remarkably, only at this point does Foucault bring in the sexual theme. It was his excess in familial relations – what Butler calls 'kinship trouble' in her book *Antigone's Claim*[53] – that contribute to his monstrosity. Perhaps because it has been so over-played by Freud Foucault wishes to bypass this aspect. Yet Oedipus's patricide and incest seem crucial to understanding both the basis of his power, and the reasons for his fall. Killing Laius opened up the need for a king, the knowledge deployed in answering the riddle of the Sphinx put Oedipus in that role, his reward was also the marriage-bed of his mother, and the resolution of the play is his realization, his coming to knowledge, of the past. Foucault continues to argue that this linkage between knowledge and power has been obscured in Western thought, through successive recastings since Plato and Sophocles. But this has blinded us to the reality of political operations because we believe that:

> There is an antinomy between knowledge and power. If there is knowledge, it must renounce power. Where knowledge and science are found in their pure truth, there can no longer be any political power. (DE#139 II, 569–70; EW III, 31–2)
>
> This great myth needs to be dispelled. It is this myth Nietzsche began to demolish by showing...that, behind all *savoir*, behind all *connaissance*, what is in play is a struggle for power. Political power is not absent from *savoir*, it is woven together with it. (DE#139 II, 570; EW III, 32)

This political claim would be clearly demonstrated in Foucault's subsequent work. It would come through in his lectures, his writings and his activism, on revolt, punishment, prisons, hospitals and health.

2

Inquiry: Revolt, Ordeal, Proof

In the summer of 1971, Foucault suggested that his 'new preoccupation' with prisons had come 'as a real escape from the weariness [he] was feeling in relation to literature' (DE# 94 II, 203). He had spent the summer doing research on 'the history of juridical practices' at his family home in Vendeuvre (C 38/47), the traces of which can be found in his extensive reading notes now archived at the BNF. The *Théories et institutions pénales* course certainly begins to discuss some of these themes. Delivered between late November 1971 and early March 1972, this was a time when Foucault was involved in some of the most radical political activism of his life, working with the GIP along with groups on health and, less directly, asylums. It was also a time of a number of prison riots in France (see Chapter 5). Indeed, on the opening page of his manuscript for the first lecture of the course, Foucault notes that he will dispense with an introduction and that the *raison d'être* for the course is simple – people should just 'open their eyes', stressing the link between what they will see and his course's content (TIP 3).

Interviews conducted around the period of this course's delivery give some sense of his political views. They include the discussion with students for *Actuel* from November 1971; the debate 'On Popular Justice' with Maoists from 5 February 1972; and the 'Intellectuals and Power' interview with Gilles Deleuze from 4 March 1972. In the first, translated as 'Revolutionary Action: Until Now', but actually published under the Nietzschean title of 'Par-delà le bien et le mal [Beyond Good and Evil]', Foucault discusses issues of repression and revolution with a group of high-school students (DE#98 II, 223–36;

LCP 218–33). He is clear about the political uses of knowledge, but suggests these have a class dimension. 'Official knowledge has always represented political power as arising from the issue of a struggle within a social class... or perhaps as the issue of a struggle generated between the aristocracy and the middle class'. But popular movements are routinely dismissed as being dependent on material conditions: 'famines, taxes, or unemployment' (DE#98 II, 224; LCP 219). He also discusses the workers' inquiries into just such conditions that were conducted in the nineteenth century, which Marx used in his analysis, and which we now know of largely through this second-hand route (DE#98 II, 225; LCP 219–20).

The 1971–2 course goes a long way to show the impact that militant activism had on his theoretical work, and vice versa, though Foucault immediately recognizes that the title of the course – penal theories and institutions – is missing a third term of 'practice' (TIP 3; see 6). The 'Popular Justice' interview, for instance, rehearses this course's analysis of shifting notions of medieval courts (DE#108 II, 342–4; P/K 4–7). His interlocutor 'Pierre Victor', i.e. Benny Lévy, is frustrated at the historian's response, saying he is interested in what happened after 1789, and pushing Foucault to address the twentieth century. Foucault, for his part, refuses to engage with a discussion of China, which he says he knows little about. As the discussion gets tetchy, Foucault questions Lévy what he means by 'the ideology of the proletariat'. When he hears the response 'I mean, by that, the thought of Mao Tse-Tung', Foucault acerbically remarks that 'Sure, but you will agree with me that what is thought by the mass of the French proletariat is not the thought of Mao Tse-Tung and it is not necessarily a revolutionary ideology' (DE#108 II, 360–1; P/K 26).

The course is comprised of two parts. The second half analyses the birth of the medieval state and associated practices of inquiry and ordeal, especially in relation to penal practice. It relates to Foucault's longstanding interest in what he called the 'politics of truth'. From courses given in Rio in 1973 and Louvain in 1981, it is clear Foucault saw the medieval period as crucial to that story. But only now do we have the sustained study of the shift from the ordeal [*l'épreuve*] to the inquiry [*l'enquête*] that those two later courses drew upon. This analysis was preceded by a number of lectures on the *Nu-Pieds* [bare feet] revolts of 1639–40 in Normandy, along with their forcible subjugation by the apparatus of the state, by Cardinal Richelieu and Chancellor Pierre Séguier. The *Nu-Pieds* were 'the salt-makers of the Avranches region, who walked barefoot on the sand'.[1] Given Foucault is often criticized for talking of the positive, productive side of power, but rarely examining it outside of antiquity, or of never showing how resistance takes place or is even possible, this course provides an important corrective, even if his focus becomes largely on its repression.

Revolt: The *Nu-Pieds*

In the detailed analysis of the *Nu-Pieds* revolt against taxation, and in particular the repression that followed, Foucault makes extensive use of documentary materials, especially an 1842 edition of Séguier's journal and an 1876 edition of the memoirs of Alexandre Bigot de Monville.[2] Much of his source material though derives from the work of earlier historians, including Roland Mousnier's *Fureurs paysans* [Peasant uprisings],[3] and most importantly, Boris Porshnev. Porshnev's *Les soulèvements populaires en France de 1623 à 1648* [Popular Revolts in France from 1623 to 1648] was originally published in Russian in 1948, and translated into French in 1963.[4]

Despite saying that there were multiple revolts in the 25-year period he was studying, and that the *Nu-Pieds* revolts were 'fairly typical, and were nothing extraordinary, neither from a quantitative nor a qualitative point of view', Porshnev devotes over 200 pages to his analysis of them. They are remarkable because they show a unified peasant and plebeian uprising, they were specifically anti-fiscal, and because there is a great deal of archival material available concerning them.[5] The archival traces include the Séguier and Monville texts, as well as a wealth of other information, archived in Leningrad, which is where Porshnev did his research.[6]

There was a debate between Porshnev and Mousnier with which Foucault is engaging throughout these lectures. Porshnev's theses were challenged by Mousnier in a 1958 article, later reprinted in his 1970 book *La plume, la faucille et le marteau* [The pen, the hammer and the sickle].[7] Foucault also makes extensive use of Madeleine Foisil's 1970 thesis *La révolte des Nu-Pieds et les révoltes normandes de 1639*.[8] Foisil was a student of Mousnier, and it would appear that contemporary Francophone debates have largely followed the lead of Mousnier and his students.[9] Mousnier's own analysis, in *Fureurs paysans*, notes that it is indebted to Foisil's work.[10] There is therefore a specifically French nature to both the material and to the debate around it: of these books, only Mousnier's *Peasant Uprisings* is available in English.[11]

Why did Foucault find these events, and to an extent the debate over their importance, of such importance that he was prepared to devote seven whole lectures to their analysis? Porshnev's claim is that the revolts were predominantly about taxation, what he calls the 'the fiscal yoke [*joug*]' and that they were spontaneous peasant-led revolts against a situation that put them in intolerable poverty.[12] The revolts were not aimed at the King, but at those who benefited from feudal rents, that is land-owners and also a significant number of the bourgeoisie, the new capitalists. Porshnev suggests that feudalism was structured on the extraction of revenue from the serfs by the land-owners, and from the sixteenth century on, the monarchical state enabled the levy, collection and distribution of this rent, and it was one of the mechanisms by which the state became increasingly centralized.[13] Thus the monarchy was not a break with the feudal system, but increasingly its agent. Capitalism, at this time was isolated and marginal, and the bourgeois class therefore existed in relation to the dominant feudal structures.[14] The bourgeoisie are thus embedded in the system, and do not play an especially important role in the class struggle at the beginning of the centralized monarchy. But on the contrary, the peasantry *do* play an active role, and the *Nu-Pieds* can be understood as a revolutionary political force. As Claude-Olivier Doron notes, in the period 1960–70 Maoism insisted on the important link to be forged between peasants and workers, and this re-evaluation of the role of the peasantry historically fitted this: it was one of the reasons he suggests it fits with Foucault's interest and analysis.[15] Porshnev's analysis fits within his wider historical work on feudalism, most of which is only available in Russian.[16]

In contrast, Mousnier suggests that while 'many of [Porshnev's] observations and conclusions have a genuine scientific value and several of the arguments in support of his theses are strong', he rejects his work in general terms because he thinks that he forces the facts and relations 'into the framework of a Marxist theory, which the topic explodes [*que la matière fait éclater*]'.[17] The key issue is class. For Mousnier, class only emerged as a central theme in the eighteenth century. Porshnev sees the *Nu-Pieds* as a kind of 'pre-proletarian' class. Mousnier characterizes his view as arguing that 'French society of the seventeenth century was a feudal society, characterized by the predominance of feudal economic forms and means of production'. Capitalist means of production were only found in isolated instances, in some towns. He thinks it is only with the French Revolution that feudalism was dealt a 'mortal blow'.[18] Nonetheless, in these revolts there are traces of kinds of struggles that would follow. Mousnier argues that 'these theses, solidly constructed, contain plenty of partial truths'.[19] But the overall picture cannot be accepted, and he thinks that the idea of a 'peasant bloc against the lords' is no less plausible than a 'class front' against the peasants.[20] He goes on to claim 'if the nobility were, as Porshnev thinks, the active guardians of the "feudal-absolutist order", it must be recognized that they played that role very badly'.[21] Rather, Mousnier emphasizes the fractures within the 'blocs' or 'fronts', stressing differences and tensions, lack of coordination and absence of ties. Sometimes, the nobles, bourgeoisie or minor royalty played an underhand role in struggles. For him, it is 'a vertical division of society, more important than a horizontal stratification',[22] which sounds odd but seems to mean that the connections were local and located, rather than general and structural.[23]

Essentially, Porshnev proposed a class analysis of this period, and gave the peasantry a major role; while Mousnier thought that seeing class-parallels with later proletarian struggles was anachronistic. This is not to say he did not recognize their impoverished position. He suggests that the rebels comprised 'representatives of all three of the main orders of society, and of many "estates", many different strata of each order', but that each of them would be at the 'very bottom' of a 'scale of wealth – the economic scale'. As he summarizes: 'This was a revolt of poor men, or men who were relatively poor, anyway, whatever might be the social esteem enjoyed by their estate'.[24] Nonetheless, this does not mean he is in anyway supportive. The overall summary is damning: 'Not only was this a retrogressive political movement, of a particularist character, aimed against the development of the modern absolutist state, with its centralizing and unifying function; we can find no trace in this anti-tax struggle of any social program'.[25]

Mousnier says that 'the Marxist synthesis of Porshnev does not seem to me to conform to the facts' and his position can only be achieved by 'abstraction from several specific facts [*faits caractéristiques*]'.[26] In sum, 'a theory can only be accepted by a historian if it can integrate all the categories of relevant facts [*fait concernés*], not when it takes only a certain number'.[27] As Doron characterizes it, for Porshnev, 'seventeenth century France remained characterized by a feudal system, and the monarchical state was a brake on the development of capitalism'. Mousnier questioned the use of the term feudalism and suggested that the ground rents collected in the seventeenth century had nothing to do with 'feudal ground rent'.[28] But the debate need not be an either/or. Perry Anderson uses both Mousnier and Porshnev in his work *Passages from Antiquity to Feudalism*, and has this to say of Porshnev: 'Contrary to the intimations of his Western colleagues, it is not a rigid "dogmatism" that is his major failing, but an over-fertile "ingenuity" not always adequately restrained by the discipline of evidence; yet the same trait is in another respect what makes him an original and imaginative historian.'[29]

Like Anderson, but with considerably more detail, Foucault steers a course between these two positions. There are archival traces of his very detailed notes on Porshnev's book, as well as Mousnier's critique of it, read in *La plume, la faucille et le marteau*, in Paris.[30] His engagement with these debates is crucial in understanding his position in relation to the material, and in seeing what he is doing that goes beyond both figures. In general terms Foucault is closer to Porshnev politically and to Mousnier historical-conceptually. Like Anderson and Mousnier, he is suspicious of the overarching themes that Porshnev develops on the basis of limited and selected evidence, and that class relations are not the major structuring force. But the emphasis on struggle, power and broader politics are things that attract him to the topic, and to Porshnev's account. His interest in the suppression develops an analysis beyond the earlier work he is engaging with, and shows a specific focus on the documentary sources. In addition, it is intriguing, given the proximity of Foucault to Maoism at this time, that his choice of focus is a peasant, rather than worker, uprising.

However it becomes increasingly clear that Foucault's principal interest is not so much in the revolt itself, but the reaction of the authorities, the subjugation of the peasants, and the emergence of a new repressive State or system. This is not a theme especially stressed by Mousnier, and Porschnev's treatment is confined to the last chapter of his analysis, despite both of them relying principally on the archives of Chancellor Séguier for their accounts.[31] There is a fuller treatment in Foisil's thesis.[32] If Foucault's analysis of a revolt seems to indicate the stakes and possibilities of resistance, it quickly becomes a study of the crushing of such hopes. Cardinal Richelieu and Séguier are the key figures here, and Foucault thinks it is important that he can discern the 'first great deployment of the "arms" of the State independent of the person of the King' (TIP 7); a characteristic Foucault describes as 'armed justice' and which links Richelieu to Louis XIV (TIP 22, 40). Richelieu is an intriguing figure because of his links between the aristocracy, the church and state. Born as Armand Jean du Plessis in the late sixteenth century, heir to the duke of Richelieu and Fronsac, he became a bishop and then cardinal of the church, and was foreign secretary and then Chief Minister to Louis XIII. His *Testament Politique* is an important text in the practice of statecraft.[33] He perhaps represents best the tangled relations between these elements of French elite society. His protégé, Cardinal Mazarin, would serve as Chief Minister to the young Louis XIV in the first years of his reign. Yet it was Séguier who was tasked by the King, Louis XIII, with putting down the rebellion in mid-December 1639, and he arrived in person in Rouen on 2 January 1640.[34] Mousnier notes that 'the king's absolute power over the armed forces and the judiciary' was delegated to Séguier. Just over a week later, several of the agitators were executed, and several more imprisoned. In February he moved onto Caen, then Bayeux and other locations until March, when the uprising was over.[35]

Foucault underlines that 'armed justice is not an institution, but an operation: a series of operations which cut across, and to a certain extent displace, existing institutions' (TIP 41). It is significant that Foucault stresses the clash of competing exercises of power: this is not power imposed simply from above. The study of the *Nu-Pieds* is one of a sequence of 'refusals of the law and struggles against power' (TIP 5). But this is not to set power and law on one side and the peasant refusals, struggles or resistance on the other. The King, the State, individuals such as Séguier, and the peasants all exercise power. 'For the *Nu-Pieds*, the rejection of the law is at the same time a law (it is like the other side of the law...); the rejection of justice is like the exercise of justice; the struggle against power is a kind of power' (TIP 30). This emphasis on power allows him to use both Porshnev and Mousnier's insights, but without being bound by either's overall framework. He takes from Mousnier the emphasis on different groups, clashing competing interests, and fragmentation; which he sees reflected in the overall contours of Porshnev's account that something fundamental is being developed here.

Foucault stresses that the army is being used to put down an internal revolt, far from a contested frontier, rather than an existing local force being used: Foucault contrasts Aquitaine, on the Spanish border, with Normandy. In Aquitaine in 1635 a revolt was suppressed by a governor with local forces already stationed nearby (TIP 42). Although Normandy is on the northern coast of France, and so close to England, the garrisons for an English invasion would have been further north, more in the Pas-de-Calais region. Because there were no troops nearby, they needed to be raised, and the resources for this had to come from the central state. A division between town and countryside, and the poor and the aristocracy begins to be clearly marked (TIP 43, 45). These might be mutually reinforcing divisions, but the existence of the rural poor challenges any simple sense of a divide, and the risk was that the poor in towns and rural areas supported each other, as they had in Aquitaine (TIP 44). Alternatively the emerging urban bourgeoisie might find common cause with the poor against the aristocratic, feudal system (TIP 46).

The events in Normandy should be followed, Foucault suggests, 'at the level of manifestations of power' (TIP 47). The armed suppression operates first, with the legal system following later. This is the gap Foucault mentioned – an unchecked use of power to assert and protect the king and the nascent state (TIP 42). How is this 'sending in of the army and the retaking of civic power' manifested? (TIP 47). Foucault stresses that the 'ceremonies, rites and gestures *mean nothing*. They are not addressed by a semiology, but by an analysis of forces (their interplay, their strategy). The marks which appear here must be analysed not [through] a semiotics of elements, but by a dynastic of forces' (TIP 47). 'Dynastic' is an important term which, at this time, though postdating the 'Nietzsche, Genealogy, History' essay, appears as a possible alternative name to genealogy to describe an approach to sit alongside archaeology (see also PS 86/83–4, and less directly PS 212/206).[36] In a September 1972 interview Foucault clarified the relation:

> What I call the 'archaeology of knowledge [*savoir*] is precisely the mapping [*repérage*] and description of types of discourse and what I call the 'dynastic of knowledge [*savoir*]' is the relation which exists between these grand types of discourses which we can observe in a culture and the historical conditions, economic conditions, [and] political conditions for their appearance and formation. Thus, *The Order of Things* led to *The Archaeology of Knowledge*, and what I am in the process of examining now is at the level of the dynastic of knowledge. (DE#119 II, 406)

Sometimes 'genealogy' and 'the dynastic' seem to be alternative names for the same process, but a detailed editorial note indicates several issues to be explored.[37] One is that the contrast with semiology is very strong, and that this approach owes more to Nietzsche, read through Deleuze, than to Roland Barthes. Nonetheless, as the note continues to suggest, 'power is still here studied as a form of *representation* (manifestations, gestures, ceremonies, symbols, etc.)'.[38] In other words, though the approach is different to a semiological one, the things being examined for the balance of forces are the same kind of material. Foucault suggests that Séguier provides both a 'political distribution of repression', and 'a theatrical representation of power: that is a development [*déroulement*] in time and space, in a visible and ceremonial form, of men, signs and discourse, through which the exercise of power takes place' (TIP 7). Foucault describes this as the 'theatre of power' (TIP 49).

Doron suggests that both Porshnev and Mousnier stress the question of time, especially the past, and long processes of 'the development of capitalism, class struggle or monarchical institutions'. Porshnev provides 'a reversed bourgeois reading'.[39] Foucault, in contrast, bases his reading on an event (TIP 41).[40] This event might be of a sequence of events, 'a continuous series of refusals of law and struggles against power' (TIP 5), but they cannot be easily grouped together as part of an overall account. The heterogeneous, singular and discontinuities between events need to be stressed. For Foucault these events give a privileged insight into relations of power, yet 'it is not a pure and simple struggle against established power' (TIP 27). A key aspect of the event is the 'chronological gap [*décalage*] between the arrival of the army and the entry of justice into the scene' (TIP 41; 57). Foucault then outlines a quite detailed chronology of the events of the repression. Foucault presents the successive elements of the repression as a ceremony, a sequence of scenes or theatrical acts (TIP 58), though it seems this was much more clearly delineated in a lecture given in Minnesota on 7 April 1972, shortly after the end of this course. That lecture, entitled 'Cérémonie, théâtre et politique au XVIIe siècle' was previously only available in an English summary made by Stephen Davidson, in relatively hard-to-find conference proceedings.[41] Foucault clearly drew on material from the first half of this course in his lecture, even though he reframed it for the specific event.

The first stage is the 'sending of the army, and the army alone', where 'power designates the population as an enemy; it disqualifies it as a subject' (TIP 58). The army executes people immediately, tortures them – the French word is *supplices*, designating spectacular, exemplary punishments, rather than the judicial practice or *torture* – and tramples on the rights of the population in terms of billeting troops (TIP 58). Power does not recognize the people as either part of the existing social order, nor '*another* (foreign) power': 'while remaining inside the kingdom, you are an "enemy"' (TIP 58). This gives rise to the idea of the 'interior enemy', the enemy within, a practice which is clearly marked before the notion itself appears (TIP 59).'Repressive practices designated certain forms of struggles for power or struggle against the exercise of power as acts of hostility', and those that conducted them as 'enemies' (TIP 59). This repressive practice forms the model for the later treatment of diverse social groups, including 'paupers, the unemployed, beggars, vagabonds, the seditious' and so on (TIP 59).

The second stage of this act is that after the military crackdown on the countryside, local dignitaries send delegations to Paris, the Archbishop of Rouen writes to Richelieu and Séguier, and there are also instances of local *parlements* 'not registering edicts and not reconstituting offices' in mild opposition to the rule of Paris (TIP 60). (*Parlements* here has a sense of regional courts, rather than parliaments.) Foucault suggests that these elements of power play a role of *freins* – checks, brakes or bridles: they can function as 'moderators of royal power' (TIP 61). Drawing on Claude de Seyssel Foucault outlines the traditional 'theory of three checks' on the King: religion, justice and the police (TIP 61).[42] (Police here should be understood in a broader sense than the modern uniformed force for the prevention and detection of crime; it is more officials and civil servants.) In this instance, local bishops, *parlements* and the town mayor could potentially act as limits on absolute royal power, but Séguier largely bypasses such processes, preventing people from going to Paris to appeal and saying decisions were already made; refusing to hear the Archbishop's petition; and denying the 'three checks' (TIP 61–2). Instead he made an appeal to the 'Final judgment', which Foucault describes as 'one of the most formidable and fantastic manifestations of power that can be understood', partly because it implied that the king was not, himself, subject to the laws of the kingdom, nor to the Holy Roman Emperor, but was directly led by God (TIP 62). It was an example of royal absolutism, a type of power that would 'sweep aside all checks, and all limitations (institutional, religious or traditional) to royal power' (TIP 63). This was a power that could make stark divisions of people, which could disqualify the rebels as political subjects and see them not as another example of power, within civil order, but as 'enemies of the king' (TIP 63). 'Power is repression before it is guaranteed' (TIP 64).

The third stage is when 'civil power' appears, when Séguier and other state officials enter Rouen. Foucault stresses it is not just the men themselves, but 'the bodies to which they belong or the social groups they represent' which are important. These figures had remained backstage [*dans la coulisse*] while the army resolved the situation; now at the beginning of the New Year, on 2 January 1640, civil power makes its entrance (TIP 67). The army falls under the control of the Chancellor, who unites 'the functions of war and justice', a 'union [*jonction*] that is marked by a series of measures, gestures, "formalities"' (TIP 68). But this is not a standard use of justice, since Séguier does not consult others in reaching judgments, hears witnesses but not the accused, and can pass sentence verbally rather than in written form: a violation of rules that was considered extremely seriously by contemporary jurists (TIP 68). It is not just that justice and the military are brought together, but that the lines between them are blurred: 'not subject to the privileges of one nor the rules of the other...Beyond the power of justice and the force of combat, something which is repressive power' (TIP 68–9). Foucault allows that this is hardly the first time that a revolt has been put down violently, but stresses there is something new here, because the violence is not employed during the struggle, but 'deployed when everything has already been returned to order', the revolt had already been put down and the people had surrendered (TIP 69). Repression thus becomes a third aspect to the traditional ones of the sovereign monarchy – justice and the army (TIP 69).'The king can and must dispense justice between individuals who are his subjects; he can and must provide the defence of his subjects against their enemies; he can and must repress sedition from his subjects' (TIP 69).

A second element of this third stage, or act, is important. While these actions of the Chancellor are a crucial moment in the development of a 'purely repression function of the State', and appear linked to the duties of the king, this function is employed without the direct involvement of the king. Séguier is exercising this power directly, even though authorized by the Conseil du Roi (TIP 70). The king becomes increasingly detached from the actual practices, and Séguier and those like him' represent or rather constitute the whole of State power...In the place of the absent king the visible body of the State appears [*s'avance*]' (TIP 71). Foucault stresses the economic elements of this exercise of power: the new people are embedded in a feudal system of ground rents, imposition of levies and taxes, distribution of rents, pensions and roles (TIP 71–2). As such, he suggests, 'a State apparatus exists, which is a fiscal apparatus' (TIP 72).[43] Functionaries and financiers take the place of the king, as the repressive state recalibrates justice and the army.

The fourth stage concerns particular actions taken by Séguier in his role, suspending existing local authorities and appointing temporary commissaries to act. While not making new institutions, new people from Paris were appointed to offices, and the reorganization changed the relation between the crown and these suspended bodies (TIP 73–5). While the *parlements* still maintained a 'feudal definition of the body politic as a "court" of the sovereign; the king already refers [to] a definition of the body politic as a State apparatus' (TIP 74). The *parlements* and the mayor shift from being autonomous agents to operatives on behalf of the central authority; their legitimacy does not come from local sources, but from the king (TIP 75). Some of the personnel changes were to do with familial relations, but others were simply to do with Paris people being closer to central power. But even when the same men were left in place, with the same functions, they would come to use them differently (TIP 76).

In the final scene of the enactment – clearer in the Minnesota summary than the Paris manuscript – Foucault gives examples of military and compensation measures that were put in place. These meant that there was a disarmament of local forces, and selective concentration of military resources, as well as a major revenue distribution towards the central state, raised by a combination of direct and indirect taxation (TIP 76–8). The military and financial 'double guarantee' enabled the state to pardon the population as a whole for the revolt – the key figures having, of course, been executed. The rich were pardoned 'because they were the financial and military guarantors of order; the poor were pardoned as taxpayers and producers of the fiscal levy' (TIP 79). This was a system which Foucault stresses was 'unstable, despite its logic, because it rested much too much on feudal structures' (TIP 79). He closes this analysis by stressing that in time 'all the functions which appeared in the course of these events, and which were exercised punctually, in temporary measures, in gestures, ceremonies, etc. – all these functions the state still entrusted to the bourgeoisie, the local nobility, to *parlements*, in the feudal form of arrangement [*l'engagement*]' (TIP 79; see 88). With the Fronde civil wars later in the seventeenth century it became clear that they needed to be centralized further, in 'a specialized State apparatus'. The control of populations was too important to be left to 'uncertain allies', and needed to be 'by an instrument solidly held in the hands of the State' (TIP 79; see 92).

The visible manifestation of power here is the State, no longer the King (TIP 86, 88). Foucault's emphasis on the visual, the ritual, the spoken performance and the ceremonial perhaps suggests that, as well as Ernst Kantorowicz's *The King's Two Bodies*, whose influence on Foucault is widely acknowledged, we should also be examining his *Laudes Regiae: A Study in Liturgical Acclamations and Mediaeval Ruler Worship*.[44] Kantorowicz shows how inscriptions, texts and music of rituals and ceremonies can shed considerable light on political and religious power. The theme returns in *Discipline and Punish*, where Foucault notes 'some of the characteristics of the liturgy of *supplice* – above all, the importance of a ritual that was to deploy its pomp [*son faste*] in public' (DP 60/49). While the visual, spectacular nature of exemplary power would play a central role in the opening scene of *Discipline and Punish*, in these lectures we can begin to see Foucault searching for formulations that traced the emergence of a less visible, more anonymous form of power. There are initial examples here, but it is developed in much more detail in the 1972–3 course, *The Punitive Society*, where de-personalized systems and relations become his predominant focus.

The events outlined in this first part of this course are, for Foucault, fundamental to the emergence of a new system of the exercise of political power, which becomes the idea of penal justice. 1639–40 marks a crucial moment in the treatment of a wide range of people in society. Foucault highlights the 'unemployed, vagabonds, adventurers [*hommes sans aveu*], the banished, brigands', and says they are subjected to conscription, imprisonment or as a labour force for major works [*les grands travaux*] (TIP 93). Foucault had, of course, discussed the 'great confinement' in relation to the mad in *History of Madness*, and these were precisely the kind of people who accompanied the mad into the new prisons, workhouses and asylums. Here he indicates that putting people to work serves the interests of nascent capitalism (TIP 94). The wealthy are protected in multiple ways, with the police becoming more and more a centralized force that could intervene directly in ways the army would find difficult; and the development of imprisonment and deportation, 'that is the *subtraction* of a fringe of the population' (TIP 95). 'The police and imprisonment are two correlative phenomena' (TIP 95), and even though the prison's 'economic role is marginal', it is still fundamental to the development of capitalist production. This is because of its role in the repressive State apparatus, and especially in terms of a centralized judicial system, its control of the kinds of seditions that took place in the sixteenth and seventeenth centuries, which could be dangerous to capitalism (TIP 96, 101–2).

Foucault suggests that this is the period when 'the juridico-military form of state power is subsumed [*relevée*] by an administrative form' (TIP 87). These two forms of the state have different relations to being their subject. In the first, being a subject meant an ability to use the judicial system but a duty to accept it, a protection from external enemies by an army, but a duty to serve in it; in the latter it means having a role in 'financial, economic, judicial and military' decisions, taken in the name of everyone and applicable to all (TIP 87). This is not to say that the administrative State apparatus only appears at this time, and its history can be traced much further back, which is what he does in the remainder of the course. But there is an explicit moment of the use of repressive force by the state at this time that is singularly striking (TIP 88–9). It illustrates the importance of the emergence of a centralized army, which could often be used for suppression of internal problems as much as to fight external ones, but it also highlights a tension between rent and tax (TIP 93–4).[45] Séguier does not resolve these contradictions, and actually makes them worse and more acute. But he highlights them, and that for Foucault is crucial: 'Séguier's repression is a suture point between a real contradiction in the exercise of power at the end of feudalism and a characteristic contradiction in the role of the State in the initial development of capitalism' (TIP 92).

Foucault therefore suggests that the popular revolts are crucial to the history of the state and economic transformation, but neither in the way that Porshnev sees them nor how Mousnier sees them. Porshnev sees them as part of wider trends and resistances in feudalism, with the nobility upholding their existing position, a class analysis indebted to Marxism; Foucault stresses a discontinuity. Mousnier sees them as relatively minor events within a wider shift to the emergence of the monarchical state; Foucault stresses their crucial pivotal role. The *Nu-Pieds* revolts are situated by Foucault at the dividing line between the 'repressive feudal system' and the 'repressive state system' – literally so, in a diagram included in the course manuscript (TIP 24).[46] The point of the diagram is that there are two overlapping transitions, each stretching across centuries. The first is from feudal justice (of the church and lord) to royal justice, its cusp is dated to the thirteenth century; the second between the repressive feudal system and the repressive state system, the transition point is 1639.

The reading of these small, perhaps marginal events, thus says a great deal about how Foucault views the emergence of the disciplinary society within the wider conjuncture of the demise of feudalism, the birth of capitalism and the emergence of the monarchical, and then the modern state. But it is read through the lens of analysis of power relations, rather than historical materialism. The 'new repressive system' is linked to the development of capitalism in a range of ways: the strategic effect of 'a counter-attack to popular seditions'; the 'jurisdictional effect of its decisions' in favour of capitalism; the 'economic effect of its functioning', which is directed towards 'production, and the mobilized capital of the bourgeoisie'; and the 'institutional effect' where many of its elements were part of the 'political system of the capitalist and bourgeois State of the nineteenth century' (TIP 105). As such, it anticipates future political forms, and both reinforces new developments and makes possible future ones. The apparatus of the repressive monarchical state 'is structurally linked to feudality (and its centralized form)...[but] is functionally linked to the development of capitalism' (TIP 105). Four key and interlinked processes are at stake: 'the requirements of the formation of capital; the disappropriation of the powers of justice; the separation between the exercise of justice and fiscal levies; the transfer of the exercise of justice to the administrative power of the state' (TIP 106).

Ordeal: From Germanic Law to the Monarchical State

This analysis of the *Nu-Pieds*, their suppression and the wider lessons to be drawn from it occupies the first seven lectures of the course. The final six lectures are on early Germanic law, the emergence of the monarchical state and the medieval practices. The second half of the course provides essential background to the 1972–3 course, and indeed for *Discipline and Punish*. While the shift from the reading of *Nu-Pieds* to the Middle Ages is rather abrupt in the manuscript (TIP 114), the point is that Foucault wants to go back and do a genealogy of the institutions that together form this repressive state apparatus, in fiscal, political and military registers. It thus forms a central element of his work. Foucault suggests that the new repressive system, in place in the seventeenth century, is opposed to the older one by a 'certain number of fundamental traits':

– Its position in regard to private property: it protects it, but it is not the object of an appropriation.
– Its position in relation to taxation: it guarantees it, but does not operate as a levy itself.
– Its position in relation to political power. It is an element of it, it derives from it, but it does not constitute an instance of it [*Il en est un element; il en derive, il n'en constitue pas une instance*].
– Its position in regard to capitalist production: while the ancient system acted as a brake, this one favours it. (TIP 111)

How did this situation arise? It becomes clear that if 1639–40 marks an emblematic moment of emergence, the lineage of the concepts and practices stretches much further back. And, of course, the system the new one replaces needs to be interrogated. What was the earlier model of the Middle Ages? To be clear, by the Middle Ages Foucault means a period from around the end of the twelfth century, sometimes called the high Middle Ages. The period before that, and after the collapse of the Western Roman Empire is what he examines through Germanic law. It is what is sometimes called 'the Dark Ages' in English. Foucault is interested in how there is a transition around the thirteenth century to the great monarchical, absolutist state. It is to that deeper history that the second half of the course turns, outlining both the system that the new supplants, but also its roots and descent into the present. That is a history that is continued in the lecture course of the following year on *The Punitive Society*. A variety of economic, political and military apparatuses emerge, to be doubled and reinforced by the repressive use of power. The seventeenth century system is comprised of two key elements: a judicial apparatus, and a state apparatus.

To undertake the genealogy of these practices, Foucault explores a wide set of themes, including legal codes, crimes and punishments, different mechanisms of rule in medieval Europe and pre-state political formations. He is especially interested in Germanic law, and its gradual replacement by Roman legal codes in the high Middle Ages. Ancient Germanic law worked on the basis of the test or ordeal. These were disputes between the accused and the injured party, the victim or a member of their family. The opposition between two sides was put to the test, a kind of duel. Law is characterized by a struggle [*lutte*] between the victim and the accused, with a formal arrangement guaranteed by the judicial apparatus, rather than the legal system making the judgment itself (TIP 115). The judicial act is 'not organized by peace and truth' but by 'a war according to rules' (TIP 116). As Foucault suggests in Rio, 'it was a law in which the system of inquiry did not exist; disputes between individuals were settled by the challenge of the proof [*jeu de l'épreuve*]' (DE#139 II, 572; EW III, 35).

Only in two cases, Foucault suggests, did the wider public get involved: 'treason, desertion and military cowardice' and sexual transgression (TIP 118). In Rio he says 'treason and homosexuality' (DE#139 II, 572; EW III, 35). Foucault's claim is based on J.J. Thonissen, *L'organisation judiciaire, le droit pénal et la procedure pénale de la loi saliques*.[47] Thonissen is actually making a narrower point about capital crimes, but with slightly wider examples. The suggestion is that the *lex antiqua* does not talk of military crimes, ones directed towards the 'security of the nation', or 'the most serious offences against morals or public decency'. Thonissen suggests that these were crimes of such gravity that they could not be addressed by making amends, and so were treated outside that system. These were crimes punished by the 'ultimate penalty [*dernier supplice*] by virtue of national custom'. This is where Foucault gets his list: 'treason, desertion, cowardice, regicide, *les moeurs infâmes*'. The latter might be narrowly understood as sodomy, but is really any nefarious or 'infamous' moral transgression. Foucault notes two parallels between political treason and sexual offence. First, that the same punishment was given to traitors and those who had violated a virgin: blinding and castration; and second that 'the crime of sodomy was joined to that of *lèse-majesté* [injured majesty] in the thirteenth century' (TIP 118).[48] Curious cases, and curious that Foucault does not make more of the sexual, given the way his work would go in just a few years time.

Foucault's point is that, outside these two exceptions, there were only individual litigants (TIP 118); legal disputes were 'a kind of private, individual war'. Justice was not at stake: the 'penal procedure was merely the ritualization of that conflict between individuals...law was thus a regulated way of making war...the ritual form of war' (DE#139 II, 572; EW III, 35). This need not involve one side killing the other, as elaborate forms of compensation could be developed to make good a wrong [*tort*], including the *wergild* (man price) and the *fredum*, a fine for obtaining pardon in place of revenge (TIP 133). The claim is that there is a distinction between a wrong and its vengeance and a transgression [*faute*]. Ritualized war could be brought to an end, 'one of the two adversaries would buy back the right to have peace, to escape the possible revenge of his adversary' (DE#139 II, 573; EW III, 36). Here, though, Foucault's point is that justice is not imposed on a dispute. Rather, justice 'is constituted by the will of the individuals in dispute' (TIP 117).

Foucault's summary of the history of the Middle Ages, with Germanic kingdoms established on the ruins of the classical Roman Empire, and the balance between old Germanic law and Roman law is necessarily brief (TIP 114; 132–3). In Rio he discusses how Roman law was dominant in the Merovingian and Carolingian empires, but that Germanic law reappeared when they collapsed (DE#139 II, 574; EW III, 36). Others could add substantial nuance to this account, and we might want to have a fuller analysis of the disrupted legacies of Roman legal codes, which existed only in fragmentary form until the rediscovery of Justinian's codifications in the late eleventh century: Foucault merely hints at how the Justinian code 'gave a theoretical model to crimes of *lèse-majesté*' (TIP 132). Foucault's point is that in, for example feudal law, it was the Germanic codes, and 'the system of the test' that was dominant (DE#139 II, 574; EW III, 37). He gives various examples of oaths by others (TIP 129), of elaborate verbal formulas, of 'magico-religious tests of the oath' and 'famous corporal, physical tests called ordeals'. Foucault gives various examples – walking on hot coals, or being thrown into water with limbs bound together (DE#139 II, 575; EW III, 38); boiling water, 'hot water, cold water, the cauldron, the hot iron, the cross', and judicial duels (TIP 129). Essentially, he suggests, all these were 'a matter of combat, of deciding who was the stronger…the trial was nothing more than the regulated, ritualized continuation of war' (DE#139 II, 574–5; EW III, 37–8). Foucault then outlines various characteristics of the test, stressing its binary characteristic: someone would win, and someone lose; victory or defeat, rather than a balanced judgment; without the need for some neutral third party or authority to arbitrate or judge. 'In its theatre, the judgment is still a struggle, an episode of war, a rivalry' (TIP 130). Crucial to all this is that the truth is not the question at stake, it was much more a case of strength determining right, with the test as a 'mechanical operator [*opérateur*] of the law, a shifter [or switcher, *commutateur*] of force into law' (DE#139 II, 576–7; EW III, 39).

Some of these duels were, in a sense, merely smaller forms of the private wars that dominated the Middle Ages. These could be wars between feudal lords and their sovereigns, which often became public wars with organized permanent armies, out of which unified and 'national' states began to emerge. But there were also wars that flared from disputes between villeins and within the bourgeoisie (TIP 130). Resistance to private wars was 'one of the most important phenomena of the penal system of the Middle Ages. Private war did not fall outside the law, while it is a "marginalized" or "isolated [*enclavée*]" form of the law, but it is a form of the law' (TIP 131). This begins to change with the dawn of the high Middle Ages, and Foucault suggests that 'the influence of Roman law was linked to the growth of royal power', because it 'gave to monarchs a technical instrument, an institutional tool, and also a theoretical justification for putting in place a public force [*puissance*] intervening in judicial matters and pursuing in its name infractions of the law' (TIP 132).

From Feudalism to Capitalism

Several things start to emerge in feudal society in the twelfth century. The first key change is that instead of legal disputes being contestation between individuals, brought by one against the other, now there is a legal process 'imposed from above...a power external to them, imposing itself as a judicial and political power'. This means a new figure emerges: the prosecutor, as a representative of 'the sovereign, the king, or the master'. This was 'a power that was injured by the mere fact that an offence or a crime had occurred' (DE#139 II, 579; EW III, 42; see TIP 188). It follows from this the nature of penality changes, no longer in terms of a wrong or harm [*dommage*] done to an individual, or a violation of feudal rights, but 'as an infraction against public order' (TIP 185). It is not that new offences are created, but that they are seen in a different way. This is, Foucault suggests, 'a crucial [*capital*] event in the history of penality' (TIP 186).

The king is thus represented twice, both by the prosecutor and the judge: 'it is as sovereign that he judges and it is as sovereign that he accuses' (TIP 189). And with the emergence of a new figure, there was also a new concept: the infraction. The infraction replaces the wrong [*tort*] committed by one individual against another. The infraction was done 'to order, to the state, to law, to society, to sovereignty, to the sovereign' (DE#139 II, 580; EW III, 43). The King is seen as 'injured [*lésé*] by all crime, he takes the position of the injured individual', and so as victim can become co-accuser. The victim is then a victim in a double sense: as a private individual and as subject of the King (TIP 188–9).

Finally, alongside these changes, there was the idea that the sovereign was not just the injured party, or the one who prosecuted, but also the one to whom compensation was owed. And with the confiscation of property, the 'great emerging monarchies' were able 'to enrich and enlarge their holdings'. Foucault says that this was achieved by the sovereign, rather than 'the state', which emerges somewhat later, though we might want to use a different term to 'sovereign' for the same reason. Nonetheless his point is clear: there is a wider 'political background' to this legal transformation (DE#139 II, 580; EW III, 43).

There is also an economic one. While stressing that seizing goods during warfare was crucial, Foucault is more interested in how 'judicial actions and contests' allowed goods to circulate. He notes again that the disputes were between individuals, and that figures of power were used to 'ensure [*constate*] the regularity of the procedure', rather than to act in judgment. 'There was no autonomous judicial power, and no judicial power in the hands of the holder of military and political power'. It was because this 'right to regulate and control' was so useful, because it allowed the accumulation of wealth, that the powerful sought to control it (DE#139 II, 579; EW III, 41–2). 'Justice is an element of capital power – because judgments fixed rights, properties, fees [*redevances*], inheritances, dependencies [subordinations] – but also because it operates in itself as an economically important levy [*prélèvement*]'. What this means is that 'the distribution of justice takes part in the circulation of goods', because of the control of a range of contracts, both civil ones such as marriage, inheritance, and so on; and criminal ones for infraction, theft, illicit earnings (TIP 133). In sum, civil justice thus 'controls the circulation of wealth', while criminal justice 'contributes to the circulation of wealth' (TIP 134).

Initially, this emergent criminal code had risks for justice, not so much for judging a serf, but certainly for a rich man or a noble, because the judgment might not be obeyed, it might precipitate a private war, or because it might be appealed and lead to a judicial duel between jurisdictions (TIP 134). Yet criminal fines could be a major source of revenue, either by making amends or confiscating goods. Confiscation was either the full penalty in the case of suicides in some regions, or certain forms of fraud, or as a supplementary penalty for a range of other offences. It 'regularly accompanied the death penalty, mutilation or banishment, and was applied if the culprit fled or escaped prison' (TIP 135). 'Confiscation and making amends [*l'amende*]...were the common denominator of all penalties...before, during, after the act of justice a major [*grosse*] circulation of wealth and goods; a series of transactions, expenses, profits and earnings' (TIP 135). In time, 'rendering justice is no longer dangerous, on the contrary it is profitable and desirable...Justice tends to become obligatory' (TIP 136). Nonetheless, to have the power to impose these decisions required political and military force, a force of coercion (TIP 136). These benefits, though, led to a proliferation of justices, which were organized hierarchically, but still tended to raise a range of questions of jurisdiction, supremacy, exception and immunity, and arbitration (TIP 136–7).

Other factors are also at stake. The penal system was linked to the feudal questions of land and rent, but became linked to population growth and movement, including growth of towns, expansion of agricultural land and reduction of forests. Land scarcity became an issue, which could lead to large uprisings, against which a central army became necessary, and 'which could soak up seditious elements of the population' (TIP 137). Plague could also have an effect, with some land not producing enough rent, dearth, the relative decline of rent, and peasant uprisings (TIP 138). The plague had been a major factor in precipitating the revolt of the *Nu-Pieds*.[49]

Foucault summarizes the distinction between this system and what comes after it, claiming the medieval penal system is fiscal, it has an economic motive of appropriation, and is 'ideologically linked to Christianity'. The system is one of compensation, taken from the old Germanic law, but now often meant to compensate the central authority, not the individual wronged. 'In brief, *exchange*'. In contrast, the modern system is carceral, 'it has a social form of "anti-sedition" ' (TIP 139), and is ideologically linked to social protection, psychology, psychiatry (TIP 140). It functions as a system of imprisonment, of disconnection. 'In brief, exclusion' (TIP 139) Foucault suggests that the Middle Ages 'taxes [*prélève*] goods (compensation [*rachat*])', while 'ours withdraws [*prélève*] people (prisons)' (TIP 140).[50]

He is here returning to a claim made at the end of the first part of the course about the 'great confinement', and indicating what will become a major theme in his next course and in *Discipline and Punish* itself: the birth of the prison. Yet some punishments could be used in both systems, though with an entirely different purpose. You could imprison someone as a pledge against a debt, or imprison them as the punishment in itself; the death penalty could be 'in recompense, [for] salvation, or definitive exclusion'; mutilation or branding either 'purificatory compensation [or] social marking' and avowal [*l'aveu*] either 'confession [or] investigation [*reconnaissance*]' (TIP 139). Having established the shift from the old economy of punishment as *talion* to the medieval economy of punishment as taxation, Foucault now has to examine the shift to the modern economy of incarceration.

He does not get there by a direct route. Instead he discusses a range of instances where penalty and money intertwine, including the practice of usury in the Middle Ages, especially with regard to Jewish creditors and the confiscation of their assets by the King. Foucault notes here that 'rather than speaking in terms of ethics, one can better speak for the first time of a penal practice' (TIP 151). He is trying to think about how money begins to take over the working of the economy generally. Foucault suggests, not entirely clearly, that the penal system that begins to emerge here 'is not yet a state apparatus, but its function is that of a state apparatus' (TIP 152). He equally suggests that a 'judicial, police and penitentiary apparatus' begins to develop here (TIP 152), even though the penal system of the Middle Ages is not itself an apparatus, but rather 'a codified means of exercising power' (TIP 153).

Out of all of this work, Foucault begins to draw some conclusions. The administration of justice by the state has three key characteristics: it is universal, obligatory, and delegated or granted to lower powers (TIP 184). But the emerging state, which Foucault dates in France to the thirteenth to fourteenth centuries, has justice and its relation to the economic partnered with the development of a standing army (TIP 183). Justice, economics and the army are thus linked. As Foucault summarizes:

- Justice, progressively linked to tax [*fiscalisée*] in the Middle Ages, exercises a pre-state function (the economic-political correlation)
- Justice as a correlate of institutions of peace appears as the reverse side of an apparatus whose other face is the army, and
- The concentration of both the tax-system and the army gives birth to a state apparatus which breaks down into two series of institutions
  - Juridical-fiscal institutions
  - Military institutions (TIP 160)

Nonetheless, while juridical forms link to economic relations, and decisions of the judicial system are essentially 'to renew the relations of production', there is another level where the economic is not the major factor: the relations of power. Justice is one of the means by which the political inserts itself into the economic (TIP 171–2). As

such, relations of power and relations of production need to be interrogated together, in their balance with the state apparatus (TIP 172).
Thus the relations help us to understand 'the constitution of the state
or at least some of its rudimentary forms' (TIP 173). Foucault provides several examples of means of keeping the peace, putting down
seditions, and balancing the competing claims of powerful families
and minimizing private wars. These are what he calls '*institutions de
paix*' (TIP 154–9). It is hard to know where Foucault is going with
this work, and the examples range so widely across centuries that
detail is conspicuously absent. In addition, the note-like form of the
material, especially with no other sources than these lectures to work
with, makes it hard to see how this fits into the overall analysis. He
suggests that the attempt is to create 'a space, time, place where
private wars are proscribed', where there is a 'singular and collective
authority' and that this authority requires that disputes are brought
before a court (TIP 167). Foucault tries to link a whole range of
revolts, civil wars and succession disputes into this narrative, but
his notes are so minimal it is hard to see how they could have been
developed in a convincing way (TIP 174).

But the general point here is important: the interlinked nature
of judicial, military, and economic concerns within a wider frame
of power relation. 'Justice as a state apparatus is developed in the
shadow of the army' (TIP 160). At another point he adds a political
institution: 'Parliament and the centralized army were born together'
(TIP 137). Foucault develops this analysis in a later lecture, where he
suggests that while it was initially a court of nobles, with the king's
entourage and counsellors, having no judicial status; it became the
highest court: a court of appeal, to mediate major conflicts, and
especially disputes between levels of the justice system (TIP 175).
'Parliament, a court of feudal origin, becomes a part [*organe*] of
sovereignty, an element of a state apparatus' (TIP 176). At one point
Foucault makes the somewhat surprising point that 'the mad king
defines absolutism' (TIP 174; see n. b). The figure here is the French
Charles VI; a couple of years later Foucault will focus on the case of
the English George III, which demonstrated a rather different understanding of power (see Chapter 4). Here, as the editor notes, Foucault
seems to mean that the system could endure the effective absence of
the key figure.[51] This was, in a sense, his point about the suppression
of the *Nu-Pieds* revolts: while the King might have appointed Séguier,
he was operating distinctly from the King.

The final lecture is the crowning glory of the course, a synthetic and
programmatic summary of power-knowledge relations in the legal

systems of the high Middle Ages. In particular, the remarks on the code of *talion* – a punishment of retribution or retaliation on the basis of equivalence – are significant in terms of the contrast with what was to follow. This lecture comes in two parts, one of which was clearly the basis for the oral delivery, and some 'Complementary Remarks', whose status seems unclear. Unfortunately six pages of that part are missing from the archive, along with several pages of the lecture itself. Given the links between this lecture and the extension of its themes and the third Rio lecture, it is possible Foucault removed them to serve as the basis for that talk. At least, the Rio lecture helps us to fill in the gaps, as the editorial notes indicate (i.e. TIP 198 n. e, 201 n. d). Nonetheless there are still some real riches here.

The most important is perhaps the clear distinction between the two systems – the Germanic and the medieval. One is based on proof [*épreuve*] as a means of addressing a harm [*dommage*[, between one who demands and one who defends; and the other is based on the problem of disorder, with a prosecutor and an accused, coming to a judgement based on truth. The means to arrive there is the inquiry [*enquête*], which can be based on witnesses, written records, and confession [*aveu*] (TIP 204). These are two different systems of knowledge. Yet the analysis is broader than this, and brings in power relations: 'By the inquiry knowledge creates power which creates knowledge [*Par l'enquête le savoir crée du pouvoir qui crée du savoir*]' (TIP 209).

It also offers the most detailed contrast between 'measure' and 'inquiry' we yet have, importantly showing how the inquiry relates to issues of proof and confession, the notion of *l'aveu*, sometimes translated as 'avowal' (e.g. TIP 205). While that notion can be found in some of Foucault's earlier texts, and takes on a significant role from the mid-1970s in his work on sexuality, through to attempts to write a book on Christianity and confession, this course is a crucial moment in his engagement with the concept and practice.[52] He draws on it explicitly at the beginning of *The Abnormals* course, with its discussion of judicial truth and proof in legal procedures (A 7–8/6–7). It returns in a related context in the *Wrong-Doing, Truth-Telling* course in Louvain in 1981. Measure and inquiry are not opposed, because 'they are not on the same level. The inquiry is perhaps a certain way of achieving measure' (TIP 209). Yet both are forms of power-knowledge, Measure is an 'instrument and form of a power of distribution', whereas the inquiry is an 'instrument and technical form of a power of information' (TIP 210). In the final pages, after some missing sections, Foucault shifts to how the measure and inquiry relate to knowledge and science, and introduces the notion of the examination as a third term. He closes by suggesting that 'from these three juridico-political matrices the sciences are born: measuring [*mesurantes*] of *kosmos*; descriptions of nature; the norms of man [*normatives de l'homme*]' (TIP 215).

By June 1972, when he wrote the summary, Foucault had done a lot of clarification on the relation between power and knowledge. He suggests that the course delivered that year was part of a broader project 'outlined the previous year: to trace the formation of certain types of *savoir* out of the juridico-political matrices that gave birth to them and act as their support' (TIP 231; EW I, 17).

> The working hypothesis is this: power relations (together with the struggles that traverse them or the institutions that maintain them) do not simply play a facilitating or obstructing role with respect to knowledge [*savoir*]; they do not merely encourage or stimulate it, distort or restrict it; power and knowledge [*savoir*] are not bound together solely through the action of interests or ideologies; so the problem is not just to determine how power subordinates knowledge [*savoir*] and makes it serve its ends or how it superimposes itself on it, imposing ideological contents and limitations. No knowledge [*savoir*] is formed without a system of communication, registration, accumulation, and displacement that is in itself a form of power, linked in its existence and its functioning to other forms of power. No power, on the other hand, is exercised without the extraction, appropriation, distribution, or restraint of knowledge [*savoir*]. At this level there is not knowledge [*connaissance*] on one side and society on the other, or science and the state, but the fundamental forms of 'power-knowledge [*pouvoir-savoir*]'. (TIP 231; EW I, 17)

Foucault suggests three ways that this work might be done. The first, which he says he covered in 1970–71 was *measure*, a form of power-knowledge examined in its relation to the Greek city-state. The second, in the 1971–2 course, was *inquiry*, and the 'formation of the medieval state'. He suggests the third, to be outlined in the 1972–3 course, was the *examination*, 'as a form of power-knowledge linked to systems of control, exclusion, and punishment characteristic of industrial societies' (TIP 231; EW I, 17–18). Note that with the first two, the Greek and medieval, it is the state that Foucault examines; whereas with the third it is societies. Interestingly, 'state' is a somewhat misleading concept to make use of the earlier political formations: but by the time it becomes the appropriate notion it is replaced. These three courses, then, are fundamentally linked. 'In their historical formulation, *measure, inquiry*, and *examination* were all means of exercising power and, at the same time, rules for establishing knowledge [*savoir*]' (TIP 231; EW I, 18).

> *Measure:* a means of establishing or restoring order, the right order, in the combat of men or the elements; but also a matrix of mathematical and physical knowledge [*savoir*]. The *inquiry:* a means of establishing or restoring facts, events, actions, properties, rights; but also a matrix of empirical knowledge [*savoirs*] and natural sciences. The *examination:* a means of setting or reinstating the norm, the rule, the distribution, the qualification, the exclusion; but also a matrix of all the psychologies, sociologies, psychiatries – in short, of what is called the 'human sciences'. To be sure, *measure, inquiry,* and *examination* are brought into play simultaneously in many scientific practices, as so many pure and simple methods or strictly controlled instruments. It is also true that at this level and in this role they are detached from their relationship with the forms of power. Before appearing together, in this clarified form, inside definite epistemological domains, they were connected to a setting in place of a political power; they were both its effect and its instrument, *measure* a function of order, *inquiry* a function of centralization, *examination* a function of selection and exclusion. (TIP 231–2; EW I, 18)

This is a crucial passage, because it locates the explicitly historical-political analysis of the courses themselves within a wider project, stretching back to *The Order of Things* and *The Archaeology of Knowledge*. There are few traces of the inquiry as 'a matrix of empirical knowledge and natural sciences' in *Théories et institutions pénales* as delivered, though Foucault was doing a lot of reading around this topic at the time.

Foucault then presents the two parts of the course in reverse. He first outlines, in some detail, what he calls the first part of the course but was actually the second. This is the analysis of the inquiry in the Middle Ages, with, Foucault suggests, a special stress on 'the domain of penal practice'. Foucault describes the focus as 'a transition from the system of revenge [*la vengeance*] to that of punishment; from accusatory practice to inquisitor practice; from the inquiry that provokes the litigation to the infraction that determines the prosecution; from the decision upon ordeal [*épreuve*] to the judgment upon proof [*preuve*]; from the combat that designates the victor and shows the just cause to the official report that establishes the fact by relying on the evidence' (TIP 232; EW I, 18). Pushing harder on a point made in the course, he sees this as tied to the birth of a stronger State, and that the sources of the inquiry were both the Carolingian administration and 'much more surely from models of ecclesiastical administration and control' (TIP 232; EW I, 18–19). He argues that 'this judicial model of the *inquiry* rests on a whole system of power; it is this system that defines what must be constituted as knowledge [*savoir*]; how, from whom, and by whom it is extracted; in what manner it circulates [*déplace*] and is transmitted; at what point it accumulates and gives rise to a judgment or a decision' (TIP 233; EW I, 19).

Foucault sees this model as not just important for penal practice, but as foundational to the empirical sciences.

> We belong to an inquisitorial civilization that, for centuries now, practices, according to forms of varying complexity but all derived from the same model, the extraction, displacement, and accumulation of knowledge [*savoir*]. The inquisition: a form of power-knowledge essential to our society. The truth of experience is a daughter of the inquisition – of the political, administrative, judicial power to ask questions, extract answers, collect testimonies, verify assertions, establish facts…empiricism forgot and covered over its beginning. *Pudenda origo.* (TIP 233; EW I, 19)

Again, little of the course as actually delivered touches on those themes: they are the essential background, and link back to earlier concerns; but they are also founded on extensive background reading.

The course summary focuses predominantly on the analysis of the inquiry in the medieval period, and says only a few lines on the theme of popular revolt and mechanisms of social control (TIP 232–3; EW I, 20). Foucault simply says this part of the course 'was devoted to the emergence, in sixteenth-century France, of new forms of social controls. The massive practice of confinement, the development of the police apparatus [*l'appareil policier*], the supervision of populations prepared for the construction of a new type of power-knowledge which would take the form of the examination' (TIP 233–4; EW I, 20). He notes that this would be developed in much more detail in the following year's course with respect to the nineteenth century. That is certainly the case for the 1972–3 course, *The Punitive Society*, but in fact, there is little in the course from 1971–2 that actually discusses this theme, and where it does, it is the seventeenth century. So, at best, this is a very partial reference to the material on the suppression of the *Nu-Pieds* revolts. It might be more accurate to say that the course as a whole serves as a historical examination of the conditions of possibility of such 'new forms of social control'.

The focus of those lines is almost exclusively to lead to the work anticipated for the following course. It is almost as if Foucault has used the analysis of the *Nu-Pieds*, Richelieu and Séguier entirely instrumentally, despite the extent of the work, and was now moving on. Yet the research conducted in this course is important both for the next one and can be traced through to *Discipline and Punish*. Indeed, Ewald and Harcourt go so far as to suggest that this 1971–2 course is almost a 'first version' of the book.[53] But it is more than this, for as they also suggest, it is one of the deepest engagements Foucault provided with multiple topics, including the already-mentioned encounter with Marxism, with the Middle Ages, with popular revolt, but also with the question of law.[54] It indicates all sorts of potential avenues for research, scrupulously documented in the editorial notes to the lectures, which are themselves heavily reliant on Foucault's own preparatory materials. It is a course that enables, and requires, multiple readings.

Inquiry: Truth and Power

Foucault began the third Rio lecture with a synopsis of the preceding two – that is of the themes of the *Lectures on the Will to Know* course. He argued that Greek thought give us three models for truth. The first two are 'rational forms of proof [*preuve*] and demonstration', found in areas such as philosophy; and the art of persuasion and convincing, that is, rhetoric. The third is the one that provides a link to the present lecture: 'a new type of knowledge – knowledge gained through witnessing, through recollection, through inquiry [*enquête*]'. This can be found in a range of disciplines, from history in Herodotus, to 'naturalists, botanists, geographers, Greek travellers'. Aristotle was the 'encyclopaedic' successor of this line (DE#139 II, 571; EW III, 33–4). Foucault suggests, very briefly and not entirely plausibly, that 'the history of the birth of the inquiry remained forgotten and was lost' for several centuries, only to be taken up in the later Middle Ages (DE#139 II, 571; EW III, 34).

> In the European Middle Ages, one sees a kind of second birth of the inquiry, which was slower and more obscure, but had much more success than the first. The Greek method of inquiry had remained stationary, had not achieved the founding of a rational knowledge [*connaissance*] capable of indefinite development. By contrast, the inquiry that arose in the Middle Ages would acquire extraordinary dimensions. Its destiny would be practically coextensive with the particular destiny of so-called 'European' or 'Western' culture. (DE#139 II, 571–2; EW III, 34)

It is then that Foucault begins to draw on *Théories et institutions pénales*. While he is summarizing several lectures in a single one, the published Rio lecture is a transcript of what he actually said, so has helped to fill out some of the detail from the manuscript. It also helps to complete the missing parts of the crucial final lecture.

Foucault suggests that the test model disappears and the inquiry model emerges between the late twelfth and the thirteenth century; a change he suggests transforms not just Europe but world history, because of the extension of the Western model through colonization – a point which is unfortunately undeveloped. The general point is, however, crucial: 'What was invented in this reformulation of law was something that involved not so much the content [*contenus*] as the forms and conditions of possibility of knowledge [*savoir*]'. Foucault sketches the transition as being dependent on a shift in feudal practices to later market societies. In feudalism only a fraction of transactions were commercial, but other mechanisms such as 'inheritance or testamentary transmission, and above all through bellicose, military, extrajudicial or judicial contestation' were more important (DE#139 II, 577–8; EW III, 39–40).

The test procedure is dropped because 'the king or his representative, the prosecutor, could not risk their own lives or their possessions every time a crime was committed' (DE#139 II, 580–1; EW III, 44). Foucault suggests that there was a moment when the society had punished without the need for a test in feudal times, which was when the offence was caught in the act, *in flagrante delicto*. But things that had happened without being discovered at the time presented a problem, so he says that what was decided upon was the inquiry model.

> When the representatives of the sovereign had to resolve a problem of law, of power, or a question of taxes, morals, ground rent, or ownership, they initiated something that was perfectly ritualized and regular – the *inquisitio*, the inquiry. The representative of power would summon the persons regarded as being knowledgeable about morals, law, or property titles. He would assemble these persons, making them swear to tell the truth, to tell what they knew, what they had seen or what they had learned from having heard it said. Then, left to themselves, these persons would deliberate; at the end of this deliberation they would be asked for the solution to the problem. (DE#139 II, 581–2; EW III, 44–5)

There are earlier medieval models for this, especially in administrative matters in the Carolingian empire, or in the generalized inquiry conducted by William the Conqueror for the Domesday Book.

The inquiry has several characteristics. 'Political power is the essential component', and it is exercised by posing questions in order to uncover the truth, which is not known prior to the interrogation. Hierarchical relations are important, with deference to 'the persons fit to know'. These notables are asked for their view of the truth, they are not coerced to reveal it (DE#139 II, 582; EW III, 45). This model had also been used by the Church, when a bishop visited places within his diocese and asked what had happened in his absence, but as well as being a spiritual exercise was now a major administrative mechanism. The Church, of course, had done both: 'a spiritual inquiry concerning sins, transgressions and crimes committed, and an administrative inquiry concerning the way in which the Church's assets were managed and the profits gathered, accumulated, distributed and so on' (DE#139 II, 583; EW III, 46). The church as a landowner required peace in order to protect its revenues (TIP 170). Though Foucault does not use this language, this is the distinction between the Church's spiritual and temporal power, which would be a major concern through the late Middle Ages. But it is the idea of the *inquisitio* that 'was taken up and adapted in juridical procedure' (DE#139 II, 582–3; EW III, 46–7; see TIP 132).

Thus, for Foucault, the inquiry has a 'dual origin': one administrative and linked to the state, and one religious, ecclesiastical. The inquiry could help to re-establish what had passed, where people could be brought together to swear what had happened, to show how it had happened and who was responsible. Thus past events could be treated as if they were *in flagrante delicto*. 'This integration of the inquiry procedure, re-actualizing what had transpired, making it present, tangible, immediate, and true, as if one had witnessed it, constituted a major discovery' (DE#139 II, 583–4; EW III, 47; see TIP 205). An 'entire ethic and theology of the avowal of the truth' emerges here, and, anticipating themes from much later in his work Foucault notes the 'ethical and religious link of the subject to truth' (TIP 207).

Foucault draws several conclusions here. First, he wants to break from the idea that the inquiry is simply a rational development from earlier 'crude, archaic, irrational systems'. The inquiry model is 'a governmental process, an administrative technique, a management method... a particular way of exercising power'. Rather than a narrative of reason's progress, 'its emergence was a complex political phenomenon', which must be analysed on the basis of power relations (DE#139 II, 584; EW III, 48). Second, if the inquiry can be linked to modes of exercising power, then the question of what it related to also shifts. From the idea of the *tort* comes the transgression, fault [*faute*] or infraction (see TIP 168). Because the religious basis of the inquiry is adopted, the infraction cannot simply be removed with making amends, but would take on a moral, religious character, that of committing a sin (see also TIP 132, 138–9). Despite the distant history of this, Foucault suggests that 'we are not entirely free of that conjunction' (DE#139 II, 585; EW III, 48–9). Third, while religious in background, and (criminal-)judicial in emergence, the inquiry becomes the basis for a reorganization of judicial practices more generally, but also for wider 'social and economic practice and domains of knowledge'. These included the question of the administration of the state, with economics and statistics, but also into much wider fields of knowledge (DE#139 II, 585–6; EW III, 49).

> Beginning in the fourteenth and fifteenth centuries there appeared types of inquiry that sought to establish truth on the basis of a certain number of carefully collected items of testimony in fields such as geography, astronomy, and the study of climates. In particular, there appeared a technique of voyage – as a political, power-exercising venture and a curiosity-driven, knowledge-acquiring venture – that ultimately led to the discovery of America. All the great inquiries that dominated the end of the Middle Ages were essentially the unfolding and dissemination of that first form, that matrix originating in the twelfth century. Even domains such as medicine, botany, and zoology were, starting in the sixteenth and seventeenth centuries, vectors of this process. The whole great cultural movement that, from the twelfth century, prepared the way for the Renaissance can be defined in large part as that of the development, the flowering of the inquiry as a general form of knowledge. (DE#139 II, 586; EW III, 49–50)

The test then, starts to disappear, only finding traces in practices that continued. One example is torture, though even this is now directed towards 'obtaining a confession [*aveu*], a test of verification'. This is what leads him to the claim that 'one could write an entire history of torture, as situated between the procedure of the ordeal and inquiry' (DE#139 II, 586; EW III, 50; see TIP 207). Foucault briefly discusses alchemy and the *disputatio* of the medieval university as two ways by which the older model of the test was replaced with that of the inquiry. Alchemy was a sequence of 'secret or public rules or procedures', not an inquiry but a test or contest between the alchemist and nature. The *disputatio* was similarly 'a form of proof, of display of knowledge, of authentication of knowledge that conformed to the general scheme of the test'. Both were progressively displaced by models that took the inquiry as their basis, with 'observations of nature', with 'authors no longer as authority but as witness' (DE#139 II, 586–8; EW III, 50–1).

The point Foucault establishes in Rio – and here he is going well beyond the specific focus of the *Théories et institutions pénales* course – is that 'the inquiry is absolutely not a content [*contenu*], but rather a form of knowledge [*savoir*] – a form of knowledge situated at the junction of a type of power and a certain number of contents of knowledge [*contenus de connaissance*]' (DE#139 II, 588; EW III, 51). In other words, the transformation is as much about a mechanism of power as it is about instances of knowledge.

> The inquiry is precisely a political form – a form of management and exercise of power that, through the judicial institution, became, in Western culture, a way of authenticating truth, of acquiring and transmitting things that would be regarded as true. The inquiry is a form of knowledge-power. (DE#139 II, 588; EW III, 52)

Preparatory Materials

It seems that Foucault is hinting at much more than he actually says, and in this respect his preparatory materials are very revealing. Back in 1994, before any of the Collège de France courses had been published, Defert described *Théories et institutions pénales* as a course that 'outlines, from antiquity to the nineteenth century, the juridico-political matrices of certain types of knowledge' (C 39/48). A strange description, given what is presented in the manuscript edited into the book, but it has some bearing on the wider situation.

At the BNF, box 32 is labelled as preparatory material for the first three courses – 'Notes de lecture pour les Cours 1970, 1972, 1973'.[55] It includes just two folders. The first folder relates to the 1970–1 course, *Lectures on the Will to Know*, and the notes are revealing of just how much reading was undertaken. Foucault read widely, in English and German secondary literature as well as French, and in journal articles as well as books, as well of course as the primary texts, which he quotes from liberally. The topics are much what you would expect from reading the course – the material is on ancient Greece, philosophers and sophists, money, rhetoric, language, law and truth. Figures include Aristotle, Homer, Hesiod, Solon and others. The notes on Nietzsche are filed with the ones on 'German Philosophy from the 1950s' archived elsewhere;[56] but there is no sign of notes on Oedipus.

But the second folder in the box does not contain the material for the next course. Instead it is a loosely themed set of quite extensive notes on puritanism, the scientific revolution of the seventeenth century, English universities of the period, projects for their reform, the Royal Society, later reforms of the nineteenth century, and so on. Foucault's sources include Michael Walzer, *The Revolution of the Saints*, Robert Merton's *Science, Technology and Society in Seventeenth Century England*, Richard Foster Jones, *Ancients and*

Moderns, and some texts of the time include Thomas Hobbes's *Elements of Philosophy*, John Wilkins the Bishop of Chester's work on discovery of new planets, William Harvey on the circulation of blood, Francis Bacon, John Webster's *The Examination of Academies* and William Petty's projects on pedagogy.[57] Foucault is interested in techniques such as medicine and anatomy, the determination of longitude, the length of a meridian, magnetism and navigation, and more generally science by means of experimentation.

Many of the notes are taken from Jones's book, and there are extensive notes on George Sarton's *The Study of the History of Science* and *Life of Science*.[58] Foucault seems struck by Sarton's observation that 'The history of mankind is double: political history which is to a large extent a history of the masses, and intellectual history which is largely the history of a few individuals... *The essential history of mankind largely in secret*. Visible history is nothing but the local scenery, the everchanging and capricious background of the invisible history which, alone, is truly ecumenical and progressive'.[59] Foucault has a lot of notes on developments in the Thermidor of the French Revolution, and the establishment of various scientific and educational institutions, including Polytechnics, the École normale, and the Bureau de longitude. Later there are notes on the establishment of the Écoles des Ponts et chausées (1740–50); École des mines (1763); École des Arts et Métiers à Liancourt. He seems especially interested in the English experience around the time of the revolution or civil war of the seventeenth century. He has notes about geology, chemistry, palaeontology, and geography and cartography. There is material on almanacs, and the navigation of the Northwest Passage. Christopher Hill's *Intellectual Origins of the English Revolution* is also used, and Foucault seems struck by his reflections on the sociological approach to intellectual history.[60] A reading list includes several works by E. G. R. Taylor, including *Tudor Geography 1485–1583* (1930), *The Mathematical Practitioners of Tudor and Stuart England* (1954) and *The Haven Finding Art* (1956) on navigation; plus her article 'The Surveyor'.[61]

There are some quite detailed notes on the Faust legend, mainly from Christopher Marlowe's play, read through Ernest Faligan, *Histoire de la legend de Faust*, rather than from Goethe.[62] Foucault briefly mentions Faust in 1971, when he contrasts him to St Anthony. Faust, for Foucault, is a figure who searches for the 'summit of knowledge', and sees it 'multiplied in the infinite power which is added to it' (LWK 115/120). Foucault would return to the Faust legend in later courses, where he mentions the Marlowe, Lessing and Goethe versions (HSu 296–7/309–10; CT 196/211). There are also some notes on Balzac which are not obviously connected, except for a telling quote from *La Peau de Chagrin* [The Wild Ass's Skin] entitled: 'Pouvoir, vouloir – et savoir' [Power, Will and Knowledge]: 'will burns us and power destroys us, but knowledge leaves our feeble organism in a perpetual state of calm'.[63] Perhaps Foucault envisioned using the Faust story as an illustrative example of the dangers of science and the quest for knowledge, or the 'power, will, knowledge' quote from *La Peau de Chagrin* to introduce a study of these themes.

It is not entirely clear what Foucault thought he was doing with this material. But the focus seems to be very clearly on the term that structures much of the *Théories et institutions pénales* course, and its retrospective presentation for the course summary and the 'Truth and Juridical Forms' lectures: 'Inquiry'. Foucault delivers a course that looks at the political inquiry of the suppression of the *Nu-Pieds* revolt, but also the juridical inquiry that emerged alongside the medieval state. But it appears that an alternative focus was the scientific inquiry. There are traces of this in the Rio lectures. But it is explicit in the 1972 course summary, where he talks of the *inquiry* as both 'a means of establishing or restoring facts, events, actions, properties, rights; but also a matrix of empirical knowledge [*savoirs*] and natural sciences (TIP 232; EW I, 18).

The nature of the notes – and comparing them to the notes for materials for which we do have a lecture record – means it is difficult to know what Foucault would have made of them. There is at least one level of analysis missing from just reading his notes. But they do give a very revealing introduction to his thinking and reading concerns. It is important to stress that the notes are undated, and that the description of the box is the BNF's, not Foucault's. It is possible that the notes are from a different period entirely, though the paper, and style of note-taking, ink and handwriting are similar to the 1970–1 course notes in folder 1 of this box. If not for an alternative 1971–2 course, they could be material for an extension of the 'Will to Know' material – these too concern related topics, measure especially, from a different historical period. There are thematic links to *The Order of Things* too, of course, though the specific sciences are quite different. How would *The Order of Things* have looked if instead of the shift from the analysis of wealth to economics, general grammar to linguistics and natural history to biology, the focus was on the transitions from alchemy to chemistry; from studies of the earth to geology and palaeontology, and the development of cartography and navigation?

The folders catalogued as the preparatory notes for *Discipline and Punish* are where material read for the 1971–2 and 1972–3 courses ended up. There are five boxes of material.[64] Many of the notes here connect directly to those two courses. In particular, box 1, folder 1, subfolders 1–3 are on 'Revolts in the Middle Ages' and urban jurisdiction questions in that period. Foucault reads widely here, including many texts referenced in the course – the editors had access to the same materials. Georges Duby's *L'économie rurale et la vie des campagnes dans l'occident mediéval* seems to have provided the background and broader context.[65] Foucault was interested in a wide range of revolts and resistances, of which the *Nu-Pieds* became his central example. Others include the fourteenth-century Jacquerie revolts; Robin Hood and uprisings in England, including Wat Tyler; and struggles in Flanders.[66] His specific notes on revolts in the seventeenth century and on the *Nu-Pieds* are filed in a much later folder in the BNF arrangement of materials.[67]

His reading notes move to look at royal power and justice in this period of the thirteenth to fifteenth centuries, including works on the inquiry which shape the later part of the course; what he calls 'institutions de paix' and then analysis of the Merovingian and Carolingian empires of the Middle Ages.[68] There are also detailed notes on criminal procedures, accusation, ordeal, and inquisition.[69] He draws extensively on a wide range of works including Esmein, *A History of Continental Criminal Procedure*, Guilhiermoz, *Enquêtes et Procès*; Adolphe Tardif, *La procédure civile et criminelle au XIII-XIVe siècle* and his *Histoire des sources du droit français, origines romaines*, and Alec Mellor, *La torture*.[70] Later folders have detailed notes on modes of punishment and torture.[71] These include much on the Middle Ages through to the early modern period, but include photocopies of pages from texts on antiquity such as Desmaze's.

These notes link, naturally, to the published book *Discipline and Punish*, to the extent that the courses were preparatory presentations of some of its ideas. But they also show research undertaken which Foucault chose not to present to his audience. In particular, the material ranges much more widely than the French focus of the first part of *Théories et institutions pénales*, and looks at a much broader range of historical instances. With *The Punitive Society* it is harder to tell where notes for the course end and ones for the book begin. With the notes on the seventeenth to nineteenth centuries in Boxes 2–5 we are back on more familiar ground. The notes show, again, the extent of Foucault's reading, and there are extensive notes on Beccaria, Bentham, Brissot, penal theories, prisons, the 1810 legal Code, parapenal institutions such as Mettray, delinquency, general surveillance in society and so on. There is also a really extensive set of notes for penal reform in the time of the Revolution and the Empire, and quite a lot of photocopied extracts from documentary sources. There is a lot of material on England and other foreign countries, rather than just France.[72] As Chapter 3 will show, *The Punitive Society* is distinct in important ways from *Discipline and Punish*, especially with its dual focus on England and France as examples. One thing that is worth stressing is that Foucault's older historical critics, who suggested his research was shallow, should perhaps grudgingly recognize that the works cited in the published book were but a fraction of those read in its preparation.

The course title for *Théories et institutions pénales* is therefore somewhat misleading as to the actual content. In the course summary, Foucault says that 'this year's course was meant to serve as a *historical preliminary* [emphasis added] to the study of penal institutions (more generally, of social controls and punitive systems) in French society of the nineteenth century' (TIP 231; EW I, 17). That seems a more appropriate description of its contents. Ewald and Harcourt describe the two halves of the course as a 'double genealogy': the latter covering multiple centuries, the former just a few short years. Together they afford, for them, a Foucauldian vision of 'the birth of the state, which he is often reproached for not having provided'.[73] For the later Foucault, the question of the state becomes subsumed within his wider inquiry. As he said in 1979, 'the state is nothing else but the mobile effect of a regime of multiple governmentalities'.[74]

Here, though, the state is a crucial focus, and it is because of this, along with its engagement with the historical debates, that Ewald and Harcourt suggest that this course is 'a decisive element' for Foucault's engagement with Marxism.[75] It is a course where the stress is firmly, as it would be for Foucault's more famous analyses of the later 1970s, on power and relations of power, yet there is due deference to the emergence of 'state apparatuses'. As Étienne Balibar indicates in his comments included in this volume, there is certainly a 'trace' of Althusser in this course.[76] The kingdom now starts to become more than just the lands controlled through feudal relations, but is constituted as:

- A place of circulation controlled by armed forces;
- A network of communications for merchandise and wealth
- A space of validity for orders, prohibitions [*interdictions*], and decisions...

It is the site [*lieu*] of an economic, military and legislative order. (TIP 185)

This is a powerful insight into the spatial dynamics of the state, where the lands of a kingdom became not the property of a ruler, but the extent of their rule. In time, as shown elsewhere, this is where the concept of territory emerges.[77] Foucault's remarks are telling especially on circulation, which anticipate later work on spaces of security. As such, the King is not just a sovereign in the sense of a supreme ruler, but 'the guardian of order, a public order character-ized by the centralized control of arms, the security of the exchange of trade, and obedience to the orders [*prescriptions*] of the sovereign' (TIP 185). Foucault links this emergence of the state to nascent capi-talism (TIP 104), but stresses that it is not capitalism that produces criminals, as many Marxist accounts suggest. Rather Foucault argues – and he elaborates this in much more detail the following year – capitalism is reliant on a repressive apparatus that produces a 'certain penality-delinquency coding' (TIP 106). While Foucault would come to distance himself from the idea of the repressive, here he indicates that this way of posing the question evades moral, sociological and psychological ways of looking at punishment (TIP 4). This too is a claim that would be substantially developed the following year.

3

Examination: Punishment, War, Economy

In October 1972 Foucault gave three lectures at Cornell University: 'The Knowledge of Oedipus', 'Literature and Crime' and 'The Punitive Society' (C 42/52). No manuscripts for the second or third have yet been published, and they are not presently available in the archive.[1] The last, in title at least, anticipates the course Foucault would deliver in early 1973 in Paris. The course was originally called 'The Disciplinary Society' (C 43/53), which is a description Foucault himself later uses of its analyses (DE#139 II, 588; EW III, 52). It is a course that ranges widely across history and politics to understand a series of linked questions. The research conducted and presented here was to be very important for subsequent works, not simply the related book *Discipline and Punish*, but also future courses at the Collège. In *The Abnormals*, for example, Foucault provides a brief overview of his argument of the transition, referring back to this course, rather than the very soon-to-be-published book (A 81/88).

The most obvious way to read the course is as an early draft of *Discipline and Punish*. Foucault gave *The Punitive Society* lectures between January and March 1973; completed a draft of the book in April 1973; and the final version in August 1974 before its publication in February 1975. There is certainly a lot of connection – the regicide Damiens appears here, there are discussions of Bentham, Beccaria and Colquhoun; and the theme of the prison is very important. However some crucial themes in *Discipline and Punish* are not highlighted here, and it is clear that Foucault elaborated many aspects that would form part of the book in the *Psychiatric Power* course and the 'Truth and Juridical Forms' lectures. In addition, Foucault discusses a number of themes that do not appear in the book, and puts a different emphasis on much that does. The course must be seen as situated within a political and intellectual context, of which the dissolution of the GIP immediately prior to this course is perhaps the most important.[2] In a sense the course is the continuation of historical inquiries into the institution that Foucault had spent a lot of effort in trying to make intelligible in his own present. It has long been known that the GIP is at least part of what is behind Foucault's comment in *Discipline and Punish* that he is not interested in writing a history of the past, but of the present. Much the same intention is at stake here, even as the timescale is more tightly compressed. But there are also contemporary references to the struggle for abortion rights, discussed in Chapter 6.

At the time, Foucault was involved in discussions with the founding editors of the journal *Libération*, Jean-Paul Sartre and Serge July. Foucault's association with Jean-Paul Sartre is intriguing throughout his activist work, given the intellectual differences between the two men and some sharp exchanges in the 1960s. But in terms of political involvement they frequently shared platforms, attended events and co-signed petitions.[3] In the paper's founding manifesto, 'written by Philippe Gavi and Benny Lévy, revised by Sartre and discussed at length by Foucault',[4] *Libération* declared that it was 'time to challenge the secret and to help the people speak [*prendre la parole*]'.[5] It is clear that this documentary model of working was important and clearly fascinated Foucault. It would characterize the work of the GIP, which also aimed to give prisoners a voice, and in the parallel seminar to the 1971–2 course he and his colleagues worked on the case of Pierre Rivière (TIP 234; EW I, 20–1), which they prepared for publication the following year (PS 269/263) (see Chapters 4 and 5). Foucault would go on to use this approach for the case of the hermaphrodite Herculine Barbin, and proposed doing something similar with his 'Lives of Infamous Men' project.[6] With *Libération* he imagined progressive political possibilities emerging from the representation of the archive.

I was thinking about chronicles from worker and proletarian memory, that is, historical fragments from the nineteenth century...Or earlier, and until recent years. For example the *canuts*, the first great revolt of the carpenters of Paris in 1855 (or 1845?). And prison mutinies. The first dates from 1829, the other from 1830. So it would be a historical chronicle related to current events. I think that would interest our readers...I suggest the idea. It would naturally be a team effort.[7]

Foucault did not deliver on this suggestion, though in his first contribution to *Libération* did repeat these ideas in a brief interview,
entitled 'For a chronicle of worker memory'. Here he suggested that
these were largely neglected stories, but could be represented, alongside more recent recollections, in a collective serial that could appear
as often as 'once or twice a week', continue until that 'vein dried up',
and then move to a new theme (DE#117 II, 399–400).[8] Such themes
recur in the lectures he delivered in 1972–3.

It is important to recognize that Foucault was delivering these as
lectures to an audience that would, at least in part, have followed
previous courses. The course sits in especially close relation to its
predecessor. As Harcourt puts it, the 1971–2 course looked at the
'repressive dimension of penality [*pénalité*]', while this course looked
at both the 'productive dimension of penality, but [also] at the more
general question of the emergence of punitive power, which he called
"disciplinary" '.[9] In a more theoretical register, Foucault explicitly
relates the analysis here to the concept of 'measure', the 'inquiry', and
the 'examination', which is introduced here and will go on to have
a significant role in *Discipline and Punish* and some of Foucault's
later courses. In some unread notes from 7 February 1973 Foucault
makes a clear distinction between inquiry and examination. Inquiry
is 'knowing [*connaître*] events – according to witnesses, according to
criteria of observation', whereas examination is 'knowing individuals
according to observation by power-holders and criteria of normality'
(PS 118/115; see 200–1/195–6).[10] Later in the course examination is
described as

> the permanent checking of individuals…like a permanent test
> [*épreuve*], without a final point. It is an inquiry, but before any offence,
> outside any crime. It is an inquiry of general and *a priori* suspicion of
> the individual. We can call *examination* this uninterrupted, graduated,
> accumulated proof [*épreuve*] which permits a control and continuous
> pressure, to follow the individual in each of their steps [*démarches*],
> to see if they are regular or irregular, ordered or dissipated, normal or
> abnormal. The examination, making this perpetual division, authorizes
> a graduated distribution of individuals up to the judicial limit. Thus
> we can see born, at this precise point of the relation of the body of the
> labourer to the forces of production, a form of knowledge which is
> that of the examination. (PS 200/196)

Both formulations link the examination to a political economy that
is so often muted in Foucault's work. His relation to Marxism is a
central theme of the course.

Modes of Punishment

Foucault begins the course noting that attempts have been made to distinguish societies on the basis of the how they treat the dead, as to whether they bury then or cremate them. Foucault wonders if we can use this to think of societies more generally through how they treat the problematic living, through mechanisms of exclusion or inclusion (PS 3/1–2), though he notes that the idea of exclusion is problematic, as is the notion of transgression (PS 4–7/2–6). If we are to use these terms we need to do this within a broader, or differently conceived, framework, 'where it is no longer a question of the law, of the rule, of representation, but of power rather than law, of knowledge [*savoir*] rather than representation' (PS 7/6).[11]

The course is more concerned with the more 'subtle [*fines*] tactics of sanction' or punishment [*punition*] (PS 8/6). He wants to map out [*réparer*] four ways that society has punished, broadly conceived: exclude; make atonement [*rachat*] or impose a compensation; mark or brand [*marquer*]; and imprison or confine (PS 8–9/6–8; see PS 256/248). These models are presented in different ways by Foucault at different times, but it is important to note the first two as alternatives to the simple binary that *Discipline and Punish* might be seen to be suggesting. Foucault confesses he is unsure that this typology is valuable, and that several objections could be raised, but he wants to examine how they relate to the question of property [*biens*] (PS 10/9). Exclusion might involve, at its extreme end, throwing someone off cliffs; compensation might be as severe as killing a relative. In his discussion of exclusion he returned to the analyses of Greece that he made in the *Lectures on the Will to Know* (PS 11–12), but a note suggests that he saw it apply to the early modern 'classical age' as well (PS 8 n. b/7 n. †). Foucault here briefly describes the figure that Giorgio Agamben would come to analyse in much more detail as the *homo sacer* (PS 11–12/10).[12] When he examines the idea of atonement (of old Germanic law) of compensation (PS 12–13/10–11, and 12 n. a/10 n. *), his analysis builds on the more detailed analysis in the previous year's course.

Foucault's outline of the third form is quite detailed, discussing a whole range of ways that bodies are marked by the exercise of power, with an emphasis on the sign, the wider social value of this. Some of these punishments link back to the idea of compensation, with the hands of thieves cut off, for example; but they are more about making visible, and especially making visible the power of the sovereign. Foucault claims 'this tactic of branding [*marquage*] is preponderant in the West from the end of the high Middle Ages until the eighteenth century' (PS 9/8). Foucault only uses the word *supplice* – a concept which would become so crucial to *Discipline and Punish* – once in the course as delivered; and once more in manuscript pages he did not read (PS 12/10, 15–16 n. a/14 n. a). The term captures a physical form of punishment or torture, perhaps conducted or displayed publically. It seems likely that the previous year's course had contained a much more comprehensive analysis of this form of torture. Here he simply indicates that 'such a lavish variety of *supplices*' was required because of the way they were calibrated to a whole series of variables including the culpable, the act and the victim: 'there is the stake for heresy, quartering for traitors, the cutting ears off for thieves, piercing the tongues of blasphemers' (PS 12/11). He then discusses the death penalty, using the example of Damiens the regicide and his spectacular public execution (PS 12/11), noting that this penalty continues to exist: it was abolished in France only in 1981. He, however, describes it as essentially the extreme form of imprisonment, not as a visible display of the marks of power on a human body. On that last broad form of punishment, imprisonment, he notes that it is the tactic that is prevalent today, becoming established at the turn of the nineteenth century (PS 9/8).

There are thus various principles of punishment including social utility and the relativity of this to societies with different needs; fine gradation of penalty to achieve social goals; infallible surveillance during the punishment; and the exemplary nature, the public face, of this punishment to dissuade (PS 68–9/67–8). These different principles can be found in earlier punishments such as infamy – making a public example of someone; compensation [*talion*] or amend; and slavery – 'forced and public labour [*travail*]' (PS 69–71/68–70). But imprisonment, which is common today and has been since the nineteenth century, is 'not collective like infamy, graduated in its nature like *talion*, reforming like forced labour' (PS 71/70). In prison – 'an abstract, monotonous, rigid punitive system' – the only graduated variable is time (PS 71–2/70). There is an economic parallel here: 'Everyone is given a salary for labour time, and inversely, time at liberty is taken as the price for violation [*infraction*]. Time is the only property possessed, it is purchased for work or it is taken for infraction' (PS 72/71). Foucault suggests that prison and wage-labour [*forme-salaire*] are 'historical twins', though he insists he is not suggesting there is a causal relation with the socio-economic model directly changing penal practice (PS 72/71). Nonetheless it is striking that both the system of capitalist power and the system of penality both show 'time exchanged against power', and it is striking how imprisonment parallels 'the organization of worker time [in] the factory, the distribution and calculation of time is wage, the control of leisure, the life of the worker, savings, pension, etc.' (PS 73/72). This is what he calls 'the global hold of power over time' (PS 73/72).

> Thus, what allows us to analyze the punitive regime over offences and the disciplinary regime of labour as a whole is the relation of life-time [*du temps de vie*] to political power: this repression of time and through time, this continuity between the factory clock, the chronometry of the chain-gang [or production line, *chaîne*] and the prison calendar. (PS 73/72).

The relation to Marx is obvious, though this is not the same as the labour-theory of value. Rather it might be described as the time-theory of labour and punishment.

Civil War and the Social Enemy

The army is a key theme in *Discipline and Punish*, and arguably the true model of the disciplinary society in that text.[13] The army receives some discussion in this course, but what is striking is the quite lengthy discussion of civil war. Foucault told Defert around the time he began the course that he wanted to understand relations of power through the 'most condemned form of war: not Hobbes, nor Clausewitz, nor class struggle, but civil war' (C 42/52). Foucault would elaborate these themes again in the 1976 course *'Society Must Be Defended'*. Additionally the 1972–3 anticipates even later lecture courses – the grain regulation from *Security, Territory, Population*, for instance, and the discussion of political economy and the government of the population from *The Birth of Biopolitics*.[14]

Foucault suggests that we need to think about penal tactics within a wider understanding of power, asking what forms of power were there that led to tactics such as exclusion, branding, making amends and imprisoning (PS 13/12). The analysis of these tactics is in order to shed light on power, not on juridical representations, morals or ideology: 'Penality as analyser of power: that is the theme of this course' (PS 14/12). Further, he wants to examine struggle, conflicts and political protests within this notion of power, which can be conceived within the frame of civil war (PS 14–15/13–14). He suggests that the idea of 'the obscuring, the disavowal of civil war, the claim that civil war does not exist is one of the first axioms of the exercise of power' (PS 14/13). He brings in Hobbes and Rousseau here and contends that in their work the idea that civil war might be positive is never considered, and that civil war is seen as something that existed before the social contract, and is really natural, rather than civil, war. 'From the contract onwards, civil war is only the monstrous prolongation of the war of all against all, in a social structure which must normally be controlled by the contract' (PS 14–15/13). In both Hobbes and Rousseau, 'civil war is the accident, the anomaly and that which must be avoided [*éviter*] to the same extent that it is a theoretical-practical monstrosity' (PS 15/13). Rather, Foucault suggests that civil war is a permanent state, which allows us to understand 'a number of tactics of struggle, of which penality is the privileged example. Civil war is the matrix of all struggles for power, of all strategies of power and, as a consequence, also the matrix for all struggles concerning, and against, power' (PS 15/13). His focus for the course is thus the 'interplay, in nineteenth century society, between permanent civil war and opposed tactics of power' (PS 15/14).[15]

These preliminary remarks lead to an outline of four themes to be discussed this year: the universal and constant war within society; that the penal system is not equally applied to all, but operates in the interests of some against others; the structure of universal and constant surveillance; and the system of imprisonment (PS 26/24). In undelivered passages of the course manuscript Foucault underlines, yet again, that his focus is not about 'in the name of which principle, and according to what scale of value', but 'how one punishes; who punishes, who is punished, by which instruments' (PS 23 n. */21 n. *). It is thus about the how, not the why. Foucault says his focus will be on 1825–48, in the context of the 1808 *Code d'instruction criminelle* or the 1810 Napoleonic penal code (PS 23/21–2). He notes that 'the overturning of spectacle by surveillance' helps to produce the modern epoch (PS 25/23).[16]

In clarifying his comments on the civil war, suggesting that it is not the same as Hobbes's war of all against all, 'but the war of the rich against the poor, the propertied against those who possess nothing, the masters/employers against the proletariat' (PS 23/22). He does discuss Hobbes's state of war here, especially in terms of the argument of *Leviathan* and the emergence of a sovereign figure (PS 26–9/24–7). But Foucault wants to reject a number of the claims Hobbes makes, especially the idea that this war precedes the establishment of power, or is exterior to power. For Foucault it is precisely a struggle of power (PS 30–1/29, 33/30): 'There is no civil war without the work of power and work on power... The everyday exercise of power must be considered as a civil war: exercising power is a certain way of conducting civil war...' (PS 33/31–2). Some of

Foucault's examples look at collective movements, and he examines 'the market riots', the *Nu-Pieds* and the Luddites – peasant revolts in Normandy, and machine-breakers in England (PS 31–3/29–1).[17] Such revolts, especially the *Nu-Pieds*, had been analysed in detail in the previous year's course (see Chapter 2), but the contemporary resonance, in particular in relation to France's *loi anti-casseurs*, a law against 'wrecking' or 'breaking', are striking. The law meant that it was an offence to attend a demonstration at which violence or damage occured.

Politics is then, for Foucault, conceived as the continuation of civil war. This civil war is not a Hobbesian war of all against all, but serving specific purposes. There is a very strong sense here of the purpose *behind* discipline and incarceration, of whose interests it serves. The supposed absence of this explanation would be one of the critiques Henri Lefebvre, among others, would level at Foucault's work.[18] It is interesting that *Discipline and Punish* offered only a partial view of what Foucault's initial researches on this topic were pointing towards. As Harcourt notes, Hobbes and Clausewitz, and indeed the theme of civil war, almost completely disappear from the book, only to reappear in a course delivered about a year after it was published.[19] We can therefore re-read *Discipline and Punish* in the light of the analyses provided here and in '*Society Must Be Defended*', of the advent of the disciplinary or punitive society as one of the strategies within a wider civil, or class, war.[20] Foucault's civil war is not simply a class war, but a war directed against the social enemy – here, the criminal, but extended in later courses to the perverse, the insane, and others who do not fit the mould. But while the direction of the analysis is, here, towards the end of better productive relations, this is not something that can be reduced to class struggle. Foucault here, as elsewhere, wants the focus to fall more on struggle than class, and suggests that class is not the only, or even the primary, division within society.

He then discusses the status of the criminal as a social or public enemy – we might say 'the enemy within' – and juridical practice as the declaration of public war (PS 34–6/32–4), especially through the use of the jury in which criminals are 'judged not by their peers, but judged in the name of society by its representatives' (PS 36/35). He looks at the effect of privileged knowledges or sciences [*savoirs*] such as psychopathology and criminal or deviance psychiatry. These have 'epistemological effects', the 'sociology of criminality as social pathology' (PS 37/35). He later notes that 'the programme of the *connaissance* of the prisoner as such becomes a central problem…the criminal as an object of *savoir*'. 'This institution therefore opens up an entire field of possible *savoirs*'; a parallel with the hospital: 'what the hospital is for the body, the prison is for the soul' (PS 93/91). In order to get there he provides more discussion of the criminal as a particular figure in this work: 'I would like to undertake a critical analysis of the sociologization of the criminal as a social enemy, a sociologization whose effects currently control penal practice, the psychopathology of delinquency and sociology of criminality' (PS 38/36). These claims develop from the analysis in the 1971–2 course:

> It is not that capitalism produces criminality…We can say that capitalism cannot subsist without an apparatus of repression of which the principal function is anti-sedition. This apparatus produces a certain penality-delinquency coding. (TIP 106)

This discussion of the criminal as the social enemy is a major theme, with Foucault looking to make a historical 'map [*epérage*] of its first manifestations' (PS 46/44). He begins with a focus on a 1789 proclamation of the National Constituent Assembly, which describes an offence being committed as one where 'society as a whole is injured by one of its members' (PS 45/43–4). His examples include Physiocrat Guillaume Le Trosne's 1764 *Mémoire sur les vagabonds et sur les mendients*, which is discussed in some detail (PS 47–53/45–52), only to be reduced to briefer mentions in *Discipline and Punish* (DP 92/76–7, 104–5/88–9). More than being merely like begging or idleness [*mendicité, oisiveté*], vagabondage is a matrix of crime and delinquency (PS 47–8/45–6), someone who disrupts production, because 'the vagabond is fundamentally someone who refuses work' (PS 51/50). Along the way he says something of how the physiocrats saw this question, seeing the turning of paupers into vagabonds, by detaching them from their home area. They do not pay taxes and they lead to labour shortages. Le Trosne proposes four kinds of measures to address this: enslavement, juridical outlawing, 'the self defence of the peasant community' through constituting an armed force that could work alongside the police against vagabonds; 'the hunt and mass conscription'. Anyone who refused to stay put could be hunted down; fixing in place was a key aim (PS 51–2/50–1). One of the discussions touches upon the use of a worker's booklet or record book [*le livret*] that they need to present to employers or show to the police: 'at the same time a contractual act between the boss [*le patron*] and the worker, and a police measure: there must be an economic and moral control over the worker. The booklet is one of the institutions which are not exactly penal but which make it possible to ensure the continuity of the punitive and the penal' (PS 199/194). Another indication of the criminal as social enemy comes in the analysis of the debate about the death penalty in 1791 (PS 63–4/61–2), but this is most striking when Foucault references Marx's articles on the theft of wood (PS 64/62). These examined the way in which the right to gather wood was curtailed as landowners asserted their complete right to landed property.[21]

His other examples of the criminal as social enemy come from literature, especially Alain-René Le Sage's early eighteenth-century novel *Gil Blas*,[22] and horror novels from the end of that century and the start of the next, including Ann Radcliffe's 1803 novel *Les visions du château des Pyrénées* (PS 55–7/53–5) – a work now known to be wrongly attributed.[23] But the point extends to her better-known works too. In these, Foucault suggests, criminality is 'localized and outside society. We find crime, no longer in the milieu of society, but in extra-social sites [*lieux*]: convents, chateaus, underground passages, mountains hollowed like a fortress. In the interior of this geography peculiar to crime we have a sort of entirely closed society, with its initiations, rites, values, and hierarchy' (PS 56/55). Out of these different threads, Foucault contends, the dualities appear as 'massive oppositions: life/death, innocence/crime, good/evil, characterizing this form of delinquency' (PS 57/55).[24]

Religion, England, France

There is a footnote in *Discipline and Punish* where Foucault says his investigation is going to be in relation to France and that a comparative analysis would be too burdensome and any analysis as a whole too schematic (DP 40 n. 1/309 n. 3). In this course there is a lengthy discussion of England as a counterpoint to France, though there are only limited indications of the very different historical-economic transformations of the two countries. Foucault examines the relation between a whole set of wider questions and the shift to 'a new punitive tactic: imprisonment' (PS 64/63), which he finds applied in England around 1790–1800, and in France between 1791 and 1820. He notes that imprisonment, somewhat surprisingly, was not a major focus before – prisons existed, but not within a general penal system (PS 65–7/63–5). One striking issue is that discourses on punishment do not, initially, work within the prison – it was a largely lawless space. Louis XVIII's adviser, Decazes, apparently wrote to say that 'the trouble is that the law does not penetrate prison' (PS 67/65). Prisons existed, not to punish, but to guard or guarantee – you might imprison a political enemy or a debtor (PS 68/66). This is the point Foucault makes in a June 1973 interview when asked if he can imagine a society without prisons. 'The response is simple', he says, because there have long been such societies, as the prison as punishment is an invention of the nineteenth century (DE#125 II, 432). This development comes from the new penal theory, which suggests that prison punishment is a mode of social defence, social protection (PS 68/67).

> I will take two landmarks [*repères*], England and France, to study
> the conditions of acceptability that made possible the generalization
> of the prison-form and the penitentiary domain in the eighteenth
> century. (PS 105/101)

Foucault is interested in various religious dissenters, including Quakers and Methodists (PS 105–6/102) and societies for the 'reform of morals' and suppression of vice who campaigned to respect Sunday, close gambling houses and brothels, and prevent indecent literature (PS 106/102–3). He also discusses 'self-defence groups of a paramilitary character', later making use of the poorest members of society to constitute a police (PS 107/103–4), which demonstrates the importance of their economic function: a private police to protect bourgeois fortune – which could be in warehouses, docks, roads (PS 107/104). This last theme is situated within a much wider range of economic transformations – population movements, new uses of capital, the division of labour and the circulation of merchandise. As 'the capitalist mode of production develops, capital finds itself exposed to a certain number of risks which were previously more controllable. Capital is exposed, in effect, not only to brigandage or pillage, as before, but to everyday depredation by those who live on it, alongside it' (PS 108/104).

The political regime in England did not provide sufficient guarantees, and so, 'due to the weakness of centralized power, there is on the one hand a micro-territoriality of judicial bodies [*organismes*] and penal instruments...and, on the other, an extremely strict penal code' which had been set up by the crown but which was inadequate to the new situation (PS 108/105). The new system of control that emerges occupies the limits of morality and penality; its aim is not so much for the detection and punishing of crime, but rather to address its conditions, to instil norms of behavior, moralizing and controlling [*maîtriser*] of the 'lower classes' (PS 109–10/105–6). Its aims were 'patience, work, sobriety, frugality, religion', a passage Foucault takes from Edmund Burke's 'Thoughts and Details on Scarcity'.[25] Harcourt notes that Burke is arguing against the language of the 'laboring poor', whereas Foucault is suggesting they go together.[26]

Nothing can be so base and so wicked as the political canting language, 'The labouring *poor*'. Let compassion be shewn in action, the more the better, according to every man's ability; but let there be no lamentation of their condition. It is no relief to their miserable circumstances; it is only an insult to their miserable understandings. It arises from a total want of charity, or a total want of thought. Want of one kind was never relieved by want of any other kind. Patience, labour, sobriety, frugality, and religion, should be recommended to them; all the rest is downright *fraud*. It is horrible to call them 'The *once happy* labourer'.[27]

Foucault notes that some important theorists of penal right like Bentham and Beccaria had separated fault and infraction: 'laws, for them, were not to punish the moral conduct of people, they were only concerned with the utility of society and not the morality of individuals' (PS 111/107). But the moralization of these issues came from these other groups at the same time, who mobilized the state more towards the requirements of moralization – 'a movement of statification [*étatisation*]' on behalf of 'the higher classes, as they controlled power...The State sees itself required to become the instrument (by the laws it defines, or by the police it introduces) of moralization of these classes' (PS 111/108).[28] Central among these figures is Patrick Colquhoun. At one point Foucault remarks that 'unfortunately, when we teach morals, when we study the history of morals, we always analyse the *Foundations of the Metaphysics of Morals*, and we do not read this person [Colquhoun], fundamental for our morality' (PS 111/108).

The central analysis is of Colquhoun's 1797 work on the police of the metropolis.[29] He stresses this work offers a stark contrast with Bentham and Beccaria on the break between law and morality. For Colquhoun there are three key principles: morality as the foundation of the penal system; the necessity of the police; the target of the lower classes (PS 111–13/108–9). From all of this Foucault draws a number of conclusions:

1. The State is an agent of morality, using the police 'to exercise a whole set of controls over everyday life...the state therefore became the essential agent of morality, of surveillance and ethical-juridical control' (PS 113/110);
2. There are important links to the development of capitalism, with the 'progressive application of this control from only the lowest classes to, finally, workers' (PS 113/110);
3. The coercive factor 'establishes a connection between morality and penality. Its target is not only the infractions of individuals,

but their nature, their character', and for that it requires 'a permanent and fundamental surveillance as instrument' (PS 114/110). The coercive is 'the condition of acceptability for prison. If the prison, with its geographical and religious features, was able to insert itself into the penal system, it is because capitalism utilized coercion in setting up its specific forms of political power' (PS 114/111).
4. The non-conformist religious groups that put pressure on the state 'bring the state into morality [*étatisé la moralite*] and make the State the principal agent of moralization' (PS 115/112).

It is important that England is a detailed example here, and Foucault spends some time discussing the prison reformer John Howard and William Blackstone. The Panopticon is briefly mentioned only once (PS 66/64), but appears in some notes prepared but unread (PS 118/115) and again in the course summary (PS 264/258), even though Bentham is discussed much more. In those unread notes Foucault stresses the role of the Panopticon 'as a form of power, but also type of *savoir*' (PS 118/115). Foucault's neologism 'panopticism' appears in some additional notes that were prepared but unread until Foucault lectured in Rio later in the year (i.e. PS 224/219; and see PS 265/262). What is interesting is that Foucault discusses the spatial characteristics of the prison late in the course, but in relation to the star design (PS 230/226). Foucault appended the comment 'Bentham → Petite Roquette' to the manuscript.[30] Petite Roquette was a prison in Paris opened in 1830 and only closed in 1974. Foucault makes the point that 'this prison form is much more than an architectural form, it is a social form' (PS 230/227). Foucault later says that he discovered the explicit design of the Panopticon, which led him to the text of Bentham's *Panopticon Letters*, when working on hospital architecture (DE#195 III, 190; P/K 146). That was a theme of the seminar running alongside his next course, *Psychiatric Power*, and indeed the Panopticon is discussed in the course itself (e.g. PP 54/52). But the Panopticon is first mentioned in Rio in May 1973, and in an October 1973 interview (DE#127 II, 437).[31] As he declares in Rio, 'today we live in a society programmed basically by Bentham, a panoptic society, a society where panopticism reigns' (DE#139 II, 606; EW III, 70). In *The Punitive Society* there are discussions of other institutions, such as religious communities, factories, Mettray (PS 209–10/204, 221/216), and so on. A key concern is the relation of the system to wealth. Towards the end of the eighteenth century, it is increasingly merchants and aristocrats – 'people linked to power' that promote this form of control, and, crucially, the target changes.

'It is no longer so much marginal or irregular individuals, but the class of workers...one social class over the other' (PS 125/122). In the manuscript: 'The State as agent or essential support of the moralization of the poor classes' (PS 125 n. b/123 n. †)

In France, things are somewhat different. It is perhaps not surprising that Foucault was to abandon this comparative analysis and focus only on France in *Discipline and Punish*, while retaining some of the texts and thinkers discussed here in relation to England. Foucault claims that in France it led not to 'a bourgeois revolution as in England, but a monarchy which finds itself confronted with specific problems of control' (PS 126/123). It shifts away from the army and justice as its 'two instruments of control and repression' (PS 126/123), whose emergence Foucault had traced the previous year, to the use of new apparatuses of *quadrillage* and control, 'on the one hand an apparatus both administrative and para-judicial: the intendants of justice, police and finance; on the other, a police apparatus, directly in the hands of the king, and relayed by the police lieutenants' (PS 127/124). Foucault mentions the kinds of mechanisms that repression requires to function: above all it must be tolerated. He mentions a repressive State apparatus, and suggests this be an explanatory schema of different political systems from the Second Empire to fascism and Nazism (PS 128/125 and 128 n. a/125 n. †). But here, as elsewhere, he is most interested in the social utilization of powers at the capillary level and gives the example of the *lettres de cachet* as a crucial element of this (PS 129/126). These were letters, bearing the king's seal, which allowed imprisonment.

Foucault discusses the *lettres de cachet* in numerous places in his work, and it was to be almost a decade before he published his co-authored study of them.[32] In this course he suggests that while they are often seen as 'the symbol of an autocratic, arbitrary power' (PS 129/127), he contends it is not so much as state power, or that of the King, but the power of the kinds of people who ask for them – 'individuals, families, religious groups, esteemed citizens [*notables*], legal persons (notaries, etc.), and corporations' (PS 130/127). So it is not just an expression of royal, state power, but a 'circular process' between people, more lowly administrators, 'localized micro-powers' (PS 131/128) and so on. Out of all these fascinating figures, he suggests we could reconstruct 'a sort of perpetual biography of infamy, a sort of anti-Plutarch: the lives of infamous men' (PS 134/132). What is intriguing, looking forward, is that these people are so silenced in the book that follows, a curious absence from a book that is so anonymous in those subjected to power. Individuals reemerge with much more explicit focus in lecture courses and the intended *dossiers* of the perverse, hermaphrodites, and other marginalized figures that Foucault collected and, only in part, published.[33] Some of these were under the explicit title of a book series entitled *Lives of Infamous Men*; elsewhere it is the category of the 'dangerous individual'. Here, Foucault discusses how the field of knowledge [*savoir*], constituted out of these biographical archives, had such an influence on the knowledges [*savoirs*] of psychiatry, criminality and sociology in the nineteenth century (PS 135/133). In an undelivered conclusion to the lecture of 14 February 1973 he outlines in some detail how this was a knowledge produced out of permanent surveillance, from dossiers of surveillance, statistics, and the knowledge of individuals, where 'individual *savoir*, clinic of transformation' (PS 138 n. f/136 n. *). In time, of course, we see the replacement of *lettres de cachet* by centralized state organs – the great houses of correction for beggars, vagabonds and the poor – in the hands of the state apparatus, and the ruling class (PS 136–7/134). In Rio he makes the broader point explicit: the 'idea of imprisoning for correction, of keeping a person prisoner until they corrected themselves – this paradoxical, bizarre idea, without any foundation or justification at the level of human behaviour – had its origin precisely in this practice' (DE#139 II, 603; EW III, 67).[34]

Foucault had another example in mind, which was that religion made a link between prison and sin. However he makes a number of distinctions, suggesting that prison as a canonical punishment had been abolished in the early seventeenth century in France and elsewhere at other times, and definitely by the time imprisonment became the key penal punishment (PS 73 n. a/72 n. *). The organization of monasteries is more complicated, and he sketches the relations between cells in convents/monasteries and in prisons, noting that this model is best found in Protestant practice, especially in the Quakers (PS 74 n. a/73 n.*). 'If there is a religious model for the prison, it is certainly in Calvinist theology and morality, and not in the monastic institution' (PS 74 n. a/73 n. *). He stresses that 'the prison is not the convent of the industrial age' (PS 88/86). If it is born out of religion it is Protestant English Dissenters and American Quakers (PS 88/86). Historically, these are better lineages for the modern use of the prison. In particular the Quaker rejection of the English penal code, and the death penalty, is important, and he suggests that the root of the prison lies in the 'Quaker conception of religion, morality and power' (PS 89/87). He gives examples from Pennsylvania after 1790, and the discussion of the text *Des prisons de Philadelphie* by La Rouchefoucauld-Liancourt (1796) (PS 91/88), and suggests that the architectural form of Walnut Street leads to workers' cities and to the great prisons of which Bentham gives the first model. 'M[onastic] F[orm] + worker city → Walnut Street' (PS 95 n. a/93 n. *).

All this perhaps makes sense of why *Discipline and Punish* – concentrating largely on French examples – also made use of English debates and theorists. Key elements within the story told by this course, such as the Quakers and English dissidents are only present in a minor role in *Discipline and Punish*.[35] That element of the course makes explicit the 'genealogy of morality' that Foucault claimed to be making a contribution towards. One further point worth noting is the almost complete absence, here, of references to Foucault's contemporaries or others who examined these questions before him, and it has taken Harcourt's bibliographic labours to fill in some of the missing details, especially Foucault's reading of E. P. Thompson. Of course, reading a text that has its basis in the transcript of Foucault's verbal presentation necessarily lacks the references that might have been provided had he worked this up for publication himself. Yet Harcourt consulted the manuscript that Foucault used as the basis for his lecture delivery, and this provides only minimal detail. Perhaps Foucault thought his audience would fill in some of these missing references for themselves: in the published form Harcourt has done much of this work.[36]

Political Economy

As this discussion suggests, the political-economic aspect of Foucault's analysis is especially striking in this course. He situates his argument within a wider set of historical transitions from feudalism to capitalism (PS 212–13/207, 235/231–2). As Harcourt suggests, 'the 1973 course reads as challenge to the great texts on the history of capitalism'.[37] In its relation of morality to economy, he goes on to suggest it can be read as a fuller engagement with Marx than Foucault's other commentaries, and in juxtaposition with Max Weber's *The Protestant Ethic and the Spirit of Capitalism*.[38] In this he makes explicit a point that should be obvious but is often neglected: that 'the Marxist theory of the accumulation of capital' is, for Foucault, 'dependent on disciplinary techniques (themselves intimately linked to capitalist production) to make "productive bodies"'.[39] *Discipline and Punish* obviously has a discussion of the 'political economy of bodies' (e.g. DP 33/25), but the stakes are not as explicit as in this course; with the recurrent discussion of the body of the worker and the body of wealth [*corps de la richesse*] (PS 178/173–4; 191–2/186–7). There is also much more on the state (with some unspoken allusions to Althusser) than in *Discipline and Punish*.[40]

Perhaps the most explicit development of themes in this course – as opposed to more explicit statements of otherwise well-known themes – concerns the treatment of popular insurrections and illegalism [*illégalisme*]. In this, Foucault's examples again range from England to France. His concern is both with the way that these movements are suppressed, but also how they are utilized. His key term is the control of popular illegalism, which he suggests is a more useful and a rather broader term than 'seditious mob' (PS 144/140).[41] The control of these may be with the direction of State apparatuses by the bourgeoisie, but Foucault contends that the notion of 'a certain popular illegalism is not only *compatible* with, but *useful* for the development of the bourgeois economy'. While the bourgeoisie demands that the judicial apparatus targets popular illegalism when it causes 'damage [*éprédation*]' (PS 144/140), on the other hand he takes Paul Bois's *Paysans de l'Ouest* as an example, which examines the case of the weavers of Maine, who helped the bourgeoisie in their struggle against feudal systems and laws (PS 144–8/141–4). [42] To make sense of these different uses or tactics he proposes a historical divide. While the bourgeoisie was trying to triumph over feudal structures the working class might be a strategic ally; once in a position of power themselves they may become the new social enemy.

> ...these means do not entirely absorb this economic illegalism (machine-breaking), social illegalism (constitution of associations), civil illegalism (refusal of marriage), [moral illegalism,] political illegalism (riots)...
>
> In the eighteenth century, illegalism functions with bourgeois illegalism in a complex relation; in the nineteenth century on the contrary, worker illegalism is the target [*cible*] of the entire repressive system of the bourgeoisie. (PS 154/151)

These shifts run alongside the move to imprisonment as the dominant penalty, with the 'birth of industrial society' partnered by the way 'the bourgeois responds by a gigantic operation which constitutes the penal and penitentiary encirclement of popular illegalism in general' (PS 165/161–2). This was not simply in terms of the perceived threat to bourgeois wealth, but that more and more resources previously held in common were becoming owned. One example is 'the forest, which had been a place of refuge and survival, became exploitable property and thus surveyed [or overseen, *surveillée*]' (PS 161/157–8; see 161 n. b/158 n.*); these techniques applied as much to the urban as the rural; the worker and the peasant (PS 164/160).[43]

Different means might be used to address these concerns. It could involve the use of prison, the army, legal regimes or mechanisms; or it might be through labelling and the work of the sciences. Some of this – anticipating themes Foucault would elaborate in much more detail in *'Society Must Be Defended'* – bought into racial categories, with the 'lower class' described as 'bastardized [*abâtardie*] and primitive' (PS 168/164; see DP 321/276). Some of it links to the labelling of particular kinds of behavior in negative ways, such as the emergence of the delinquent as someone who is savage, immoral, but reformable [*régénérable*] by surveillance. Some of it was on more straight-forward class-based lines. Foucault provides the example of Guy Jean-Baptiste Target's moralization of the two classes as 'one as the bearer of virtues, the values of the good [*bien*, also property], and the other characterized by vices which drive it, its immorality, by the fact it can be considered as foreign to the very body of society, as forming a sort of exterior nation connected to the real nation' (PS 175/170); 'a division of society into two classes' (PS 175/171).

Foucault suggests that the fear at the beginning of the nineteenth century is not just of urbanization and the new modes of production but also a fear of the worker, their desire and their body; and fear of the working (labouring) class. This fear has a foundation, in that bourgeois wealth is under threat from the working class and the limits of its poverty, with the working class portrayed as the 'dangerous' class (PS 176–7/172).[44] Foucault's point, made very explicit here, is that the bourgeoisie establishes the penal code to support property, providing a framework for the regulation of the body of the worker in relation to wealth, profit and law, not so much a contract as a habit [*habitude*] (PS 178/174). As such, the capitalist regime is supported through law and war; through the penal system watching over the body, desire and needs of the worker, and criminal law codes with their direction towards the social enemy (PS 182/178); and through the use of military force, to directly protect the apparatus of production (PS 180/175). Much of this concerns the training of the body, to ensure that bodies are available for work, and their force is applied in the right direction for the necessary task, but also to ensure that bodies are used for the reproduction of the forces of work. Foucault's key text to show how the disciplinary apparatus is brought to bear on the body of workers is Alphonse Grün's *De la moralization des classes laborieuses* from 1851 (PS 192/187).[45] This is not a text that Foucault discusses elsewhere, but the arguments made are important.

Foucault also sketches the outline of a history of laziness, from the classical idleness of the seventeenth to eighteenth centuries; and collective and organized refusal to work in the nineteenth century (PS 193–4/188–9). There are various mechanisms used to deal with this – in the first it is local pressure, almost on an individual level; in the second, 'at the state level', it is tied up with 'the obligation to put everyone to work to augment production as much as possible – the instruments being the police and intendants' (PS 194/189). He discusses how dissipation and degradation go together, and the three institutions of dissipation – festival, gambling, cohabitation (PS 197/192). Different means may be used to address each of these, but broadly the mechanisms are those familiar from Foucault's books: a graduated, continuous, cumulative system; with the continuity and capillarization of justice into everyday life; general surveillance; the form of the examination. What is explicit here, though, is just what the purpose of all this is. If the dominant example in *Discipline and Punish* is the army, then the key reference here is the factory, the workshop, and the figure of control in those institutions – the boss in the factory and the foreman in the workshop (PS 211/206). Foucault spends a lot of time examining different work institutions. His examples include a whole range of institutions of imprisonment – pedagogic 'crèches, schools, orphanages', corrective institutions such as 'agricultural colonies, reformatories, prisons', and therapeutic institutions of 'hospitals, asylums' (PS 209/203). In sum, there are the explicit instruments of 'prison, colonies, army, police'; the construction of the 'social enemy'; and the moralization of the working class (PS 154/151).

Two Methodological Issues

The course is also invaluable for tracking Foucault's developing thinking on two methodological issues: first, the understanding of power, and second, the genealogical approach. Concerning power, Foucault continually stresses the relation between knowledge and power. He contends that as a knowledge-power, 'the prison-form is much more than an architectural form; it is a social-form' (PS 230/227). This means that 'we can thus map [*repérer*] which images symbolize the form of power' – the medieval throne 'the place of listening and judging', 'the magistral form of power', or the head which commands the body, such as in the frontispiece to *Leviathan*. The modern form, in contrast, is a centralized form, 'from which the surveying and controlling gaze radiates' (PS 230–1/227). It is therefore an issue of asking 'in which system of power does the prison function?' (PS 231/227).

This leads Foucault to some summary claims concerning his general analysis of power, and, in particular, of four schemas to reject when trying to understand it:

1. The appropriation of power. 'Certainly, the formula "which class has power" is a politically useful formula, but it does not help a historical analysis' (PS 231/228). Power is not possessed, it is exercised (PS 231–2/228). 'Power is not monolithic', it is 'never stable, suffered once and for all', but always mobile (PS 232/229).
2. The localization of power. Power is not strictly localized in State apparatuses, and 'it is not even sufficient to say the State apparatuses are the stake of an interior or exterior struggle' (PS 233/229). 'that is, practically, neither the control nor the destruction of the State apparatus will suffice to transform or get rid of a certain type of power, in which it functions' (PS 233/229). Rather the grounding [*ancrage*] of power is much deeper, and 'we must therefore distinguish not only systems of power from State apparatuses, but also, in a more general way, systems of power from political structures' (PS 234/230).
3. The subordination of power to the mode of production, to maintain or reproduce it: 'Power can no longer therefore be understood as a guarantee of a mode of production, as that which allows the constituting of the mode of production. Power is in fact one of the constitutive elements of the mode of production, and it functions at its heart' (PS 234/231). Break with the idea that work is crucial to humans – instead we should consider 'pleasure, discontinuity, festival, rest, need, moments, chance, violence, etc.' (PS 236/232) 'Rather, it is all this explosive energy which must be transformed into continual labour power and continually offered on the market' (PS 236/232). These are the tactics necessary to enable the strategy that Foucault is examining.
4. Power as ideology. For Foucault, 'all points of the exercise of power are at the same time a site of formation, not of ideology but of knowledge [*savoir*]; and, on the other hand, every knowledge formed enables and assures the exercise of a power' (PS 237/233). Thus 'it must be shown how knowledge and power are effectively bound up together, not at all in a mode of identity – knowledge is power, or the reverse – but in an absolutely specific way and according to a complex interplay' (PS 237/233). All knowledge permits the exercise of power, but cannot be reduced to it, and Foucault provides the example of administrative surveillance, the

knowledge of management; a knowledge of inquiry; a knowledge of police inquisition (PS 237–8/233–4).

Foucault is therefore getting closer and closer to his mature view of power, and is beginning to sketch the broad contrast between sovereign power and a type of power he alternatively calls disciplinary power, punitive power, or the power of normalization (PS 240–2/237–9, 240 n. b/237 n. *).

> In other words, the discourse which speaks of the king and his majesty [*royauté*] disappears and gives way to the discourse of the master, that is to the discourse of the one who surveys, prescribes the norm, makes the division between the normal and abnormal, (the 'deviant' and the 'ill',) assesses [*apprécie*], judges, decides: discourse of the schoolmaster, judge, doctor, psychiatrist. Linked to the exercise of power, we therefore see the appearance of a discourse which takes over the mythical discourse of the origins of power – which periodically recounted the genealogy of the king and his ancestors – that is the normalizing discourse of the human sciences. (PS 243–4/240–1)[46]

Linking his analysis to the previous course, and the 1972 Minnesota lecture (see Chapter 2), Foucault suggests 'the role of the ceremony of power in the seventeenth century is taken now by what can be called the social consciousness' (PS 243/240). The latter form of power is, in this course at least, very explicitly tied to the wider political-economic frame, suggesting that the apparatus of confinement [*séquestration*] fixes individuals within the apparatus of production, because it fabricates the norm and produces the normal. 'We therefore have a series which characterizes modern society: constitution of a labour force; apparatus of confinement [*séquestration*]; permanent function of normalization' (PS 242/239).[47]

In an earlier lecture Foucault had summarized this in relation to the broader themes he was elaborating: 'it is a society which links to the permanent activity of punishment a connected activity of knowledge, of registration... (Recall that we live in a punitive and examining [*examinatoire*], a *disciplinary* society)' (PS 201/196).[48] Of course, the original French title of *Discipline and Punish* was *Surveiller et punir* – more literally 'survey, supervise or surveil and punish'. The pairing of these terms, as part of a wider system of discipline, first emerges in this text, albeit within a somewhat broader and more explicitly economic analysis:

> The pair survey-punish [*surveiller-punir*] is imposed as the indispensible power relation for fixing individuals within the apparatus of

production, for the constitution of productive forces, and characterizes the society that we can call *disciplinary*. (PS 201/196)

There is also some interesting discussion of the relation between archaeology and genealogy here, among other theoretical asides. The idea of genealogy, being developed here and in previous courses as a complement to archaeology, is seen as equivalent of a dynastic analysis. This is necessary, he contends, because an archaeological focus on discourses alone will not enable an understanding of the emergence of the prison in its modern form. Foucault phrases his inquiry in a way reminiscent of genealogical analyses conducted by himself and his followers:

The problem is precisely to find this apparatus [*appareil*] of power and to see how the prison-form could effectively be inserted and become an instrument in power relations. Until now we have been studying the threads of possible derivations: for example, how ideas and institutions join up with each other within the theoretical and practical penal system. Now it is a matter of discovering the relations of power that made possible the historical emergence of something like the prison. After an analysis of the archaeological type, it is a question of making a dynastic, genealogical type of analysis, tracing the filiations on the basis of relations of power. (PS 86/83–4)

The relation between the dynastic and the genealogical, and in turn their relation to the archaeological, was discussed in Chapter 2 (p. 53 above). In sum, his analysis is of asking 'why this strange institution that is the prison?' (PS 229/225). At an earlier moment in the course when he had phrased a related question, he cautioned how such an analysis should proceed:

...in such a domain as the history of ideas, it must certainly be recognized that influence can never be considered as a cause. (Rather the conditions that made these transfers and exchanges possible must be researched.) It is only a determining phenomenon...(PS 104/101).[49]

In Rio, in a discussion following the final lecture, Foucault made it clear that his current work was extending the archaeological analysis, rather than abandoning it. Archaeology is defined as 'a historico-political attempt which is not grounded on relations of resemblance between the past and the present, but rather on relations of continuity and on the possibility of defining currently the tactical objectives of the strategy of struggle, precisely according to that' (DE#139 II, 644). He is also asked if archaeology is 'a miraculous machine?' His answer is telling, not in relation to the questioner's unclear concept, but in relation to the question of power: 'Archaeology is a machine, certainly, but why miraculous? A critical machine, a machine which puts in question certain relations of power, a machine which has – or at least tries to have – a liberating function' (DE#139 II, 644).

In addition, Foucault is broadening his analysis of the *episteme* to encompass all practices as well as discursive ones (see AK 259/191). Power forces him to develop his earlier conceptualization:

> There are therefore two ensembles [*ensembles*]: the penal *ensemble*, characterized by the prohibition and the sanction, the law; and the punitive *ensemble*, characterized by the coercive penitentiary system. The first *ensemble* carries with it a certain theory of infraction as an act of hostility towards society; the second carries with it the practice of imprisonment. (PS 114/111)

He links the first explicitly to 'the state institutionalization of justice' tracing it back archaeologically to a 'practice of justice organized for the exercise of sovereign political power since the Middle Ages' (PS 114/111). The second comes 'formed in a movement of development, not of the State itself, but the capitalist mode of production; in this second system we can see the mode of production provide itself with the instruments of political power, but also moral power' (PS 115/111). This makes sense of an earlier discussion of the role of the penitentiary as a dimension of all contemporary control societies. The prison existed before, but something additional was added: the penitentiary. 'The penitentiary would be the corrective element of the prison' (PS 103/99). 'The penitentiary is therefore the prison's associated field' (PS 104/100).

Foucault's question, however, extends beyond an archaeological one. 'Thus the genealogical problem is to know [*savoir*] how these two ensembles, of different origins, come to be added together and function inside the same tactic' (PS 115/111). It appears, on this reading, that the notion proposed here of the *ensemble* is an early version of what he would come to call a *dispositif*, a complicated term in Foucault's work which is developed in *Discipline and Punish*, and, most explicitly, in the first volume of the *History of Sexuality*. The concept is discussed in more detail in Chapters 4 and 5, and in *Foucault's Last Decade*, but this course is an important early marker.

In Rio in May 1973 Foucault elaborated on this distinction. The inquiry, which was most fully discussed in Chapter 2 above, is found in philosophy and science, and remains 'a rather characteristic form of truth in our societies' in political, administrative and juridical practice (DE#139 II, 541; EW III, 4–5). But it is not the only such model:

> Other forms of analysis were invented in the nineteenth century, from the starting point of juridical, judicial, and penal problems – rather curious and particular forms of analysis that I shall call *examination*, in contradistinction to the inquiry. Such forms of analysis gave birth to sociology, psychology, psychopathology, criminology, and psychoanalysis...they arose in direct conjunction with the formation of a certain number of political and social controls, during the forming of capitalist society in the late nineteenth century. (DE#139 II, 542; EW III, 5)

In addition, at the end of his final Rio lecture, Foucault makes explicit the links between the inquiry and examination and the Marxist analysis he is utilizing and going beyond:

> It cannot be said that these forms of knowledge [*savoirs*] and these forms of power, operating over and above productive relations, merely express those relations or enable them to be reproduced...Power and knowledge are thus deeply rooted – they are not just superimposed on the relations of production but, rather, are very deeply rooted in what constitutes them...The inquiry and the examination are precisely those forms of knowledge-power that came to function at the level of the appropriation of wealth [*biens*] in feudal society, and at the level of capitalist production and hyperprofit [*sur-profit*]. It is at that basic level that forms of power-knowledge like the inquiry or the examination are situated. (DE#139 II, 623; EW III, 87)

While the focus in these lectures is on institutions such as the prison, factory and school, Foucault also anticipates his next project: 'An entire history could be written of the knowledge [*savoir*] of sexuality', analysing how the old inquiry into dissolute behaviour was taken over by psychiatry and organic medicine, especially with debauchery, syphilis and hysteria (PS 135/133).[50] He briefly mentioned sexuality in schools, and outlines the relation between heterosexuality and homosexuality (PS 219–21/213–16), and the relation of normal and abnormal (PS 221–2/216). This is followed by comments about sexuality and the family (PS 234/230) and Catholic confession (PS 220–1/215; 221 n .a/215 n. †). In themselves these are passing remarks, though with the benefit of hindsight we can see the beginning of future concerns. Some of Foucault's notes from this time focus on nineteenth-century concerns about homosexuality in prisons.[51] In addition, this course opens up themes of civil war and the social enemy that return in later courses including '*Society Must Be Defended*' and the ones on governmentality.

By the time Foucault wrote the course summary around June, he had delivered the Rio lectures, additional ones in New York and Montreal, worked 'on Colquhoun and Bentham in the New York Public Library', and drafted a complete version of *Discipline and Punish* (C 43/54).[52] The course summary, therefore, is a product of his thinking at that time, rather than necessarily a summary of where he was in late March. Reading the course, the Rio lectures and the summary in sequence is interesting as he shows some sense of the movement in his thinking towards the book, with some telling shifts in emphasis. Foucault's summary of this course is his most extensive. He notes that there have been four different strategies of 'punitive tactics', which might be summarized as banishment and dispossession; compensation or debt; physical torture or branding; and confinement. How is it that Western societies, since the end of the eighteenth century moved to the last of these? This is the question that Foucault sought to answer in the 1973 course (PS 255–6/248–9). He goes into some detail about how this might be the case, and there is a confidence to the assertions that comes from the work he has clearly done. Yet that remains a partial sense of the course itself, and there are already some things being underplayed.

Additionally, in the course summary Foucault shows how a focus on the prison in the specific sense is part of a much wider inquiry. Why did Western societies move to 'the strange institution of the prison, why this choice of a penalty whose dysfunction was denounced so early?' (PS 269/263). The answer, in part, is because it has other benefits: 'prison has the advantage of producing delinquency, an instrument of control over and pressure on illegalism, a not insubstantial component in the exercise of power over bodies, an element of that physics of power which gave rise to the psychology of the subject' (PS 269/263). In this focus, rather than others available, the summary is, in some ways, closer to the book to come than the course just delivered. Yet Foucault would continue to work on the manuscript until 26 August 1974, almost eighteen months later, making extensive changes in March–April 1974 while in Montreal, so there was much more development to come (C 44–5/55–6). Crucial here is that by that time, though, he had also delivered another Collège de France course, *Psychiatric Power*.

4

Madness: Power, Psychiatry and the Asylum

Early Seminars and the Case of Pierre Rivière

In the candidacy presentation for his chair at the Collège de France, Foucault had stressed the importance of working with archives to uncover practices alongside scientific discourse (DE#71 I, 842–3; EW I, 5–6). He closes that academic manifesto with the suggestion that:

> Today the history of thought requires, perhaps, a readjustment of the same order: between the constituted sciences (whose history has often been written) and the phenomena of opinion (which historians know how to deal with), it would be necessary to undertake the history of systems of thought. By bringing out the specificity of knowledge [*savoir*] in this way, one not only defines a level of analysis that has been overlooked up to now, but one might well be forced to re-examine knowledge [*connaissance*], its conditions, and the status of the knowing subject [*le sujet qui connaît*]. (DE#71 I, 846; EW I, 9–10)

As well as marking a mild self-critique of his work of the 1960s, this characterized some of his working practices at the Collège de France. His first seminar, running in parallel with *Lectures on the Will to Know*, was on 'penality in nineteenth century France', with a focus on 'the first developments of penal psychiatry in the Restoration period', predominantly using 'the text of medico-legal expert opinions given by Esquirol's contemporaries and disciples' (LWK 221/228). The seminars were held on Mondays, and one of Foucault's colleagues in the seminar, Jean-Pierre Peter, describes the rhythm of 'two meetings a month, rarely more, from December to March – the normal *tempo* of the Collège'.[1] Tellingly for future concerns, in interviews around this time, Foucault notes that 'in the eyes of a lawyer in 1835 there is no difference between prison and internment in an asylum' (DE#105 II, 299; see DE#107 II, 317).

In that seminar, Foucault and his colleagues uncovered a number of fascinating cases. Most of these were found in the *Annales d'hygiène publique et de médecine légale*.[2] One of these was the story of Pierre Rivière, a story of a young Normandy man who had killed his mother, sister and brother, and was later arrested and imprisoned. He committed suicide in prison.[3] Foucault later recalls that the case was discovered by chance when 'making a study of the evolution of the penal system and the relations between psychiatry and penality'.[4] The *Annales* piece provided 'a summary of the facts and the medico-legal experts' reports'. But there was more information than normal, and more importantly a remarkable memoir by Rivière existed (PR 9/vii-viii). The case fascinated them so much that the next year's seminar, which 'continued the study of medico-legal practices and concepts of the nineteenth century' (TIP 234; EW I, 20), concentrated on it in detail. Foucault and his colleagues made an analysis of the documents, which included witness accounts alongside the medical and legal reports. Foucault recounts that 'Riviere's statement, partially published in 1836 in a medical journal, was rediscovered in its entirety by Jean-Pierre Peter, along with most of the documents from the dossier. It is this set that was prepared for publication, with the participation of Robert Castel, Gilles Deleuze, Alexandre Fontana, Jean-Pierre Peter, Phillippe Riot, and Maryvonne Saison' (TIP 234; EW I, 20–1).

Peter was a crucial figure in gathering the materials for the seminar. Foucault had asked him to do much of the archival work, including finding the original of Rivière's memoir at the Archives du Calvados in Caen (PR 13/xii, 15/xiv). Peter thought he may have discovered the Rivière case himself had he continued working on his own research,[5] though Foucault did some archive work in Caen himself.[6] As Macey notes, it was incredible that this material had somehow survived the Second World War bombardment of the Normandy town.[7] Peter had little time in Caen, so made notes, and asked for the materials to be transferred to the Archives nationales in Paris so he could work on them there. He made a transcription of the document, which the seminar participants used – Peter notes the discrepancies in the analysis, a result of the use of his unfinished, incomplete and often faulty work.[8] Foucault suggests that the case was of interest for multiple reasons. Rivière's own memoir combined being 'a remarkable document of peasant ethology' with explanation for his acts; there were several 'relatively detailed' witness depositions; 'a series of psychiatric reports' from a country doctor, a regional physician, and several Parisian experts; and its timing, where the case coincided with the 'beginning of criminological psychiatry', debates between psychiatrists and jurists about monomania and mitigation, and the emergence of 'the great criminal in literature'. Foucault links this explicitly to the publication of Pierre-François Lacenaire's *Mémoires*, which was the account of his crimes and the rationale behind them (TIP 234; EW I, 20–21; see DP 331–3/283–5; SP 183–4). The *Mémoires* were an influence on Dostoyevsky and Balzac.[9]

The following year's seminar was entitled 'Pierre Rivière et ses oeuvres' (C 42/52) and was focused on continuing the work of preparing the dossier for publication (PS 269/263). The work ran into logistical problems. Foucault had wanted to restrict the seminar to a small group of committed contributors, asking them to commit to its work in writing, but the Collège authorities did not allow this. He had to open up the seminar and Peter was scathing about those who then attended, describing the discussions as 'immediately overwhelmed by a vampire horde of knowledge consumers'.[10] The seminar was in danger of becoming effectively a second lecture course, with the attendant tape recorders and a risk of unauthorized transcripts circulating. Indeed, there was a rumour that someone was going to publish a version of the seminar discussions, which precipitated the official publication – more swiftly than was intended and without the care Peter wished.[11]

In the collection, Peter and Jeanne Favret note that 'if the peasants had a Plutarch, Pierre Rivière would have his chapter in the *Illustrious Lives*' (PR 243/175; see PS 134/132). Foucault would go on to use this idea for his 'Lives of Infamous Men' project.[12] While they took the Rivière case as the basis for this work, it was not the only interesting case Foucault and his seminar colleagues discovered. Peter published other instances himself in two articles.[13] These included the anonymous woman of Sélestat who killed and ate her daughter at the time of a famine in Alsace in 1817, the shepherd Léger who killed and ate a young girl, and Henriette Cornier who murdered her neighbour's daughter. Foucault then used those cases as illustrative examples in *The Abnormals* lecture course a few years later, and returns to them in a 1976 radio interview and in the 'About the Concept of the "Dangerous Individual" in 19th Century Legal Psychiatry' lecture in 1977.[14]

Foucault also had peripheral involvement in the production of a 1976 film based on this memoir, directed by René Allio.[15] Foucault was to play the role of a judge, but the scene did not make the final cut. The BNF has a copy of the 'Press-book' of the film, including a synopsis, cast list and multiple press reviews; as well as some correspondence between Foucault, Allio and Claude Gallimard concerning the rights to the film.[16] The BNF also includes notes in Foucault's handwriting including archives to consult, planned contents of the book and drafts of his own contribution.[17] With the exception of this volume on Rivière, and the one on Herculine Barbin, Foucault did not end up publishing many of the dossiers of case studies which he frequently promised, nor the volumes of the *History of Sexuality* on women, children and perverts where such cases might have found a natural home. But it is possible that such examples helped him to formulate his late work on technologies of the self and the ethics of self-formation.[18]

Rewriting the *History of Madness*

While Foucault's courses of this period show how he was developing a major interest in penal practice, the institution of the prison and its wider social setting, the work of his seminars shows how he connected this work to his earlier interests in mental illness and psychiatry. These concerns came to the fore in the 1973–4 Collège de France course *Psychiatric Power*. Reading the course summary, probably from June 1974, is revealing. Here Foucault discusses urban medicine, hospitals, diseases, Pasteur and anti-psychiatry – although there is little about these themes in the course as a whole. Seen in a wider context, however, of the work of his seminar at the Collège de France and lectures in other locations, especially in Rio in late 1974, the summary makes more sense. It seems likely that – as with *The Punitive Society* – the work in the seminar and the material prepared for Rio may have shaped the retrospective presentation of *Psychiatric Power*, of which the analyses are complementary in a number of ways.

Foucault's development of the question of power and the genealogical mode of analysis in the early 1970s, as previous chapters have shown, partnered rather than replaced knowledge and archaeology. If archaeology was concerned with a historical excavation of the conditions of possibility of statements of knowledge within specific discourses, genealogy examined the relation between knowledge and *power*, a more explicitly politicized approach that looks at the practices that partner, produce and depend on discourses. But *History of Madness* is a text that certainly does this already, as indeed does *Birth of the Clinic*. As Foucault remarked in June 1976:

When I think back now, I ask myself what else it was that I was talking about, in *History of Madness* or *Birth of the Clinic*, but power? Yet I'm perfectly aware that I scarcely ever used the word and never had such a field of analyses at my disposal. (DE#192 III, 146; P/K 115; see DE#216 III, 402–3)

In 1978 he makes a similar point:

In writing *History of Madness* and *Birth of the Clinic*, I meant to do a genealogical history of knowledge [*savoir*]. But the real guiding thread was the problem of power. (DE#281 IV, 82; EW III, 283)

In a sense then *Psychiatric Power* is a return to *History of Madness* with the word and the field of analyses at hand, just as the Rio medicine lectures could be said to be a similar return to *Birth of the Clinic*. The guiding theme in both, as indeed it is in *Discipline and Punish*, is a historical, institutional and social analysis of how 'knowledge functions as power' (PP 187/190). Yet tellingly, Foucault says that while the book *History of Madness* is read as political in the early 1970s, this was not the case when the book first came out in the early 1960s (DE#136 II, 524).

One of the things that emerges from reading the full version of *History of Madness* (as opposed to its abridged form as *Madness and Civilisation*) is how much the later Foucault was prefigured by this text.[19] That is, there is a general concern with themes such as health, confinement, sexuality and classification, which would be deepened and discussed in *Birth of the Clinic*, *The Order of Things*, *Discipline and Punish*, and *The History of Sexuality*. Indeed, in a 1978 interview Foucault suggested that *History of Madness* was the 'first chapter', the beginning of a programme of study (CMPP 124/113). In this course what we find is not just a development of material on these kinds of themes, but an explicit reworking of ideas in that book, especially its final parts. As well as the emphasis on power there is an attempt to go beyond institutional analyses to examine the impact of psychiatry and medicine in society more broadly. This reassessment of previous work makes sense: both the *History of Madness* and *Birth of the Clinic* were reissued in 1972, with some important additions and amendments. With *History of Madness*, Foucault replaced the preface and added two appendices. One of those was the reprint of a 1964 text, 'Madness, the Absence of Work', and the other a reply to Derrida's criticism of the passage on Descartes in the original text.[20] With *Birth of the Clinic* the changes were mainly to remove structuralist language from the original, and to be more precise on issues of knowledge in the light of *The Archaeology of Knowledge*. At the same time, Foucault was redrafting his book manuscript *Discipline and Punish*, which was completed on 26 August 1974, and published in February 1975. *Discipline and Punish* functions as an indispensable counterpoint to *Psychiatric Power*: it was a book for which the research appears to have been done at the time of the course's delivery, although the final writing was not completed until the summer. There is some material shared between the two, but not nearly as much as might be expected given their temporal proximity. As such, division of themes here is to an extent arbitrary. The remainder of this chapter discusses the rereading of questions concerning madness and psychiatry; Chapter 6 discusses the work on medicine; Chapter 5 the work on prisons and *Discipline and Punish*.

Psychiatric Power develops a number of themes, including topics that were not mentioned in the summary, particularly some very revealing work on the question of sexuality in relation, especially, to women and children. The sexuality theme is analysed in *Foucault's Last Decade*, chapter 1, because it anticipates work planned for volumes of the original, thematic, *History of Sexuality*. Here the analysis situates *Psychiatric Power* in relation to Foucault's earlier researches into madness and psychiatry, particularly looking at three methodological problems he identifies in that earlier work which he seeks to correct. It then discusses three key themes: the sources of power, particularly looking at the role of the army and religion; the emergence of the individual; and the role of spatial control in disciplinary power. To varying degrees these are all familiar themes in Foucault's work, but they are enriched, altered and contextualized by their presentation in this course. In reading this course we can gain a clearer picture of how Foucault's thought developed, and see ways in which his ideas might be applied. The course can be seen both as a reworking of *History of Madness* in the light of the extensive research already done for *Discipline and Punish*, and as leading towards the *History of Sexuality*.

When Foucault explicitly suggests that he wants to rework the themes of the last part of *History of Madness*, he says this will be with a certain number of differences. That book provides the 'background' for the new work being undertaken, but 'it has a certain number of things which are entirely open to criticism, above all in the final chapter where I ended up precisely with the power of the asylum [*pouvoir asilaire*]' (PP 14/12). *Psychiatric Power* only returns to the latter part of the earlier book, at the point where the analysis 'was interrupted' (PP 14/12), essentially the discussion of Tuke and Pinel and the 'liberation' of the mad for moral imprisonment. In the *History of Madness* this is followed by a concluding chapter that supposedly valorizes or romanticizes the mad: discussing Nietzsche, Artaud, Van Gogh, Hölderlin and others. While Foucault developed literary themes in much of his work of the 1960s, by the time of this course he had shifted focus. Foucault says to his audients at the beginning of *Psychiatric Power*, this course is 'a little bit different [*un petit peu en discontinuité*] in relation to what I have spoken to you in the last two years, but not completely' (PP 3/1). This makes sense: the specific focus is different, because it concerns psychiatric expertise and asylums rather than theories of punishment; but the interpretative lens is the one he has been developing in previous courses.

There are three displacements that he wants to make in relation to *History of Madness*.

1. A shift from analysis of representations to an analytic of power
2. From violence to the microphysics of power
3. From institutional regularities or state apparatus to 'dispositions' of power

First, in *History of Madness* Foucault accords a privilege to questions of 'perception of madness', to representations, traditional or other images, to phantasms, to knowledge as *savoir*. In part this is a response to the more literary work, but this 'second volume', as he explicitly calls it, rather than offer a 'history of mentalities, of thought' instead undertakes an analysis of 'a *dispositif* of power'. *Dispositif* is one of the most difficult words in Foucault's work to translate adequately, meaning straight-forwardly 'apparatus' but also the arrangement or set-up of a web of practices and their attendant discourses (DE#206 III, 298–329; P/K 194–228).[21] Foucault's question is how this *dispositif* of power produces a certain number of *énoncés* (scientific statements), discourses, and forms of representation? (PP 14/13; see DE#206 III, 300–2; P/K 196–8) In this sense the *dispositif* of power – a broader development of the *episteme* of knowledge, and the *ensemble* of 1973 (PS 114/111) – should be seen 'as a productive instance of discursive practice' (PP 14/13).

> The discursive analysis of power would be, in comparison with that which I call archaeology, at a level (the word 'fundamental' doesn't appeal to me much), let's say at a level which enables us to grasp the discursive practice at the precise point where it is formed. This formation of discursive practice, to what must it refer, where must we search for it? (PP 14/13)

This work therefore opens up various questions of power, and the relations of this power to discursive practices (PP 15/13). We see here

Foucault working through in rough, schematic form the central theses he would advance in books and other writings in the period from 1975 on, and to which he would continually return in interviews.

Second, Foucault admits he was very ignorant of the anti-psychiatry and psycho-sociological literature in the period of writing *History of Madness* (see DE#160 II, 773–4). In part because of this, he made implicit or explicit appeal to three notions, which appear to him as 'rusted locks [*serrures rouillées*]' which prevented him from advancing, at least at that time. These were violence, the institution and the family. In relation to violence he states that this was an attempt to combat the hagiographies of mental health reformers, and to stress the physical force they used. Now he considers that this would have been better analysed through power, and the role of the body: 'All power is physical, and there is a direct connection [*branchement*] between the body and political power' [PP 15/14). Rather than some totalizing understanding of violence this work requires an attempt to grasp the capillary nature or level of power, a species of the microphysics of bodies (PP 16/14). Foucault suggests that what John Haslam calls the 'moral treatment' of the mad is *discipline* (PP 10/9). Knowledge becomes revealed as power. As well as violence, Foucault reconsiders the reading given of the institution. In 1973 he suggests that rather than some unified thing called an institution, of which the asylum took a privileged place, he should instead consider relations of individuals and the group, and the rules which regulate them (PP 16/15). Again then, issues of power arise – 'relations of force in the tactical dispositions that permeate institutions' (PP 17/15, see 34/33). Foucault had argued this earlier in the course: 'You have therefore a tactical functioning of power, or rather, it is this tactical disposition which permits power to be exercised' (PP 8/6). Finally, the family as analysed in *History of Madness* strikes him as problematic. The suggestion there that Pinel or Esquirol introduced the family model into the institution of the asylum seems wrong to him on rereading their works. He now suggests that the father figure in the space of the asylum is produced later, only really in the twentieth century (PP 17/15–16). Foucault therefore suggests that violence is not the right word; that the institution is not the correct level of analysis; and we should not speak of the family (PP 17/15).

The third point is related. Although we should turn our attention away from the institution to wider issues of individual and collectivity, we should not use this as a reason to turn to an analysis of state apparatuses, such as Althusser had proposed in a famous essay.[22] Foucault notes that: 'it is clearly the institution – as a place, a form of distribution, and a mechanism of these power relations – that antipsychiatry attacks' (PP 350/344). This will be one of the themes of the 1974 Rio lectures. The course manuscript has an important paragraph on this that was not delivered:

> We should not use the notion of state apparatus, because it is much too broad, much too abstract to indicate these immediate, miniscule, capillary powers, which are exercised over bodies, the behaviour, actions, and time of individuals. The state apparatus doesn't take this microphysic of power into account. (PP 17 n. */16 n. *; see DE#139 II, 622, EW III, 86–7; DE#160 II, 772)

In sum, Foucault suggests there are three replacements necessary in relation to *History of Madness*: a microphysic of power for violence; tactic for institution; strategy for family model. He notes that this is an attempt to avoid psycho-sociological vocabulary, and recognizes that he is now using 'a pseudo-military vocabulary' (PP 18/16). According to the manuscript, examples like that of George III (discussed below) are not 'theatrical episodes but a ritual, a strategy, a battle'.[23] Given the two previous courses, and the turn his work took – notably in *Discipline and Punish*, 'Questions on Geography' and *'Society Must Be Defended'* – to questions of war and the military model this is perhaps not entirely surprising.

The Sources of Power

Much of the work discussed elsewhere in this book shows how Foucault proposed a move from an understanding of power on the Hobbesian model of sovereignty to a more dispersed and less centralized model, an understanding of power that is less possessed than exercised and which works throughout society rather than from a centralized source. In this course he provides a related yet strikingly different example. This is the story of King George III of England and his madness (PP 21–33/19–32). The transfer of power from a monarch to the doctors is symptomatic of a more generalized shift from a macrophysic of sovereignty to a microphysic of power. Foucault argues that what we have is not a transition from one sovereign power to another, but from sovereign power to another type of power. 'In place of this decapitated and dethroned [*decouronné* – literally uncrowned] power, an anonymous, multiple, pale, colourless power, is installed which is basically what I will call disciplinary power' (PP 23/22). This is power as discipline, not power that is 'concentrated in a named and visible individual, but that only produces an effect on its target, on the body and person of the dethroned king, who must be rendered "docile and submissive" by this new power' (PP 23/22; the quote is from Pinel).[24] In this new discipline, the figure of the doctor (Willis) is eclipsed (PP 24/23), because the shift is less from one figure to another, but from sovereignty to disciplinary power (PP 28/27). It is for this reason that the deposition or fall of the King is not comparable to a Shakespearean drama, such as *Richard III* where it is a question of a rival sovereign (a common theme in the history plays) or even *King Lear* where the dethroned king wanders in the wild (PP 23/21). Rather than the replacement of one power with another, it is a replacement of a *kind* of power.

The understanding of a new mode of power, as disciplinary power, is for Foucault a certain way in which political power touches and affects bodies, in all their actions and reactions, even down to the 'soft fibres of the brain' (the quote is from Servan).[25] Foucault elaborates: 'To put it another way, I believe that disciplinary power is a quite specific modality of what can be called the synaptic contact of body-power' (PP 42/40) Once again the manuscript includes a critique of Marxist (specifically Althusserian) approaches: 'methodologically this entails that we leave to one side the problem of the State, the State apparatuses, and that we get rid of the psycho-sociological notion of authority' (PP 42 n. */40 n. *). This is clearly a development of the critique proposed in *The Punitive Society*.

The source of this new form of power is twofold in this course: religious practices and the military. Foucault suggests that this kind of power was 'not completely marginal to medieval society, but it was certainly not central either'. Religious communities were crucial here, and through the fourteenth to fifteenth centuries Foucault suggests we can trace the emergence of disciplinary measures of everyday life, in pedagogy, and the generalized discipline of the convent and asceticism (PP 42–3/40–1). These increasingly spread through society as a whole in the following centuries, taking centre stage in the nineteenth. Foucault discusses the *Brethren of the Common Life*, earlier models from the eleventh to twelfth centuries, Cistercian monasteries, and the orders of Cluny and Cîteaux (PP 54/52, 66–72/64–70).[26] He also looks at colonization by the Jesuits in South America, and suggests that the republics that were set up in particular in Guaranis, in Paraguay, known as 'communist', 'were in reality disciplinary microcosms' (PP 71/69).

The importance of these models is in the control of time, the general surveillance and individualization of the people within them, and a permanent penal system. This penal system was in a sense very indulgent compared to Europe at the time: there was no death penalty, no *supplice* and no *torture* but instead an absolutely permanent system of punishment, which continued throughout the life of the individual (PP 71/69).[27] Although Foucault also makes reference to the grand confinement of the classical age, which he analyses in both *Discipline and Punish* and *History of Madness*, in this course these religious models allow him to raise a whole range of general questions about politics, surveillance and discipline that are in many ways the key themes of this course. His analysis therefore is of the contrast between sovereign power (without his being entirely happy with the word) and disciplinary power (PP 44/42).

Sovereign power is power shot through with asymmetry, founded on some anterior event that it always carries with it, such as divine right, conquest, victory, act of submission, an oath of fidelity, rights of blood etc. (PP 44/43). On this model, 'the other side of sovereignty is violence, it is war' (PP 45/43), a claim that Foucault makes in *The Punitive Society* and would pursue in detail in the 1975–6 '*Society Must Be Defended*' lecture course. Relationships within sovereignty are not isotopic (the same in all places), they are not organized rationally by relations of classification, not a hierarchical table of elements (PP 45/43). Disciplinary power on the other hand, does not work on asymmetry, nor on one-way relations, but is more totalizing and organizing. The example given is military discipline, which Foucault claims did not really exist before the Thirty Years War (1618–48), armies being more agglomerations of disparate forces and mercenaries. Of course, as he would later recognize in *Discipline and Punish* classical Rome provided the model for this later disciplinary model. From the middle of the seventeenth century then, and it is not unrelated that this is the same era as modern states start to emerge, with the allowing of standing armies in the Peace of Westphalia for the territorial princes, a system of discipline emerges in the army, based around career soldiers. These soldiers are not only engaged during war, but also in peace, except for periods of demobilization. Foucault notes that they receive a pension, and thus continue to think of themselves as a retired soldier (PP 48/46–7).

Once again the same kinds of issues as in the religious communities emerge: 'Military discipline commences as a general confiscation of the body, time, life' (PP 48/47). Generalizing this point, Foucault contends that 'all disciplinary systems, I believe, tend to be an occupation of the time, the life and the body of the individual' (PP 49/47). Somewhat problematically Foucault contends that disciplinary power does not need ritual or ceremony to function, but more convincingly notes that it is not discontinuous but continuous (PP 49/47). The army is again used as example, with exercises of discipline and so on (PP 49/47–8), and the Prussian army under Friedrich II is used as an example of corporal exercise, and dressage, training and breaking-in, of the body (PP 50/48). Here again we find the generalized regulation and surveillance, punishment of the minor transgression (PP 52–3/51). Foucault notes that before the regulated army there was no such thing as a deserter as there was no disciplinary structure (PP 55/53). Although Foucault gives a parallel example of the regulations in the Gobelins tapestry factory in Paris (PP 51/49, 53/51), the army here plays a major role in the analysis.

Foucault suggested that war was the verso of the relations of sovereignty, whereas the other side [*le verso*] of the relations of discipline is punishment [*la punition*], a kind of 'punitive pressure' that is 'at the same time minuscule and continuous' (PP 53/51). *Le verso* in this sense seems to mean more than simply reverse, but rather also the limit case, the extreme form. Foucault uses this model of discipline throughout the course, as the following sections of this chapter will demonstrate. As well as these extreme forms, often centred in institutional settings despite his earlier admonition, Foucault also goes on to look at the generalized surveillance of populations, and of regimes of medicine and health (PP 247–8/247–8). As in the Rio lectures from later in the year he moves between analyses of hospital based medicine and wider concerns for public health. Here he suggests that pathological anatomy, analysed of course in *Birth of the Clinic*, and the appearance of statistical medicine (a medicine of large numbers) are the two main epistemological instruments of the nineteenth century in medicine (PP 248/248). What we have here, just as he would later analyse through sexuality, is a juxtaposition of individual bodies and collective bodies.

One of Foucault's key points is that we usually trace the emergence of the individual in thought and European political reality as an effect of capitalist economy and the claiming of political power by the bourgeoisie, along with a philosophical-juridical theory that comes from Hobbes in the seventeenth century and can be traced through to the French Revolution. Foucault argues rather that the constitution of the individual is a product of a certain technology of power, namely discipline, 'specific to the power which is born and develops from the classical age, which isolates and divides, which comes from the game of bodies' (PP 59/57). Capitalist economy and power, and the philosophical-juridical theory need to be seen against this backdrop. There are two types of individuals according to this analysis: the juridical individual, an abstract subject with individual rights that no power can remove, except they consent by contract; and the individual as a historical reality, an element of 'productive forces, as an element also of political forces; and that individual is a subjectified body [*corps assujetti*], held in a system of surveillance and submitted to procedures of normalization' (PP 59/57). A couple of years later he enforces the point, showing how his work develops Marxist themes: 'You cannot understand the development of productive forces unless you perceived in industry and society a particular type or several types of power at work, at work inside the productive forces'.[28]

Foucault goes on to argue that the human sciences – in French the *sciences de l'homme* as well as the *sciences humaines* – have their express purpose to conjoin, *jumeler*, to twin, or to pair, the juridical and disciplinary individual (PP 59/57). There is a strong relation here to the analysis of the birth of 'man' in *The Order of Things*, an argument that is expressly politicized here: 'From this oscillation between the juridical individual, ideological instrument of the demand for power, and the disciplinary individual, real instrument of power's physical exercise, it is of this oscillation between the power claimed and the power exercised, is born this illusion and this reality which we call Man' (PP 60/58). This course also provides some important indications to how Foucault would think of women and children, discussed in the first chapter of *Foucault's Last Decade*.

Space and the Panopticon

In the course summary Foucault talks about 'the example of medicine, with the space connected to it, the hospital' and sees the latter as 'a birthplace of the true disease' (PP 341/335). He goes on to discuss the idea of a hospital as a place where all the misleading and confusing contexts of disease could be removed so that it could be seen in its pure state: 'a botanical site for the contemplation of species, a still-alchemical place for the elaboration of pathological substances' (PP 342/336). As is well known, Foucault, who regularly used spatial language, did not use this vocabulary merely as metaphor, but made several concrete analyses of the geographical aspects of the issues he studied.[29] As he said in 1978, 'what I study is an architecture, a spatial disposition' (CMPP 114/105).

The hospital is 'a place of observation and demonstration, but also of purification and testing'. The key issue therefore is 'should the hospital, a reception structure for the disease, be a space of knowledge [*connaissance*] or a place of testing [*épreuve*]?' (PP 342/336) In other words is the hospital a place where disease should be stopped (for the purpose of cure) or cultivated (for examination and learning)? In the summary there is an interesting aside on Pasteur and the way his work on contagion showed that physicians did not merely produce the truth of disease (i.e. an intellectual project of truth) but through ignorance of truth, had spread and thereby produced disease *itself*. 'Up to that moment, the hospital space and the physician's body had had the role of producing the "critical" truth of disease; now the doctor's body and the overcrowded hospital appeared as the producers of the disease's reality' (PP 343/337; see PH 97, 99–100).

> By determining the agent of the sickness and by pinpointing it as a specific organism, it enabled the hospital to become a place of observation, diagnosis, and clinical and experimental identification [or mapping, *réperage*], but also of immediate intervention, of counterattack against the microbial invasion. (PP 342/336-7)

This is the 'other story', that Foucault does not treat in detail (nor does he refer to it in the course itself), but about which 'a few remarks may help us to understand the position of the madman and the psychiatrist in the space of the asylum' (PP 343/337). Extending the medical issue, the role of psychiatrist is that of 'producing the truth of illness in the space of the hospital' (PP 347/342). Once more, *Birth of the Clinic* provides a useful background, but instead in the course itself there is extensive discussion of, among other themes, the 'organization of the space of the asylum' (PP 13/12). It is once again in the Rio lectures of later that year, and in his concurrent seminar that Foucault really explores the issues he suggests in the summary (see Chapter 6).

The course itself begins with a description of the ideal asylum of Fodéré in 1817 – an asylum that is not altogether dissimilar from the château of Sade's *One Hundred and Twenty Days of Sodom* (PP 3/1-2). But despite this magical and romantic setting, in the inside 'order reigns, law reigns, power reigns' (PP 4/2). There is the 'perpetual, permanent regulation, of time, activities, actions; an order which surrounds bodies, which penetrates them, makes them work, is applied to their surface', but also bears its mark on the nerves and soft fibres of the brain (PP 4/2). For the workings of power, bodies appear as 'surfaces to cross and volumes to work' (PP 4/2; see DE#84, II, 143; EW II, 375). Foucault also discusses the use of the medical gaze, which is 'constitutive of medical knowledge [*savoir*] and the criteria of its validity, [and] has as its effective condition of possibility a certain relation to order, a certain distribution of time, of space, of individuals' (PP 4/2-3). Discipline is, in this sense, a distribution of bodies, of their actions, comportments, of speech (PP 4/3). There is a twofold issue here: this disciplinary order is both necessary for exact observation and the condition for permanent recovery (PP 4/3).

In an anticipation of the analysis of *Discipline and Punish*, Foucault notes the crucial elements of the disciplinary system:

1. Spatial fixation
2. Optimal extraction of time
3. Application and exploitation of bodily forces
4. Constitution of constant surveillance and an immediate punitive power
5. Organization of regularity power which is anonymous and non-individual in its operations, but which allows a *repérage*, a mapping or location of subjectivized individuals (PP 73/71).

Foucault's analysis here shows the accumulation of people alongside accumulation of capital, a particular distribution of the work force, presented in 'all their somatic singularities' (PP 73/71, see 74/72). We have here another recognition of the workings of capital in the disciplinary society. 'Discipline is a tactic, a certain manner of distributing singularities according to a non-classificatory schema, a way of distributing them spatially, of making possible the most effective temporal accumulations at the level of productive activity' (PP 74/72–3).

In discipline, as opposed to earlier models which are both exceeded by and the condition of possibility of this new organization, 'tactics, and with it man, the problem of the body, the problem of time, etc. replaces taxonomy' (PP 75/73). In this course we find an idea that would be the subject of further analysis by Foucault and a research team at the Collège de France: the hospital as a 'curing machine' (see Chapter 6).

> That is to say, the architectural character itself, the organization of space, the way in which individuals are distributed in that space, the way in which they circulate, the manner which they observe [*regard*] and in which they are observed, it is all this which has therapeutic value in itself. In the psychiatry of this period, the curing machine is the hospital. (PP 103/102)

Foucault later describes the asylum as a 'curing *dispositif*' (PP 163/164). The institution is therefore 'a large single body where walls, wards, instruments, nurses, the supervisors [*surveillants*] and the doctor are the elements which have, of course, different functions to perform, but the essential function of which is to bring about an collective effect'. This naturally works in different ways at different times: sometimes the key role is played by the general system of surveillance, sometimes by the doctor and sometimes by spatial isolation (PP 163/164; see DE#146 II, 697–8).

It is here that the Panopticon emerges in the text, as disciplinary power takes an 'absolutely generalized social form' (PP 43/41). This and the confrontation between George III and his servants are, for Foucault, two near-contemporaneous 'historic and symbolic points of the emergence and definitive installation of disciplinary power in society' (PP 43/41). This power goes beyond what can be analysed in the functioning of the institution of the asylum: 'it is from the functioning of disciplinary power that we can comprehend the mechanism of psychiatry' (PP 43/41). Foucault's general analysis of the Panopticon and the panoptic character of disciplinary power (PP 54/52) is well known, and will be returned to in the discussion of *Discipline and Punish* in Chapter 5 below. What is important is that Foucault notes the importance of this 'spatial disposition' (PP 103/102) in the functioning of a hospital rather than a prison. In this course, the one of the previous year and the attendant seminar research discussed in Chapter 6, we can now recontextualize a remark in an interview where Foucault noted that he had discovered the Panopticon in a study of hospital architecture (DE#195, III, 190; P/K 146). The other context for the Panopticon in this course is the discussion of Jesuit missions in Paraguay, the army, workshops, and workers' cities (PP 65–88/63–87).

Nor should we forget that, even in Bentham, the Panopticon was never *merely* a prison. Bentham's text is the place where Foucault finds a 'very clear formalization, very remarkable, of the microphysics of disciplinary power'. We are accustomed to thinking of the Panopticon as a prison, but 'in fact, Bentham's Panopticon is not a model for a prison, or it is not only a model for a prison; it is a model, and Bentham says this very clearly, for a prison, but also for a hospital, for a school, a workshop [*atelier*], an orphanage. It is a form, I would say, for all institutions' (PP 75/73–4). And yet, even this formula may be misleading. Bentham does not even say that it is a schema or diagram for institutions, but a mechanism, by which power in an institution is magnified and multiplied. It is the idea of the Panopticon as constituting a 'Herculean force, but also a way of giving mind power over mind'. This is both the specific mechanism of the Panopticon and what is found in the 'general disciplinary form' (PP 76/74). His remark is followed by a reading of the space of the Panopticon (PP 76–80/74–8, see DE#139 II, 594–5; EW III, 58; DP 233–9/200–9).

The point being made is that if the hospital is such a 'curing machine' then it is not on the model of the family, but as a 'panoptic machine', it is 'as a panoptic apparatus [*appareil*] that the hospital cures' (PP 103/102).

> It is, in effect, a machine to exercise power, to induce, distribute, and apply power according to the Benthamite schema, even if, obviously, the specific architectural arrangements [*dispositions*] of Bentham's design are modified. (PP 103/102)

This is important. Foucault is sometimes criticized for generalizing Bentham's ideal plan into a model for institutions that do not look like it. Here he is making it clear that hospitals often utilized the general idea rather the exact model. There are several crucial elements of this, of which he highlights four. First, the idea of permanent visibility is retained, but instead of the circular Panopticon of cells, or a dormitory model, hospitals substitute an *architecture pavillonaire*, of small individualized units (PP 103–4/102–3). Second, the centralized surveillance is not in the form of a tower of anonymous power, but a managerial building, which allows analysis of the other buildings, what we might call 'the pyramid surveillance of observation [*la surveillance pyramidale des regards*]', of the 'guards, nurses, supervisors, physicians, who all makes some connections according to a hierarchical model, and which culminates in the chief-doctor, only responsible to the asylum'. In this the administrative and medical power cannot be disassociated, we have the explicit coupling of 'knowledge-power' (PP 104/103). Third, the principle of isolation and individuation with therapeutic value is followed. Just as Bentham's cells have a double opening and backlighting, so too does the model of Esquirol (PP 105/103). Fourth, constant examination, continual punishment of each and every minor transgression.

In the last of these Foucault notes the principle of 'no restraint' put forward by some reformers, with the abolition of means of physical constraint, the removal of the chains and the decrease in physical violence. Ultimately Foucault does not think this is all that important in terms of the policies actually being employed, suggesting that punishment continues. In one of the more gruesome parts of the course he does however go into some detail about various mechanisms utilized – such as fixed chairs which people were locked into, handcuffs, the mufflers that keep hands in front of the body [*les manchons*], straitjackets, finger-glove garments tight from the neck down to make the hand pinned to the thighs, wicker caskets that people were locked into, dog collars with spikes under the chin (PP 106/105). He is clearly fascinated by these 'corporeal apparatuses [*appareils corporels*]', and indeed he comes up with a three-part typology for them.

1. Apparatuses of guarantee and proof [*épreuve*] – things which prevent certain types of behaviour, prohibit certain desires. The chastity belt is the ideal type.
2. Apparatuses for extracting truth, through gradual intensification, quantitative growth, such as water-torture or the *strappado*. The latter is a form of torture with a rope tied around the hands, thrown over a beam, the individual hoisted up and left hanging, or occasionally dropped a certain distance. It was used on Machiavelli among others.
3. Means of marking the force of power on the body such as branding, torture [*tenailler*] or burning the regicide. (PP 106–7/105)

There is a fourth kind, which appears in the nineteenth century, particularly in the asylums, which includes the various 'orthopaedic instruments' used for the straightening [*redressement*] and dressage of the body. These are instruments of continuous action, with a progressive effect, which ultimately make themselves unneeded. So, for example, a collar with iron spikes, which if the wearer keeps their head straight and upright then they do not feel it (PP 107/105–6). The model for this is clearly not the family, but the barracks, with its parades and inspections; the workshop; certain types of agricultural practice in the colonies; and schools (PP 108/106). It is remarkable that prisons are not mentioned, though of course they had been extensively discussed in previous courses. It is also worth noting, given the impact of Foucault's work on post-colonial studies, the references he makes to colonial disciplinary regimes (see, for example, PP 110/108, 127/127).

As well as being a disciplinary space, 'the asylum is a space which is marked medically' (PP 176/178; see also 186/188). Psychiatric knowledge [*savoir*] plays a particular role, but there is a very material, corporeal element involved. Differences such as the curable or incurable; the calm or agitated; the obedient or non-submissive; those capable or not of working; those to be punished or left alone; and the level of surveillance required (continual, from time to time, not at all), are related to the spatial organization of the institution itself. It is this distribution which striates the internal space of the asylum rather than medical nosographies (PP 177–8/180). Struggles in the space of the asylum are a grappling between bodies – the subjectified body of the mad and the institutional body, 'the psychiatrist's body extended in the dimension of the institution' (PP 186/189). Foucault makes much of this point:

> The asylum must be conceived as the psychiatrist's body; the institution
> of the asylum is nothing other than the set of regulations that this body

effectuates through its relation to the body of the subjectified madman in the interior of the asylum. (PP 186/189; see 214/216)

If the machinery of the asylum and the organism of the psychiatrist are the same thing (PP 180/182), we can see all sorts of material elements of the production of *savoir*, the power relations of the space of the asylum as a body – the ears, eyes, speeches, gestures, the cogs in the machine (PP 185/188). Foucault claims that in this we can 'identify [*repérer*] one of the fundamental traits of what I call the microphysics of the power of the asylum' (PP 186/189).

> The body of the psychiatrist must be present everywhere. The architecture of the asylum…was always calculated in such a way that the psychiatrist can be present virtually everywhere. He must be able to see everything with a single glance [*regard*], and with a single walk oversee [*surveiller*] the situation of each of his patients; he must be able, at each moment, to make a review of the entire establishment, of the patients, the personnel; he must see everything, and everything must be reported to him: that which he does not see himself, the supervisors, entirely under his command [*à sa docilité*], must tell him, such that he is continually, at every moment, omnipresent inside the asylum. He covers the entire space of the asylum with his gaze, his ears, his actions. (PP 179/182)

The psychiatric hospital is therefore a 'space of inquiry and inspection, a kind of inquisitorial place' for the production of truth. Disciplinary space is also used in the education and moral treatment of the idiot children. 'Learning the linear distribution of bodies, individual places [*emplacements*], gymnastic exercises – the full use of time' (PP 215/217). The mechanisms for training and putting these children to work is also the second striking image of *Discipline and Punish*, Léon Faucher's House for Young Prisoners (DP 12–13/6–7).

The Group Information Asiles

Foucault's re-engagement with these questions of mental illness in the early 1970s, and the occasional remarks he makes about antipsychiatry might suggest that it would be a focus of his political activism. Indeed, on the model of the GIP, discussed in detail in Chapter 5, a Groupe Information Asiles (GIA) was established.[30] Yet Macey reports that Foucault's involvement with the latter group was limited to attending a single meeting along with Robert Castel in late 1971. Castel recalls that the meeting was attended by two hundred people, but was 'shambolic', and that he and Foucault concluded that nothing useful could be done.[31] Nonetheless a group was set up, and one of the group's founding statements was published in the journal *Psychiatrie aujourd'hui* in early 1972, in an issue on the theme of 'Psychiatry and the penitentiary universe'. Entitled 'Non, l'asile n'est pas fait pour soigner' [No, the asylum is not to treat], this statement describes the poor conditions in asylums – 'overcrowded dormitories, dirty, unhygienic conditions and "disgusting" food' – the lack of qualified medical personnel, the use of prison uniforms, low pay for work and high charges for everyday essentials, and so on. It notes that the asylum is not to find a way 'to reintegrate people into society... but to exile those who disturb it'.[32] Further activities of the GIA were reported, among other topics including the work of the Groupe Information Santé (GIS), in the twenty issues of a journal or newsletter, *Tankonalasanté*, between 1973 and 1976, with a compilation of material published as a book in 1975;[33] and the *Psychiatrisés en Lutte* newsletter begun in 1975.[34] *Tankonalasanté*'s general principle was that 'illness [*maladie*] is a language, a phenomenon which is both individual and social, that reflects the world within which it is situated: illness is political'.[35]

The GIA continues to exist today. In Macey's account 'it was founded and functioned without any help from Foucault'.[36] Yet in November 1971 Foucault mentions the groups he is working with as involved in 'the struggle against repression, in the penal system, in psychiatric hospitals, and in the police and judicial systems' (DE#98 II, 228; LCP 223). Later in the same interview he adds that 'we have already started interventions in the asylum, using methods similar to those employed in the prisons: a kind of aggressive inquiry formulated, at least in part, by those who are being investigated' (DE#98 II, 232; LCP 228). This involvement may have gone nowhere, but the intent was clearly there, and of course the group undoubtedly owed much to Foucault's earlier writings, especially *History of Madness*, as well as to the working practices of the GIP.[37] This group was close to the anti-psychiatry movement, allied to a more explicit class politics that came from its links to the *Gauche prolétarienne*. In 1976 a conference was held which brought different groups together as the 'Reseau Alternative à la Psychiatrie [Alternatives to psychiatry network]'.[38] As the GIA's founding manifesto stated, 'the objective of the GIA is not to find a new form of approach to madness, but to demonstrate that psychiatry is more than a simple branch of medicine, in a society based on profit and the exploitation of man by man'.[39] It noted that the language of psychiatry was a specialized and mystifying means of exercising power, and that 'psychiatry was an instrument of repression of the oppressed class'.[40] The power rela-tions at stake, while important in *History of Madness*, were brought more explicitly to the fore in the *Psychiatric Power* course. Notably though, despite the tone of previous courses, in *Psychiatric Power* Foucault does not especially pursue the class approach.

Nor, there, does he develop the relation of his work to anti-psychiatry. Anti-psychiatry is a major theme in the summary, but is barely mentioned in the course itself. At the end of the first lecture of this course Lagrange notes that the manuscript has a lengthy discus-sion (ff. 11–23) but this was not delivered (PP 18 n. */16 n.); see also an omitted remark at 137 n. */137 n. *). Foucault returns to these themes in the first medicine lecture in Rio in late 1974 (see Chapter 6). Nonetheless in this course Foucault notes that he prefers the term 'institutional critique' to 'anti-psychiatry' (PP 41/39). For Foucault's fullest treatment, we can look at a lecture delivered on 9 May 1973, at a colloquium organized by Henri F. Ellenberger in Montreal on the theme of 'Faut-il interner le psychiatres?' Foucault's lecture was entitled 'Histoire de la folie et antipsychiatrie'. Foucault is clear he wants to take a distance from anti-psychiatry, claiming that he is a historian and that as a historian he may be able to trace 'the birth of this anti-psychiatry' (HFA 95). He frames this in general terms as part of what he calls 'a cultural geography of truth' (HFA 95), part-nered by a 'differentiated chronology' (HFA 96). He has clearly been reading David Cooper, Ronald Laing and Lucien Bonnafé and notes the research of Franco Basaglia and Félix Guattari (HFA 102).[41] Yet, strikingly, Foucault does not mention contemporary French political activism around these issues, and much of the lecture shifts register to look at the hospital generally, rather than the psychiatric hospital (HFA 96). This would be paralleled in the analysis of anti-medicine, rather than anti-psychiatry, in the first Rio lecture of 1974.

The GIA later worked with the Comité d'action prisonniers (CAP) – a successor group to the GIP – and other groups on the rela-tion between mental health and incarceration.[42] A 1976 'Charte des internés', authored by the GIA and related groups, explicitly stated that its goal was not the 'improvement of psychiatry, but the complete destruction of the medical-police apparatus [*appareil*]'.[43] It went on to list a series of demands concerning the abolition of specific laws, notably the 1838 law requiring the establishment of facilities for the insane, prohibition of irreversible treatments such as electric shocks and chemicals, better provision for release, and condi-tions within asylums and hospitals.[44] It also challenged 'ergotherapy (treatment by work)'.[45] The Group also published guides for people hospitalized, setting out their rights and challenging the traditional narrative.[46] The partnership with CAP and the cross-pollination of ideas and publications with the GIS show that Foucault's influence can be found in multiple ways.[47] And given that the group had been active for over two years, the choice of focus in *Psychiatric Power* was not just a continuation of the interests shown in the early Collège de France seminars, but an engagement with contemporary debates. That parallel was even more striking when it came to the question of prisons.

5

Discipline: Surveillance, Punishment and the Prison

The Groupe d'Information sur les Prisons

The GIP had its beginnings in late 1970.[1] Defert suggested a group looking at prisons to the Maoist *Gauche prolétarienne* (GP - Proletarian left) and proposed Foucault's name.[2] The GP had been dissolved in May 1970, so membership was now clandestine and illegal.[3] Foucault agreed to lead a prison group, named it GIP, and later said that it

> is at heart a kind of group that is not of a theoretical nature but a group focused on attacking the repressive system in the way it works in France and probably also in other countries. However, our attack is centered of course on what surrounds us right here and now, that is to say, the system, if you will, justice-police in the way it maintains, extends, perpetuates, all the imperatives, and all the moral, social and judicial limitations in our society.[4]

But rather than the group setting itself up to stand in judgement on prisons, Foucault and his colleagues decided on a different tactic (see C 37/45–6). A circular letter was sent to prisoners and families of prisoners in January 1971 announcing that a committee of inquiry was being set up. They asked that reports of conditions in prisons be sent to Foucault at his Paris apartment on the rue de Vaugirard (AL 42). The group was formally announced on 8 February 1971, at a press conference held to mark the end of a 34-day hunger strike by prisoners. Foucault later recalled that it was the hunger strikes that sparked his interest: 'this movement came from the prisons and developed outside them' (DE#94 II, 204).[5] The founding 'manifesto' of the GIP was read by Foucault and signed by him, the editor of *Esprit* Jean-Marie Domenach, and the classicist and historian Pierre Vidal-Nacquet. Other key figures involved included Defert, Claude Mauriac, Jacques Donzelot, Jean Genet, Hélène Cixous, Danielle Rancière, Catherine von Bülow and Christine Martineau.[6] The text was published showing the aim of the group was both knowledge and what can be done with it:

> None of us is certain to escape prison. Today less than ever. Police control [*quadrillage*][7] over day-to-day life is tightening: in city streets and roads; over foreigners and young people; it is once more an offence to express opinions; anti-drug measures are increasingly arbitrary. We are kept under 'close observation' [*Nous sommes sous le signe de la 'garde à vue'*].[8] They tell us that the system of justice is overwhelmed. We can see that. But what if it is the police that have overwhelmed it? They tell us that prisons are over-populated. But what if it was the population that was being over-imprisoned? Little information is published on prisons. It is one of the hidden regions of our social system, one of the dark zones [*cases noires*] of our life. We have the right to know; we want to know [*Nous avons le droit de savoir, nous voulons savoir*]. This is why, with magistrates/legal officers [*magistrats*], lawyers, journalists, doctors, psychologists, we have formed a *Groupe d'Information sur les Prisons*.
>
> We propose to make known [*de faire savoir*] what the prison is: who goes there, how and why they go there, what happens there, and what the life of the prisoners is, and that, equally, of the surveillance personnel; what the buildings, the food, and hygiene are like; how the internal regulations, medical control, and the workshops function; how one gets out and what it is to be, in our society, one of those who came out.
>
> This information is not found in the official reports. We will ask those who, for some reason, have an experience of the prison or a relation to it. We ask them to contact us and tell us what they know [*ce qu'ils savent*]. A questionnaire has been compiled which can be requested from us. As soon as we have sufficient responses, the results will be published.
>
> It is not for us to suggest reform. We merely wish to know [*connaître*] the reality. And to make it known almost immediately, almost overnight, because time is short. This is to inform opinion and to keep it informed. We will try to use all means of information: daily [newspapers], weeklies, monthlies. We therefore appeal to all possible platforms.

Finally, it is good to know what threatens us, but knowledge is also good to defend oneself. One of our first tasks will be to publish a small *Manuel du parfait arrêté* (Complete Arrest Guide), paired of course with an *Avis aux arrêteurs* (Note for Arrestors).

All those who want to inform us, be informed or participate in the work can write to the GIP at 285, rue de Vaugirard, Paris-XVe. (DE#86, II, 174–5)

The manifesto was published in at least three places: in Jean-Paul Sartre's journal *J'accuse*, together with a short text by him entitled 'Violence et grève de la faim', and some other texts in a two page spread on 'Le scandale des prisons'; in *L'esprit*; and in *La Cause du peuple*.[9] *La Cause du peuple*, originally founded by George Sand in 1848, had been relaunched by the *Gauche prolétarienne* in 1968. It had previously carried pieces on imprisonment. In 1970 the journal was made illegal, at which point Sartre became its editor – effectively daring the police to arrest him – and he, Simone de Beauvoir and Jean-Luc Godard sold it in the street.[10] In 1971 it was fused with *J'accuse*, and the first joint issue of 25 May 1971 carried a piece by the GIP (written by Defert) whose title declared 'when information is a struggle' (AL 69–73). Much needed to be brought to light. Foucault and his colleagues had a will to know and to make known. As Foucault and Vidal-Nacquet put it in an interview:

> The prison institution is much like an iceberg. The visible part is the justification: 'there must be prisons because there are criminals'. The hidden part is the most important, the most formidable: the prison is an instrument of social repression. (DE#88 II, 179)

The point, however, was not just to 'raise consciousness'; it was 'to attack an institution at the point where it culminates and reveals itself in a simple and basic ideology, in the notions of good and evil, innocence and guilt' (DE#98 II, 231; LCP 228).

In order to examine the conditions within prisons, the group's first inquiry [*enquête*] was announced in March 1971 in *J'accuse*. 'This is not an inquiry of sociologists. It is rather letting those who have experience of prison speak' (DE#87 II, 175; see DE#94 II, 204). Over the next few months they spoke to prisoners, ex-prisoners and their families, standing outside prisons on Saturdays distributing the questionnaire.[11] Foucault recalls the level of police harassment they received in this work (DE#90 II, 193–4). The resulting information was published as the first of the group's pamphlets, all under the title of *Intolérable*. (All the group's pamphlets were reprinted in a collection in 2013.) The first was entitled 'Inquiry in Twenty Prisons' (IN 15–81).[12] Subsequent pamphlets examined the model prison of Fleury-Mérogis, including its architectural design (IN 83–148), the assassination of Black Panther leader George Jackson in San Quentin jail (IN 153–213), and prison suicides (IN 271–334). These were the four numbered pamphlets, but an unnumbered one was published examining the recent prison revolts and compiling prisoner demands (IN 221–66). Authorship of pieces in those pamphlets can be disputed, as the texts were generally unsigned, but Defert provides a helpful indication.[13] Foucault arranged the material and wrote the preface to the first; Jacques-Alain Miller and François Régnault produced the second. Genet took the lead on the Jackson pamphlet, signing the preface, though an English translation of the key interpretative essay credits Foucault, von Bülow and Defert,[14] and Defert also notes Deleuze's involvement. Cixous and Jean Gattègno produced the unnumbered pamphlet on prisoner demands; while the final pamphlet, on suicides, was the work of Gilles Deleuze and Defert, and was co-signed by CAP and the Association de Défense des Droits des Détenus (ADDD; Association for the Defence of the Rights of the Detained).[15] Another connected study was written by Martineau and Jean-Pierre Carasso, looking at work in prisons.[16] There were also a range of statements, interviews and commentary pieces in newspapers.

While some of the work was concerned with headline issues such as Jackson and suicides, they were more generally concerned with everyday living conditions – food and hunger, the temperature in the cells, exercise, visiting rights, sexual repression, payment for work and costs of essentials, and access to books and other educational materials (DE#88 II, 179, 180–1).

> Let's take stock. The person condemned to six months or two years of prison no longer has – so to speak – any rights. As citizen they are naked before justice. As a prisoner they cannot be allowed what remains of their rights. As a worker they are overexploited; they rarely have the possibility to study. Man or woman, they have no rights concerning their sexuality. (DE#88 II, 181)

Yet Foucault clarifies that the aim was not simply to improve these details – 'to extend the visiting rights of prisoners to thirty minutes or to procure flush toilets for the cells' – but to raise far more fundamental questions: 'to question the social and moral distinction between the innocent and guilty' (DE#98 II, 231; LCP 227). As a GIP tract put it: 'Who steals bread goes to prison; who steals millions goes to the Palais-Bourbon!' (AL 161).

While the group was initiated with general concerns of raising the question of prisons and of generating intolerance to the intolerable, the circumstances in France gave it a more pressing focus. In September 1971, two prisoners took a prison guard and nurse hostage and then killed them at Clairvaux prison. Claude Buffet and Roger Bontems were tried for murder, convicted, and executed in November 1972, even though it was accepted that Buffet alone was the murderer. Foucault wrote about this in a short piece entitled 'Pompidou's Two Deaths', where he raises a number of the GIP's concerns – the death penalty of course, but also the effects of imprisonment, especially on young offenders; the prison at Fleury-Mérogis; the risk of suicide; the violence of prison guards. Foucault suggests that President Pompidou may have used the deaths for electoral advantage, but more importantly that to execute Buffet alone, and spare Bontems, might have meant the end of the death penalty. He suggests that the prison officers' unions had clamoured for the death of both (DE#114 II, 386–9; EW III, 418–22; see DE#98 II, 230; LCP 226–7). The best account of the case comes from Robert Badinter, who was the lawyer for Bontems. Badinter went on to be Minister of Justice under Mitterrand, abolishing the death penalty in 1981.[17] In addition, as a collective punishment for the Clairvaux events and other prison deaths, and again to placate prison officers, Justice Minister René Pleven had cancelled prisoners' Christmas food parcels in 1971.[18] That was the spark for much more widespread prison riots and occupations.[19] The Toul situation and riot, the GIP declared, was 'not an exception'.[20] Prisons were not just a deprivation of liberty, but 'degradation, humiliation, beatings and lack of work' (AL 144). These revolts continued into 1972, and Foucault wrote a text for a press conference on 5 January 1972, which was during the winter break of his *Théories et institutions pénales* course (AL 151–5). The prison situation was one of the key issues behind his invitation to his audience in that course to 'open their eyes' if they wanted to see the purpose of his academic focus (TIP 3).

The point of giving prisoners a voice was important, though not the group's only aim. The use and limitations of questionnaires, problems concerning literary and French language competence, and the unequal relation between prisoners and the GIP have been rightly highlighted.[21] But we might ask what the alternative was, at least in early stages. The GIP produced a film, *Les prisons aussi*, in 1972, in which ex-prisoners spoke of their experience;[22] the *Cahiers de revendications* devoted itself to printing texts produced by prisoners, and once initial goals were reached, the GIP dissolved itself at the end of 1972, to be replaced by a more radical and prisoner-organized group, the *Comité d'Action des Prisonniers* (CAP). In 1975 Foucault also wrote the preface to the French edition of a collection of transcribed interviews with prisoners in Texas.[23] These were other means of giving prisoners a voice. But the initial GIP attempt to convey prisoner demands was not just a case of presenting their answers to questions, as in the first *Intolérable*, or of compiling their demands into the unnumbered pamphlet. It was also using the position Foucault and his colleagues had as free citizens with a profile that brought media attention. On 17 January 1972, for example, the group, accompanied by Sartre, held an unplanned press conference at the Ministry of Justice, Place Vendôme, in Paris, where a statement from prisoners at Melun was read (DE#105 II, 301) and Foucault and others spoke (AL 195–200).[24] According to Philippe Artières it was the first time the group had 'inspired a collective statement from prisoners'.[25] That same day there was a call by a Socialist party deputy and vice-president of the Assemblée Nationale, René Chazelle, for a parliamentary commission of inquiry into prisons.[26] Foucault reflected on this event and said how hard it was to get the media to report prisoner demands. He noted that even *La Cause du peuple* had censored texts by prisoners, or failed to report the press conference. The media were more interested in prisoners on the roofs, or the idea of Foucault himself writing about the prison he wanted (DE#105 II, 302). The point of having named figures such as Foucault involved was also to provide a visible target for political authorities. In a 1971 interview Foucault suggests that the group is largely anonymous, but 'we have to make public some of the names of the members of the group because we have lawsuits filed against us from the Ministry of the Interior. The penal administration and the police file lawsuits because of our attacks'.[27]

One of the other key things that the group was concerned with was breaking down any distinction between different prisoners. The earlier hunger strikes had been conducted by 'political prisoners', and it was a group of former inmates, labelling themselves as such, who produced the 1970 pamphlet *Le combat des détenus politiques*. While Foucault notes that he was inspired by this struggle, for the GIP it was politically important that Communists or Maoists did not insist on their difference from 'common' criminals. This was because, in Foucault's words, 'common law is politics, it's after all the bourgeois class which, for political reasons and on the basis of its political power, defined what is called common law' (FL 119; DE#137 II, 533). The connection of this claim, made in 1972, with the lecture courses of this time is clear. Yet while Foucault framed the work in those general terms, Bourg rightly identifies the day-to-day concerns and the practical politics he was enacting: 'Whereas for Sartre engagement was a response to collective oppression mirrored on each side of the prison wall, for Foucault, it was a series of strategic alliances among those affected by and concerned about imprisonment'.[28] The GIP was also concerned with the notion of a criminal or judicial record [*casier judiciare*], which in France is held on all citizens and available on request to employers. They suggested this meant there was 'no liberation', only 'a reprieve' for those released (IN 20; see AL 89; DE#105 II, 303).[29]

The group illustrated what Foucault meant about the role of intellectuals. He suggested that May 1968 had shown that intellectuals should not presume that they know more than the people, but while the people have a potential voice, 'there exists a system of power which blocks, prohibits, and invalidates this discourse and knowledge' (DE#106 II, 308; LCP 207). The point then, was in part to enable that voice. As a result, he and Deleuze refuse the idea that the GIP was an application of theory. As Foucault states, 'theory does not express, translate, or apply practice: it is practice. But it is local and regional...and not totalizing...A "theory" is the regional system of this struggle' (DE#106 II, 308–9; LCP 208). More generally, the idea of a specific intellectual was proposed (DE#192 III, 154–7; P/K 126–9): someone who made interventions on the basis of their specialized professional knowledge, not in the general way that Zola, Sartre or, despite his protestations, Foucault himself had made. One example he had in mind was the Toul prison psychiatrist Dr Edith Rose, who reported on the treatment of prisoners and was sacked as a result. Foucault spoke out on her behalf in *Le nouvel observateur* and paid for her statement to be published in *Le Monde*.[30] Another was Charles Dayant, who wrote the book *J'étais médecin à La Santé* [I was a Doctor at La Santé], recounting in novelistic form his experience during a year at the prison, and who went on to play a role in discussions of the politics of health (see Chapter 6).[31]

The group made other information available, publishing leaked documents provided for the training of prison warders in *Le nouvel observateur*, intending a future volume of documentation that never appeared.[32] In the founding manifesto Foucault and his colleagues had said that the GIP would publish a *Manuel du parfait arrêté* [*Complete Arrest Guide*]. It was again promised as forthcoming in the first *Intolérable* pamphlet (IN 84), and published in 1972 by some lawyers working with the GIP as the *Manuel de l'arrêté*, signed with the collective name of the 'Defence Collective'.[33] The text was a guide for individuals in their encounters with the police and judiciary, with a strong political flavour: 'These rights were won by the popular masses: they must be known and used to counter bourgeois repression'.[34] The manual continued:

> Mere knowledge of the rights that we recall is not sufficient to counter-act arbitrary [power]. But many experiences prove that their ignorance creates an attitude of submission which forcefully strengthens [that power].The objective of this manual is to provide the resources which allow taking the offensive against police and judicial repression.[35]

1972 also saw the publication of lawyer Denis Langlois's *Guide du militant*, which provided details concerning arrest and the legal system.[36] These were further instances of information provision, where information itself was key to the struggle.

In April 1972, during one of his lecture trips to the USA, Foucault visited Attica prison with John K. Simon, his host at SUNY Buffalo (C 41/51). Foucault says that it was his first time inside a prison, though this discounts his psychiatric work of the 1950s.[37] Attica, in upstate New York, had been the scene of a riot and hostage situation in September 1971, following the killing of Jackson. After four days of negotiation, police stormed the prison under the orders of state governor Nelson Rockefeller, resulting in the deaths of ten prison officers and about thirty prisoners. Foucault was clearly struck by the experience of Attica, and of speaking to a former prisoner there. He notes that the version of the prison which they saw was only part of the story – the Disneyland-style fortress and the workshops mask a different situation, the prison as machine, but one that produces nothing, a 'machine for elimination'. He notes that while they were told about and saw corridors A, B, C and D within the prison, there was a fifth corridor, E, which was 'the machine of the machine, or rather the elimination of the elimination, elimination in the second degree...the psychiatric wing' (FL 113–14; DE#137 II, 526–7).

Foucault notes that the visit to Attica forced him to confront a question which had been there but which 'the visit surely precipitated'. He had begun to realize that negative reasons alone did not make sense of the prison:

> prison is an organization that is too complex to be reduced to purely negative functions of exclusion; its cost, its importance, the care that one takes in administering it, the justifications that one tries to give for it seem to indicate its possesses positive functions. The problem then is to find out what role capitalist society has its penal system play,

what is the aim that is sought and what effects are produced by all these procedures for punishment and exclusion? What is their place in the economic process, what is their importance in the exercise and maintenance of power? What is their role in the class struggle? (FL 115; DE#137 II, 528)

Indeed, he goes on to force the class issue still further, declaring that 'crime is "a coup d'état from below"', a phrase he takes from Victor Hugo's *Les misérables* (FL 121; DE#137 II, 536). Nonetheless Foucault was quick to recognize the enormous differences between French and American prisons, both in terms of proportion of population (he cites a million prisoners from 220 million population in the US; 30,000 from 50 million in France – i.e. 4.5% compared to 0.6%), and race, with 'one out of thirty or forty black men in prison: it is here one can see the function of massive elimination in the American prison' (FL 116; DE#137 II, 529). A note in the French edition of the text suggests Foucault's figures do not match official figures in the *Statistical Abstract of the United States*, and that they likely derive from his reading of the Black Panthers.[38] Foucault had been reading the Black Panthers from 1968 (C 33/40), and von Bülow and Genet provided another link (C 38–9/47). Nonetheless Foucault's comments certainly come at the time of a sharp increase in the proportion of the population imprisoned in the US: if not strictly accurate at the time, his figures soon would be.[39]

In this interview, Foucault stresses that the GIP was 'not primarily concerned with the reform of prisons. Our project is, I think, even quite radically different' (FL 117; DE#137 II, 531). In a retrospective interview he suggested that it was 'a venture of "problematization", an effort to make problematic, to call into question, presumptions, practices, rules, institutions, and habits that had lain undisturbed for many decades' (DE #353 IV, 688; EW III, 394). Indeed, at the end of 1972, just as it seemed that the information-gathering and agenda-setting work had been done, the group dissolved, replaced by CAP (C 42/56). One of the founders of CAP was Serge Livrozet, who had been involved in the Melun prison uprising, and became friends with Foucault on his release. He and Foucault launched the *Journal des prisonniers* in 1972, which ran until 1981;[40] and Foucault wrote a preface to Livrozet's memoir *De la prison à la révolte* in 1973, in which he compares his testimony to that of Lacenaire.[41] Generally with this new group, and the related ADDD, Foucault takes a much less active role, thinking that the aim of giving prisoners a voice has been attained (C 42/52).[42] The opening editorial of *Journal des prisonniers*, signed by the CAP and the GIP explained:

Why the GIP and now the CAP? Our view is that the GIP was essential for the unreserved support that it brought prisoners in making known our demands and struggles, and for making the prison population aware. But we equally think that it is impossible for prisoners who want to take responsibility to be content with a simple adherence to the GIP. Prisoners and ex-prisoners should organize themselves as a force for struggle. A struggle against the current penal system, and all the injustices which it creates and develops; a struggle against the prison regime, the arbitrariness that dominates, and the consequences for the life of those freed. The newspaper must be the link and the instrument of these struggles.

There is no incompatibility between the GIP and the CAP. There may be a fusion of the two, or at least a close coexistence.[43]

Yet the question of prisons did not go away. In early 1973 Foucault began *The Punitive Society*, his course examined in Chapter 3 above. The course was, as the analysis there indicated, clearly presenting work destined for his next book, *Discipline and Punish*, though he would continue working on it for some time. As Foucault notes in 1979, responding to a critique of the GIP, the influence was important: rather than him shaping the GIP in the light of his concerns, the book 'owes a lot to the GIP and if it contains two or three good ideas they came from the GIP' (DE#282 IV, 97). As historian Audrey Kiefer suggests: 'What the GIP established in struggle, *Discipline and Punish* inscribes in history'.[44]

The Punitive Society ended in March 1973, and the Rio 'Truth and Juridical Forms' lectures were delivered at the end of May. Defert recounts that Foucault finished a first draft of the 'book on prisons' before leaving for North America, where he gave some talks in Montreal and New York before heading to Brazil (C 43/54). Defert and Ewald have suggested that Foucault delayed publication of the book for two years to avoid any suggestion that his activism with the GIP had been motivated solely by an academic, theoretical interest.[45] But the published book certainly developed from the 1973 draft. As Chapter 4 showed, the next Collège de France course *Psychiatric Power* connected to the future book in important ways, though largely used the theoretical tools developed to return to earlier concerns. Shortly after the end of that course, Foucault gave some lectures in Montreal in March–April 1974, the title of which was 'L'épreuve et l'enquête [Proof and Inquiry]'. The lectures remain unpublished, but Donald Bouchard describes them as as focused on the question: 'is the general conviction that truth derives from and is sustained by knowledge not simply a recent phenomenon, a limited case of the ancient and widespread belief that truth is a function of events?'[46] It would appear that Foucault was returning to earlier Paris material, but Defert notes that he rewrote 'several parts of his "book on punishment"' in his apartment on this trip (C 44/55). In particular, the Panopticon becomes a focus in his lectures after April 1973, as does the contrast between leprosy and the plague. The manuscript was finally completed on 26 August 1974, and published in February 1975 (C 45–6/56–7).

Survey and Punish

Surveiller et punir appeared in English translation as the misleadingly titled *Discipline and Punish*. A more accurate translation would be *Survey and Punish* – capturing in 'survey', or perhaps 'surveil', the dual sense of to oversee and to catalogue. The whole point is that discipline is made up of two elements – surveillance and punishment (see DE#161 II, 793; FL 140). It is important to note that the English title is a compromise, suggested by Foucault himself to the translator, Alan Sheridan, but nonetheless somewhat misrepresentative of the argument. It has distorted readings of the text. Sheridan explains the choice in the translator's note, and discusses various possibilities for *surveiller*, but not, strangely, 'survey' or even 'watch' (DP -/ix). The danger of the current title is that it makes it look like discipline and punishment are discrete, when really one is contained within the other in the modern system.

Reading this book in the light of the lecture courses preceding is revealing, as important elements of the analysis can be seen in a new way. The text is well-known in many respects, and widely discussed, but some key elements bear some discussion here.[47] Towards the end of the first chapter Foucault provides some useful guidance as to how we should read the book.

> Objective of this book: a linked history [*une histoire corrélative*] of the modern soul and a new power to judge; a genealogy of the present scientifico-legal complex from which the power to punish takes its basis, receives its justifications and rules, extends its effects and masks its exorbitant singularity. (DP 30/23)

The prison of the subtitle is *both* the prison in a literal sense *and* the soul, Foucault stating he wants to examine 'the soul, effect and instrument of a political anatomy; the soul, prison of the body' (DP 38/30). Foucault then says the purpose of the study is the following: 'It is of this prison, with all the political investments of the body that it assembles within its closed architecture, that I would like to write the history. By a pure anachronism? No, if one understands by that to write the history of the past in the terms of the present. Yes, if one understands by that the history of the present' (DP 39–40/30–1).

Foucault is clear he wants to write the history of *this* prison, not *the* or *that* prison (DP 39/30–1). Earlier he makes it clear his study is 'a genealogy or an element in a genealogy of the modern "soul" ' (DP 38/29). It is also important that Foucault says he does not want to write 'the history of the past in the terms of the present', not 'the history of the past in terms of the present' as the translation has it. That obscures the way that terminology and vocabulary, supposedly a remnant of his earlier 'archaeological' work, remains a crucial concern in his later, 'genealogical', writings. Foucault wants us to avoid reading the past with the conceptual terms of the present, which would indeed be 'pure anachronism', importing those terms back into a past that worked with different categories.

Tellingly, and any careful reading of the book has long revealed this, even in terms of institutions the book is not just about the prison. It certainly discusses prisons, of course, and was an attempt, Foucault later recalls, to build on the practical work with a historical study, though he wondered if the book came too late.[48] But the book is about much more. As Foucault notes: 'I will choose examples from military, medical, educational and industrial institutions. Other examples might have been taken from colonization, slavery, and early childhood care' (DP 166 n. 1/314 n. 1).[49] More generally, there is the concern with the disciplinary society and the wider context. Some of these broader concerns become more apparent in the light of the lecture courses. As Foucault notes, 'discipline is no longer simply an art of distributing bodies, of extracting and accumulating time from them, but of composing forces in order to obtain an efficient machine [*appareil*]' (DP 192/164).

Three Moments

In examining this history, Foucault outlines three moments. The earlier model of spectacular public displays of punishment and torture – what Foucault calls *supplice* – and the model of discipline are the first and third of these moments. The second is the dream of the reformers. This is underplayed, but it is a direct opposite or contrast to the first, aimed for but never actually achieved. As Foucault notes, 'Beccaria did not want to replace *supplices* and *tortures* with the prison' (DE#153 II, 726). In contrast to the aim, the third retains elements of the first within a modified version of the second – 'a torturous sediment [*un fond "suppliciant"*]' remains (DP 23/16). These are therefore the 'three ways of organizing the power to punish'. The first is the old, monarchical law; the other two are the alternatives – the reformers' dream and what actually happened. These 'ways' are described in an important passage which suggests there are three *dispositifs* contrasted throughout the book. Here Foucault provides three-way comparisons on separate points.

> The sovereign and his force, the social body, and the administrative apparatus [*l'appareil*]. Mark, sign, trace. Ceremony, representation, exercise. The vanquished enemy, the juridical subject in the process of requalification, the individual subjectified by immediate coercion. The tortured body [*le corps qu'on supplicie*], the soul with its manipulated representations, the trained body [*le corps qu'on dresse*]. We have here the three series of elements that characterize the three *dispositifs* that face one another in the second half of the eighteenth century…three technologies of power. (DP 155/131)

The problem, for Foucault, is why the third, and not the second, was adopted as the alternative to the first. In the dream of those like Mably, 'Prison as the universal [penalty] is incompatible with this whole technique of penalty-effect, penalty-representation, penalty-general function, penalty-sign and discourse' (DP 135/114–15). That was the project of making the link between the crime and punishment, a carefully graded and equivalent process: 'a link of resemblance, analogy, proximity' (DP 124/104). There are many moments when Foucault stresses the failure of the reformers' dream: 'have we really entered the age of non-corporal punishments [*châtiments*]?' (DP 120/101); 'the semiotechnique of punishments [*punitions*]' that was desired is replaced with a 'new political anatomy', a 'new politics of the body' (DP 122/103); 'the art of punishing, then, must rest on a whole technology of representation' (DP 123/104). Foucault keeps asking how prison could become the most generalized form of punishment despite multiple criticisms (e.g. DP 141/120). This is the question he wants to investigate. 'How did the coercive, corporal, solitary, secret model of the power to punish replace the representative, scenic, signifying, public, collective model? Why did the physical exercise of punishment [*punition*] (which is not *supplice*) replace, with the prison that is its institutional support, the social play of the signs of chastisement [*châtiment*] and the chattering [*bavarde*] festival that circulated them?' (DP 155/131).

He returns to this three-way contrast right at the end of the book.

> We are now far away from the country of *supplices*, dotted with wheels, gibbets, gallows, pillories; we are far, too, from that dream of the reformers, less than fifty years before [i.e. around the time of the French Revolution]: the city of punishments in which a thousand small theatres would have provided an endless multicoloured representation of justice in which the chastisements, meticulously produced on decorative scaffolds [*échafauds*], would have constituted the permanent festival of the Code. The carceral city, with its imaginary 'geopolitics' is governed by quite different principles. (DP 307/359)

Additionally, in one more of his striking contrasts, he reflects on the replacement of the chain gang with the police cell-carriage. In the first people are linked together, dependent on each other; in the second they are isolated and dependent on their solitude. The first was a means of collective punishment; the second was 'an apparatus [*appareil*] of reform'. Foucault stresses the contrast: 'What replaced *supplice*, was not mass incarceration [*enferment*], but, at least in principle, a carefully articulated disciplinary *dispositif*' (DP 308/264).

The use of the key term *dispositif* is also significant here. Foucault is building on the analysis in the *Psychiatric Power* lectures. At times the meaning is one that appears close to a mechanism or apparatus, but there are clear indications of its more philosophically complicated sense that would be stressed much more clearly in the first volume of the *History of Sexuality*. The word appears in several instances in this work – the Panopticon is described as a *dispositif;* as are the army, the hospital and other institutions; but it is here, in the contrast between three different *dispositifs* of punishment that Foucault most clearly articulates the way he will use the term in future work. In these three alternative systems he is articulating what Chapter 4 described as the arrangement or set-up of a web of practices and their attendant discourses.

Supplice

The term *supplice* is the title of the first part of the book, and a crucial concept in his work. The second chapter of the book is entitled 'L'éclat des supplices', translated as 'The Spectacle of the Scaffold'. *Le supplice* is torment or ordeal, so it is a form of torture, but of a particular kind: potentially a public version. *L'éclat* is fragment – coming from *éclater*, to burst, explode or shatter – or perhaps the splendour, brightness or brilliance. Foucault makes a contrast between *le supplice* and *la torture*, both of which might be translated as 'torture'. Indeed, the existing English translation renders *le supplice* as 'torture', 'public execution' or 'scaffold'; sometimes as the phrase 'public torture and execution' (DP 37/28) or even 'the process of torture and execution' (DP 56/45). Scaffold is also used for the literal French term, *l'échafaud*. The one to whom *supplice* is applied is *le supplicié*, which Sheridan renders as the 'tortured criminal' (e.g. DP 296/254), and there is also the verb *supplicier*. *Supplice* is absolutely crucial to the analysis because Foucault's first claim of what the book is about focuses on this term. He outlines the contrast between Damiens and the house of prisoners in the opening pages and then says: 'We have a *supplice* and a time-table...Among so many changes, I shall consider one: the disappearance of *supplice*' (DP 14/7). It is clear that this term is fundamental to his analysis.[50]

The discussion of *supplice* that follows is absolutely fascinating, and rewards close reading. At times it seems Foucault is compressing what he had treated in much greater detail in *Théories et institutions pénales*. Indeed, there is a general sense of a confidence in broad assertion here that is in contrast to, but dependent upon, the more hesitant and improvisational claims in the lecture courses. Foucault situates his analysis of *supplice* within a wider discussion of medieval sovereignty. 'Sovereignty' is strictly speaking the wrong word, and it should be really be 'supremacy' or other terms that are actually used in texts of the time,[51] and Foucault seems to see this as continuing up to the Revolution, as many of his sources are eighteenth century. His nuanced analysis of the 'classical age' – as found in *History of Madness* – is somewhat lacking here. But there are some very pointed analyses. Crucially Foucault argues that 'we must conceive *supplice*, as it was still ritualized in the eighteenth century, as a political operation' (DP 65/53). The ceremonial aspect is tied up with the public demonstration of the power of the sovereign (DP 61/50), with the body of the condemned as 'the place when the sovereign vengeance was applied, the anchorage point for a manifestation of power' (DP 67/55).

> Now this meticulous ceremonial was quite explicitly, not only legal but military. The king's justice shows itself as an armed justice. The sword [*le glaive*] that punished the guilty was also the sword that destroyed enemies. A whole military machine surrounded *supplice*: cavalry of the watch, archers, guardsmen, soldiers. (DP 61/50)

Foucault provides a helpful discussion which makes it clear that *supplice* is a technique, which cannot be 'assimilated with the extremity of lawless rage', and that not all punishments are *supplice*. To be *supplice* punishment must, first, be 'calculated, compared, hierar-chized...a quantified art of suffering'; second, it must be regulated, set in correlation between the 'corporeal effect, quality, intensity and duration of suffering with the gravity of the crime, the person of the criminal, the rank of his victims'; and third, be part of a ritual, 'an element in the punitive liturgy' that marks the body of the victim or the memory of the observer. *Supplice* must be stunning, spectacular or explosive [*éclatant*], almost like a Roman triumph (DP 42–4/33–4). As Foucault notes, perhaps trading on Kantorowicz (see Chapter 2, p. 57): 'This enables us to understand some of the characteristics of the liturgy of *supplice* – above all, the importance of a ritual that was to deploy its pomp [*son faste*] in public. Nothing was to be hidden of this triumph of the law' (DP 60/49). Triumph is a term Foucault uses a few times and has a strong resonance with the analysis later, when he notes that discipline is not a triumph, nor triumphant (DP 200–1/170; 220/188).

As Foucault summarizes:

> Penal *supplice* does not cover all corporal punishment: it is a differenti-ated production of suffering, an organized ritual for the marking of victims and a manifestation of the power which punishes; and not the point of exasperation of a justice which, in forgetting its principles, loses all restraint. In the 'excess' of *supplices*, an entire economy of power is invested. (DP 44/34–5)

The body then is the key to the interrogation:

> In sum, try to study the metamorphosis of punitive methods from a political technology of the body in which might be read a common history of power relations [*rapports de pouvoir*] and object relations [*relations d'objet*]. Thus, by an analysis of penal leniency as a tech-nique of power, one might understand both how man, the soul, the normal or abnormal individual has come to duplicate crime as objects of penal intervention; and in what way a specific mode of subjectifica-tion was able to give birth to man as an object of knowledge for a discourse with a 'scientific' status (DP 31/24).[52]

The Search for Truth – Measure, Inquiry, Examination

Yet this book is not simply concerned with power relations. One of the key arguments of the book develops claims Foucault made in his earliest courses at the Collège de France, especially *Théories et institu-tions pénales*. This is especially the case in the discussion of evidence and proof (DP 44–5/36–7), and subsequent discussion of proof and confession. In particular he stresses the important relation between *épreuve* as ordeal or test and *preuve* as proof.

> The search for truth through interrogation [*la 'question'*] was certainly a way of obtaining evidence [*un indice*], the most serious of all – the confession [*la confession*] of the guilty [*coupable*]; but it was also the battle, and this victory of one adversary over the other, that ritually 'produced' truth. In torture [*la torture*] employed to produce an avowal [*pour faire avouer*], there was an inquiry [*l'enquête*]; there was also a duel. (DP 52/41)

As he continues:

> In the eighteenth century, judicial torture [*la torture judiciaire*] func-tioned in that strange economy in which the ritual that produced the truth went side by side with the ritual that imposed the punishment. The body interrogated in *supplice* constituted the point of application of the chastisement and the locus of extortion of the truth. And just as presumption was inseparably an element in the inquiry and a frag-ment of guilt [*culpabilité*], the regulated pain involved in interrogation [*la question*] was a measure both of punishment and taking of evidence [*un acte d'instruction*]. (DP 53/42)

The dual use of avowal and confession mirrors the two French terms *l'aveu* and *la confession*, which is a distinction Foucault would develop in subsequent courses, *Wrong-Doing, Truth-Telling* and *On the Government of the Living* in 1980 and 1981.[53]

As the analysis of the courses in Chapters 1 to 3 showed, the relations between measure, inquiry and examination are central to Foucault's work of the first half of the 1970s. They are key themes, respectively, to his first three courses at the Collège; they are treated in some detail in the 1973 'Truth and Juridical Forms' lectures; and they are crucial to this book. The first term, 'measure' appears in rela-tively few instances here: 'Penal chastisement [*le châtiment penal*] is therefore a generalized function, coextensive with the social body and each of its elements. This gives rise to the problem of the "measure", the economy of the power to punish' (DP 107/90). The second, 'inquiry [*enquête*]', is discussed especially in the chapters 'L'éclat des supplices' and 'Panopticism', and Foucault contrasts 'inquisitorial' justice with 'examinatory' justice later in the book (DP 356/305). 'Examination [*examen*]' is treated in much more detail, especially in the third section of the second chapter of Part III, which has 'Exami-nation' as its title. It is crucial to the operation of disciplinary power, which utilizes 'simple instruments; hierarchical gaze, normalizing sanction and their combination in a procedure that is specific to it, the examination' (DP 201/170).

> The eighteenth century invented the techniques of discipline and the examination, rather as the Middle Ages invented the judicial inquiry. But they did so by different means. The procedure of inquiry, an old fiscal and administrative technique, had primarily developed with the reorganization of the Church and the increase of the princely States in the twelfth and thirteenth centuries. At this time it permeated to a very large degree the jurisprudence first of the ecclesiastical tribunals, then of the lay courts. The inquiry as an authoritarian search for a truth observed or attested was thus opposed to the old procedures of the oath [*serment*], the ordeal, the judicial duel, the judgment of God or even the transaction between private individuals [*particuliers*]. The inquiry was the sovereign power arrogating to itself the right to establish the truth by a number of regulated techniques. Now, although the inquiry has since then been an integral part of western justice (even up to our own day), one must not forget either its political origin, its link with the birth of States and of monarchical sovereignty, or its later extension [*dérive ultérieure*] and its role in the formation of knowledge. In fact, the inquiry has been the no doubt crude, but fundamental element in the constitution of the empirical sciences; it has been the juridico-political matrix of this experimental knowledge, which, as we know, was very rapidly released at the end of the Middle Ages. It is perhaps true that, in Greece, mathematics was born from techniques of measure; the natural sciences in any case, were partly born at the end of the Middle Ages from the practices of inquiry. (DP 261–2/225–6)

The examination then receives more detailed treatment in the last section of this chapter (DP 217–27/184–94). 'For in this slender [*mince*] technique are to be found a whole domain of knowledge [*savoir*], a whole type of power' (DP 217/184). The key example in this section is the school, but Foucault also relates it once more to the army, and to medical examination and the hospital, deriving not just from his work in *Birth of the Clinic* but also the 1974 Rio lectures on medicine (see Chapter 6). So, the inquiry, of which the Inquisition and *supplice* were its inevitable outcomes, is replaced with the examination, and the prison.

This theme is important, among other reasons, for its conjunction of power and knowledge: 'The examination brings with it a whole mechanism that links a certain form of the exercise of power to a certain type of the formation of knowledge' (DP 219/187). The key themes are the link between visibility and power; the accumulation of records; the placing of individual case within a raft of documentation. And in a telling comment, Foucault links this inquiry to the work of *The Order of Things* from a decade before: 'Is this the birth of the sciences of man? It is probably to be found in these inglorious archives, where the modern play of coercion over bodies, gestures and behaviour is elaborated' (DP 224/191). In sum, then, 'the examination is at the centre of the procedures that constitute the individual as effect and object of power, as effect and object of knowledge' (DP 225/192).

Marxism and the Productive Body

The comparison between the lecture courses and the published book is also telling in terms of Foucault's relation to Marxism. While *Théories et institutions pénales* and, especially, *The Punitive Society* had framed their politics within Marxist categories and with engagement with Marxist authors, the book is more muted. There are also some significant changes to the framing of the analysis. One of the striking claims of this book is the examination of the ' "political economy" of the body' (DP 33/25).

> This political investment of the body is bound up, in accordance with complex and reciprocal relations, with its economic use; it is largely as a force of production that the body is invested with relations of power and domination; but, on the other hand, its constitution as labour force [*force de travail*] is possible only if it is caught up in a system of subjectification (in which need is also a political instrument meticulously managed, calculated and utilized); the body becomes a useful force only if it is a productive body and a subjectified body. (DP 34/25–6)

It is for this reason that Foucault's work relates to some Marxist themes. In the opening part of the book he mentions the important work of Georg Rusche and Otto Kirchheimer.[54] Why had the medieval period found bodies so expendable, and why was the modern age so concerned with their use? It could not be down just to peculiarities of specific legal codes:

> There is no doubt that the existence of *supplices* is connected to something entirely other than this internal organization. Rusche and Kirchheimer are correct to see it as the effect of a mode of production where the labour force, and thus the human body, do not have the utility or market value that they are given in an economy of the industrial kind. (DP 66/54)

The theme of illegalism, developed in *The Punitive Society* is not so evident here, but is still explicitly linked to 'the development of capitalist society' (DP 103/86–7). The aim, then, is 'to constitute a new economy and a new technology of the power to punish [*punir*]' (DP 106/89). The link between the disciplinary society and the wider 'historical processes of which it forms part' (DP 253/218) deserves some attention. These processes are economic, juridico-political, and scientific. Foucault quite clearly puts his analysis within a wider history of economic transformation, stating that 'neither the residual forms of feudal power, nor the structures of the administrative monarchy, nor the local mechanisms of supervision, nor the unstable, tangled mass they all formed together could carry out this role' (DP 254/218). The 'apparatus of production' (DP 254/218) requires new techniques, which discipline provides. The economic development of the West was made possible by the accumulation of capital, but Foucault wants to trace the closely related accumulation of bodies, which cannot be separated from the narrowly economic process, and also makes possible 'a political development in relation to traditional, ritual, costly, violent forms of power, which soon fell into disuse and were superseded by a subtle, calculated technology of subjectification' (DP 257/220–1). The relation is not simply one-way, but mutually reinforcing: 'the technological mutations of the apparatus [*appareil*] of production, the division of labour and the elaboration of the disciplinary techniques sustained an *ensemble* of very close relations. Each makes the other possible and necessary; each provides a model for the other' (DP 257/221). Foucault explicitly references Marx's *Capital* here, and also the analysis provided by François Guéry and Didier Deleule's *The Productive Body*.[55]

Foucault uses the training of bodies in the army as his model, suggesting that

> the great book of Machine-Man [*l'Homme-machine*] was written simultaneously on two registers: anatomico-metaphysics, of which Descartes wrote the first pages and which the physicians and philosophers continued; and the technico-political, which was constituted by a whole set of regulations relating to the army, the school and the hospital, and by empirical and reflexive [*réfléchis*] methods for controlling or correcting the operations of the body. These two registers are quite distinct, since it was a question, on the one hand, of submission and utilization and, on the other, of functioning and explanation: there was a useful body and an intelligible body (DP 160/136).

L'homme-machine, while clearly a reference to bio-mechanics generally, is also a 1748 book by Julien Offray de la Mettrie, usually translated as *Machine-Man* or *Man, A Machine* (DP 160/136).[56] The striking thing here is not just that the Marxist language is more muted than in *The Punitive Society* lectures, but that the corporeal is much more explicitly stated: 'the historical moment of the disciplines was the moment when an art of the human body was born' (DP 162/137); or further: 'the human body enters a machinery of power...a "political anatomy" that was also a "mechanics of power"...Discipline thus makes submitted and practised bodies, "docile" bodies... Discipline is a political anatomy of detail' (DP 162–3/138–9). There is a clear purpose here: 'the growth of a capitalist economy called for the specific modality of disciplinary power, whose general formulas, techniques of submitting, forces and bodies, in short, "political anatomy", could be operated in the most diverse political regimes, apparatuses or institutions' (DP 258/221).

The corporeal is also significant in a spatial, geographical register. Foucault is explicit that 'discipline proceeds, initially, from the distribution of individuals in space' (DP 166/141), using several techniques, of which Foucault discusses enclosure, portioning, functional sites, and rank (DP 166–75/141–9).[57] This has implications in several registers, including his ongoing interest in medicine, suggesting that 'a medically useful space' is 'born of discipline' (DP 144/169). He then moves to an analysis of time, and the use of the time-table to regulate activity, soldiers being trained to march to the beat of a drum, and 'the correlation of the body and the gesture', the relation of the body to an object, and the exhaustive use of time (DP 175–83/149–56). After this summary outline of modes of spatial and temporal discipline, he discusses in more detail the specifics of how the Gobelins tapestry and dye-works factory in Paris functioned, and what he calls 'the composition of forces' – how armies and work-forces were regulated to ensure that their 'effect had to be superior to the sum of elementary forces that composed it' (DP 192/163). Foucault cites a long passage from Marx's *Capital* at this point (DP 192/163), and notes how 'on several occasions, Marx stresses the analogy between the problems of the division of labour and those of military tactics' (DP 192 n. 2/163).

> In summary, it might be said that discipline creates out of the bodies it controls four types of individuality, or rather an individuality with four characteristics: it is cellular (by the play of spatial distribution), it is organic (by the coding of activities), it is genetic (by the accumulation of time), it is combinatory (by the composition of forces). And, in doing so, it puts to work four great techniques: it constructs tables, it prescribes movements, it imposes exercises; lastly, in order to obtain the combination of forces, it arranges 'tactics'. Tactics, the art of constructing, with located bodies, coded activities and trained aptitudes, apparatuses in which the product of the various forces is increased by

their calculated combination are no doubt the highest form of disciplinary practice. (DP 196–7/167)

This he immediately describes as a '*savoir*' (DP 197/167).

One example, is the design of a military camp, 'the short-lived, artificial city', which is 'the diagram of a power that acts by means of general visibility. For a long time this model of the camp or at least its underlying principle – the spatial nesting [*l'emboîtement spatial*] of hierarchized surveillance – was found in urbanism, in the construction of working-class estates [*cités*], hospitals, asylums, prisons, schools' (DP 201–2/171–2). Foucault then goes into detail on hospital architecture (deriving from work in his 1974 seminar and in *Psychiatric Power*), on schools, on the city and saltworks built at Arc-et-Senans, workshops, factories, and orphanages. (On the 1974 seminar see Chapter 6.) He uses these to exemplify not just the spatial organization, but also the broader rules of disciplinary power discussed in the previous chapter – control of time, bodies, gestures; punishment of minor infractions; the corrective nature of these punishments as meaning of training; privileges and rewards. 'The perpetual penality that traverses all points and controls every instant in the disciplinary institutions compares, differentiates, hierarchizes, homogenizes, excludes. In a word, it normalizes' (DP 215/183). Foucault then links this to the emergence of the norm, and the normal, and references Canguilhem (DP 216/184), a theme he was developing in *The Abnormals* lecture course at the same time this book was published (A 29–48/31–52).

The references to Marx are then scattered throughout. For example, he mentions Marx's *Eighteenth Brumaire* in passing (DP 327/280) and uses him to support claims about the importance of surveillance of the production process: 'Surveillance thus becomes a decisive economic operator both as an internal part of the production machinery and as a specific mechanism in the disciplinary power' (DP 206/175). Foucault cites Marx at this point (the interjection is the term in Foucault's translation): 'The work of directing, superintending [*surveillance*] and adjusting becomes one of the functions of capital, from the moment that the labour under the control of capital becomes co-operative. As a specific function of capital, the directing function acquires its own specific characteristics'.[58]

Panopticism

The famous 'Panopticism' chapter begins with a discussion of two figures of medical intervention – the quarantining of a plague town, and the earlier treatment of lepers.[59] These are also discussed in some of Foucault's lectures – in Rio in 1974 and Paris in 1975. They exemplify two forms of the utilization and control of space – exclusion and inclusion-organization; two forms of political power – negative and positive. Lepers were immediately expelled from the shared space of the community, for the purification of the urban environment. The sickness could be separated, removed: this is a negative use of power. The positive form of power is the birth of administrative and political strategies (A 44/48), where its four modes are selection, normalization, hierarchization, and centralization (see SMBD 161/181). The discussion of the plague town is therefore detailed, because it provides a clear example of spatial partitioning, disciplinary mechanisms, legal ordinances, trained bodies, inspection and reports, registration and records. Accordingly, the 'emergency plan' [*plan d'urgence*] for epidemic disease comprised the following measures:

1. All people must remain at home in order to be isolated in a particular place, even in a single room;
2. The town is divided into distinct sectors or regions, inspectors patrol the streets, and a system of generalized surveillance is used to compartmentalize and control;
3. To accompany the detailed reports that come from these sectors, there will be a centralized information system;
4. People who do not show themselves for the inspectors at their windows will undoubtedly have contracted the plague, and therefore must be transported to a special infirmary, outside the town. Statistics can be derived from the reports that follow;

Houses need to be disinfected and sterilized (DE#196, III, 217–18; EW III, 145; see DE#153 II, 728; DE#229 III, 517–18; SKP 148; A 41-2/44–6). In this 'disciplinary *dispositif*',

> The plague is met by order; its function is to sort out every possible confusion: that of the disease, which is transmitted when bodies are mixed together; that of the evil, which is increased when fear and death become prohibitions. It lays down for each their place, body, disease and death, their well-being…Against the plague which is mixed [*mélange*], discipline brings into play [*fait valoir*] its power, which is one of analysis. (DP 230/197)

Leprosy gave rise to 'rituals of exclusion', the plague to 'disciplinary diagrams [*schémas*]' (DP 231/198).[60] The key contrast is thus spatial: 'The leper and its separation [*partage*]; the plague and its segmentations [*découpages*]' (DP 231/198). Foucault notes that the leper is an exemplar, a symbol of other forms of exclusion. Recall the opening scenes of the *History of Madness*, where the leprosaria or lazarettos are reused to house first the venereally diseased and then the mad (HM 16–18/6–8). Here Foucault also notes this treatment was given to beggars and criminals as well – exile or exclusion from the community. Similarly the plague is a symbol of how 'all forms of confusion and disorder' and the measures taken to combat them were dealt with from the late eighteenth century (DP 232/199). The responses to them are different schemas, different political dreams, of the pure community and the disciplined society; two 'ways of exercising power over men'; but they are not incompatible. Foucault's point is that what happens is a mix of the two: the former model of exclusion has the grid of order and discipline superimposed on top of it. The model for the disciplinary society is not the prison – as is often assumed – but a combination of the military dream and the mechanisms for treatment of the plague. The prison, in one of its striking architectural designs, is an outcome of this process. The emergence of the disciplinary model is one that takes as its injunction to 'treat "lepers" as "plague victims"', project the subtle segmentations of discipline onto the confused space of internment, combine it with the methods of analytical distribution proper to power, individualize the excluded, but also use procedures of individualization to mark exclusion' (DP 232/199). The binary division of 'mad/non-mad; dangerous/harmless [*inoffensif*]; normal/abnormal' – itself nothing new – is part of the double mode, partnered by the new modes of disciplinary order. This can be found, 'from the beginning of the nineteenth century in the psychiatric asylum, the penitentiary, the reformatory, the surveyed educational establishment and, to some extent, in the hospital' (DP 232/199). Foucault brings this analysis to a close, suggesting that: 'all the mechanisms of power which, even today, are disposed around the abnormal, to brand them and to alter them, are composed of those two forms from which they distinctly derive' (DP 233/199–200).

He then begins the next section immediately with the claim that 'Bentham's *Panopticon* is the architectural figure of this composition' (DP 233/199–200). The Panopticon is, therefore, an example of a wider process, not itself the model from which others derive. The spatial analysis of the Panopticon is perhaps most important for the process of subjectification that it implies: the individual observed, or thinking themselves observed from the central tower, begins to discipline themselves, meaning that power can be absent and still be effective. By turning the focus from the external to the internal, the true emergence of disciplinary power can be seen, 'to induce in the inmate a state of conscious and permanent visibility that assures the automatic functioning of power...surveillance is permanent in its effects, even if it is discontinuous in its action' (DP 234/201). The Panopticon is 'an important *dispositif*, because it automatizes and individualizes power...a marvellous machine which, from diverse desires, produces homogeneous effects of power. A real subjectifica-tion born mechanically from a fictional relation' (DP 234/202).

Foucault quickly shows that there are multiple uses, not simply for convicts, but also the mad, the worker, the pupil, the patient (DP 234/202). It is not just a prison, it 'functions as a sort of labo-ratory of power', where 'an increase of knowledge [*une accroisse-ment de savoir*] can be established on all the advances of power, discovering objects to know [*à connaître*] over all the surfaces on which it [power] is exercised' (DP 238–9/204), 'a figure of political technology that can and must be detached from any specific use' (DP 239/205). In addition, Foucault spends the rest of this chapter in a detailed discussion of how these disciplinary mechanisms are rolled out through society. There are three key elements within this analysis: the way that measures previously to deal with extreme events become part of the normal functioning of things; the spread of these mechanisms beyond institutions to the wider social context; the role of the state in providing and supporting these mechanisms, characterized by the question of the 'police' (DP 244–50/210–214). The police is subject to an especially interesting analysis, especially when he links its functioning not just to the king or the state, but also the workings of power from below in the use of *lettres de cachet*, which may have borne the king's seal, but 'were in fact demanded by families, masters, local notables, neighbours, parish priests' (DP 250/214).[61]

Only in part IV does Foucault refer to prisons as his main focus, and makes the point that while the prison form had existed before, only with the shift to the disciplinary society did it take on its central role. This is a product of 'new class power' (DP 267/231). Again he stresses how a society that privileged liberty so much almost had to have prison – the removal of liberty – as its main punishment; something that would have equal value to all, as opposed to the dif-ferentiation of the fine (DP 269/232). The contemporary resonance of this claim is hard to escape – both in Foucault's time and in our own. The prison builds on other institutions like schools, factories and hospitals, and 'carries to their greatest intensity all the procedures to be found in the other disciplinary *dispositifs*' (DP 273/236). It is char-acterized by three key principles: isolation; the strict control of time, especially for labour; the ability to modulate the sentence in terms of time-served, duration (DP 274–88/236–48). These accord to 'three great schemata: the politico-moral schema of individual isolation and hierarchy; the economic model of force applied to compulsory work; the technico-medical model of cure and normalization'; characterized by three institutions that it derives these principles from: 'The cell, the workshop, the hospital', the first to be understood in the monastic sense (DP 288/248). The second is especially important in understanding the political economy angle of Foucault's work: 'What is the use of penal labour? Not profit; nor even the formation of a useful skill, but the constitution of a relation of power, an empty economic form, a schema [*schéma*] of individual submission and of adjustment to a production apparatus' (DP 282/243).

This is central to Foucault's interest in power relations:

> The individual is no doubt the fictitious atom of an 'ideological' representation of society; but it is also a reality fabricated by this specific technology of power that we can call 'discipline'. We must cease once and for all to describe the effects of power in negative terms: it 'excludes', it 'reprimands [*réprime*]', it 'represses [*refoule*]', it 'censors', it 'abstracts', it 'masks', it 'conceals'. In fact power produces; it produces the real; it produces domains of objects and rituals of truth. The individual and the knowledge [*connaissance*] that may be taken from this belong to this production. (DP 227/194)

And alongside this is the creation of specific subjectivities:

> Behind the offender, to whom the investigation of the facts may attribute responsibility for an offence, stands the delinquent whose slow formation is shown in a biographical investigation. The introduction of the 'biographical' is important in the history of penality. (DP 292/252)

The emergence of the delinquent is important, Foucault claims, because it is not just the act but their life that is examined. And different models are applied to them: 'the legal chastisement [*châtiment*] bears upon and acts; the punitive technique [*la technique punitive*] on a life' (DP 292/252). This is Foucault's first use of the term 'dangerous' individual, which he would examine in some detail later (DP 293/252).[62] 'The correlative of penal justice may well be the offender [*l'infracteur*], but the correlative of the penitentiary apparatus is someone other; the delinquent, a biographical unity, a kernel of "danger", representing a type of anomaly' (DP 295/254). Foucault notes that prisons produce, rather than just confine, delinquency, and that this can be turned to the advantage of society.

A Wider Audience

The social aspects are crucial to the final chapter, on the notion of 'the carceral'. This is where the disciplinary institution becomes the disciplinary society. The opening of Mettray in 1840 is a key moment, because 'it is the disciplinary form in its most extreme state, the model in which are concentrated all the coercive technologies of behavior. In it were to be found "cloister, prison, school, regiment" ' (DP 343/293). From Mettray and similar settings comes the extension beyond the institution: 'this great carceral network reaches all the disciplinary *dispositifs* that function throughout society. It has been seen that, in penal justice, the prison transformed the punitive procedure into a penitentiary technique; [while] the carceral archipelago transported this technique from the penal institution to the entire social body' (DP 349/298). In an interview published at the time of the book's publication he linked this to bourgeois liberalism: 'Discipline is the underside of democracy' (DE#152 II, 722), or here: 'the real and corporeal disciplines constituted the foundation of the formal and juridical liberties...the Enlightenment, which discovered the liberties, also invented the disciplines' (DP 258/222). Once more, the wider setting is framed within a political-economic narrative.

> The carceral 'naturalizes' the legal power to punish, as it 'legalizes' the technical power to discipline...the carceral makes it possible to effect that great 'economy' of power whose formula the 18th century had sought, when the problem of accumulation and the useful management of men first emerged. (DP 354/303)

The discussion in the opening part of this chapter demonstrated the contemporary, political environment in which Foucault's work operated. And it is clear that the book was written with that purpose in mind. As he said in early 1974: 'the small volume that I would like to write on disciplinary systems, I would like it to serve as an educator, a guard, a magistrate, a conscientious objector. I do not write for a public, I write for users, not for readers' (DE#136 II, 524). In a 1975 discussion of the book Jacques Revel suggests that he anticipated a militant book, found instead a work of history, but one which had a political effect.[63] As Arlette Farge, who worked with prison educators, reports, the book did have that effect, sending 'shock waves' through their groups and those of social workers.[64] Foucault ends the book with an allusion to the contemporary moment: 'In this central and centralized humanity, effect and instrument of complex power relations, bodies and forces subjectified by multiple *dispositifs* of "incarceration", objects for discourse that are themselves elements for this strategy, the rumble of battle must be heard' (DP 360/308). And then in a final footnote, elevated to the main text in the English translation, Foucault again stresses the way his historical study is intended to link to the contemporary moment: 'At this point I end a book that must serve as a historical background [*d'arrière-plan historique*] to various studies of the power of normalization and the formation of knowledge [*savoir*] in modern society' (DP 360 n. 1/308).

After the book was published Foucault returned to this theme of addressing a wider public:

> Yes, that was certainly a very important aspect of it. I believe and hope that *Discipline and Punish* is not a difficult book to read – even if I try not to sacrifice precision or historical detail. Anyway, I do know that many people who are not academics in the strict sense of the term or who are not intellectuals in the Parisian sense of the term have read this book. I know that people concerned with the prisons, lawyers, educators, prison visitors, not to mention the prisoners themselves, have read it; and it was precisely such people I was addressing to begin with. For what really interested me in *Discipline and Punish* was being read by a wider public than one made up of students, philosophers, or historians. If a lawyer can read *Discipline and Punish* as a treatise on the history of penal procedure, I'm pleased. Or, if you want another example, I'm delighted that historians found no major error in *Discipline and Punish* and that, at the same time, prisoners read it in their cells. To make possible these two types of reading is something important, even if it isn't easy for me to hold the two together. (PPC 101)[65]

Yet if Foucault was writing for a broader audience it is perhaps surprising that the tone of the book is so different from his public pronouncements and, especially, his lectures. This book, in particular, is composed in a very specific style. Foucault writes the book largely in the passive voice, with few active subjects of verbs. The English translation does not always respect this. Some, though not all, instances of Foucault's first-person voice appearing in the text are also a choice made by Sheridan: Foucault tends to write in a more detached way. Given the argument of the book, of how subjects are made into objects, personalization and activation are quite fundamental issues. Foucault's very deliberate choices are a question of stylizing an important argument. This has reinforced many of the criticisms of Foucault's account of agency, his denial of resistance, and his failure to account for the interests discipline actually served. Additionally, some of Foucault's use of the impersonal pronoun '*on*' and locutions such as '*il faut*' become 'we'. One example is the book's final lines, quoted above: '*Il faut entrende le grondement de la bataille*', which Sheridan renders as 'we can hear the distant roar of battle' but probably should be 'the rumble of battle must be heard' (DP 360/308). That has generally been taken to refer to the GIP and contemporary political struggles, but is perhaps also an allusion to the civil war of the 1973 course, a theme that would return in the 1976 course '*Society Must Be Defended*'.[66] As he says in this book, 'the right to punish has been shifted from the vengeance of the sovereign to the defence of society' (DP 107/90). This was also an important aspect of the final chapter of the first volume of the *History of Sexuality*, which was apparently the first part of the text composed, entitled 'the right of death and power over life'. Here, among other places, Foucault provides an anticipation of this argument: 'the right to punish, therefore, is an aspect of the sovereign's right to make war on his enemies: to punish belongs to "the right of the sword, of that absolute power of life and death which Roman law calls *merum imperium*, a right by virtue of which the prince sees that his law is respected by ordering the punishment of crime"' (DP 59/48).[67]

In addition, there is an anticipation of the famous reversal of Clausewitz to be found in the 1976 course and book:

> It may be that war as strategy is the continuation of politics. But it must not be forgotten that 'politics' has been conceived as the continuation of, if not exactly and directly of war, at least of the military model as a fundamental means of preventing civil disorder. Politics, as a technique of internal peace and order, sought to implement the *dispositif* of the perfect army, of the disciplined mass, of the docile and useful troop, of the regiment in the camp and in the field, on maneuvers and on exercises. (DP 197/168)

The army was thus both a 'technique and a *savoir*' – a practice and a knowledge. Foucault continues: 'if there is a politics-war series that passes through strategy, there is an army-politics series that passes through tactics. It is strategy that allows an understanding of war as a manner of conducting politics between States; it is tactics which allows an understanding the army as a principle for maintaining the absence of war in civil society' (DP 197–8/168). Foucault claims that social relations are actually shot through with relations of war, both in 1973 and 1976 lectures, and in the *History of Sexuality*. Those themes are both repeated and anticipated here. As James Miller reports Defert saying in 1990, Foucault began writing the *History of Sexuality* on the very day he finished writing *Discipline and Punish*, 26 August 1974.[68]

6

Illness: Medicine, Disease and Health

The Groupe Information Santé and the Biopolitics of Birth

In *The Punitive Society*, on 7 February 1973, one of the examples Foucault gives of the moralization of questions is a contemporary one. He suggests that there is 'a kind of historical symmetry' between the eighteenth-century questions he has been examining in relation to dissidence and 'the present-day movement of "moral dissidence" in Europe and the United States'. His examples in the lecture are movements that 'struggle for the right to abortion, to the formation of non-familial sexual groups, to idleness', which are joined in the manuscript by 'the right to homosexuality' and the 'right to drugs' (PS 115/112, 115 n. e/112 n. ‡). In the eighteenth century, the period of his historical examination, 'morality, capitalist production, and the State apparatus' had been linked together: 'the function of present-day groups is to undo this'. Their work is broader than just breaking the rule, it is to challenge it, 'to attack this connection, this coercion' (PS 115–16/112). His main example in the present is the following.

> Think of the manifesto by abortion doctors and of the response of the Minister, Foyer, who made this quite extraordinary statement: it is altogether regrettable that the doctors' manifesto appeared during the election, because the problem of abortion is a problem of legislation and so must be dealt with in calm and reflection; since it is a problem of legislation, it cannot be raised during the election campaign. (PS 116/113)

Foucault is referring to Jean Foyer, Minister of Health, who had declared on 6 February 1973 that 'it is deplorable that a political operation be launched on such a serious problem during an election'.[1] President Georges Pompidou had previously made a similar point. Foyer was reacting to a letter signed by over 300 doctors, published in *Le nouvel observateur* on 5 February 1973, declaring that they had performed abortions illegally.[2]

Foucault suggests that Foyer's view is that such legislation must be decided upon by legislators alone, and that Foyer 'does not want the problem to be addressed by those who elect the legislators'. It is indicative of a wider point:

> This is precisely because a moral distance is introduced regarding abortion: what power [*le pouvoir*, i.e. the government] means when it says that only elected deputies are able to take care of this issue, but not those who elect them, is that the ethical-juridical problem of abortion is not a matter for the explicit choice of individuals, not a matter for the national will itself...To say that the deputies can change the law without their electors having any control over this, is to say that the change can be a matter only for power and those elected, not as representatives of a real national will, but as agents of a power that precisely exceeds their mandate, since it cannot be fixed by electoral mandate. So it is only at the level of the exercise of power that something like abortion legislation can be modified. (PS 116–17/113)

The intertwined nature of 'the system of morality and the actual exercise of power' has, for Foucault, existed in present form since the nineteenth century. It continues to have an effect in the present. Morality 'is inscribed in power relations and only the modification of these power relations can bring about the modification of morality' (PS 117/113).

Foucault's interest was not as a detached observer, using a contemporary story to situate his historical analysis. He is thinking of the current campaign for abortion rights, with which he was involved through the specific work of the Groupe Information Santé (GIS).[3] This was a group, like the GIA, formed on the model of the GIP. The GIS was officially created on 14 May 1972. Its founding manifesto states that the group was 'constituted of militants concerned by the problem of health in France and contesting the health system in its current state. It gives itself the task: of developing an intolerance of this system, of unblocking and correcting [*débloquer ou redresser*] information on health problems, struggling against false propaganda about health [*la propagande mensongère accrochant la santé*] which attributes a more or less mythical progress to health, confusing the increase in medical consumption with an improvement in health conditions'. Health in France was seen as directly linked to the benefit of the class of power, from local practices to hospitals and the pharmaceutical industry. It was not for the group to provide better information itself, but to 'help the masses express themselves, to define their needs and find their solutions', which could only be found within a wider 'struggle against exploitation... an essential element in the workers' combat in a revolutionary perspective'.[4]

The group caught a public mood post-1968 for seeing medicine as part of a wider political struggle, and followed from the earlier Comité d'action santé in challenging the power of the medical profession.[5] On 7 May 1968, the Centre National des jeunes médecins issued a statement supporting the students in Paris. They wanted to raise the question of the kind of teaching they received, and the 'ideology that underlies it'. In their longer statement entitled 'Medicine and Repression' they expanded their concern. Doctors were not just being trained in 'an exclusively biological conception', but to be of 'service to capitalist oppression'. This could be through neglect of 'socio-economic dimensions' of illness, or more active involvement where the medical profession is 'charged with keeping the population in a status of work and consumption (e.g. workplace medicine), and in making people accept a society which has made them ill (e.g. psychiatry)'.[6] The Comité d'action santé had suggested that 'medicine', rather than doctors, was the enemy.[7] The GIS membership indeed comprised many doctors, including Dayant, alongside sociologists and philosophers. It described its focus as 'industrial medicine, health of immigrants, abortion, medical power' (DE#128 II, 445; EW III, 423).[8] It was based in Paris but regional groups were set up in cities across France.[9] Its aim was partly to decentre the medical profession from its position of power in medicine, and give people back the control over their bodies and lives. Some of their work concerned workplace medicine and industrial injuries or disease.[10] Two such campaigns concerned lead poisoning in the manufacture of car batteries in the Penarroya factory in Lyon and silicosis in miners.[11] They provided health input into *autogestion* projects, such as the worker takeover of the Lip watch factory. They were also involved in supporting immigrant hunger strikes and the use of non-trademarked drugs, and in challenging the profits of big pharmaceutical firms and the way doctors used specialized knowledge in oppressive ways (MD 7–9).[12] The journal *Tankonalasanté* published some of their collected information sheets, such as one on lead poisoning;[13] a report on their first general meeting in Bordeaux; and their three key campaigns on abortion, factory health, and immigrant workers.[14]

In a text published in the journal *La Nef*, in a special issue on 'medicine, the ill and society' from late 1972, the group discusses the political nature of the inquiry, the need for marginalized groups to assert their power and claims that medical issues are at the forefront of class struggle. This was a piece that came from discussions, which were recorded and transcribed, and then instead of being presented as a round-table, were merged into a piece with a single voice as an 'article-manifesto' (MLC 69 n. 1). It appeared with the authors named as Michel Foucault and the members of the GIS. The group stressed that class relations did not just happen 'in the factory or workshop' (MLC 68), and that 'medical texts do not occupy a neutral position in relation to class struggle' (MLC 71). While they did mention the financial arrangements around the French medical system, the system of social security and challenge the 'medicine of profit' (MLC 72), their point is broader than this, and has to do with the division between intellectual and manual labour. Foucault's involvement gave intellectual and organizational experience, but the group was especially interested in the mobilization of specialized knowledge being put to progressive political ends: what Foucault would call the 'specific intellectual'.[15]

Part of the group's aim was to 'break the secrecy' around professional and expert knowledge in medicine. They aimed to 'challenge the *division* [*coupure*] between *scientific knowledge and everyday practice*, between *manual and intellectual work*' (MLC 68). The doctors recognized that they 'may already be too conditioned by the system' to be sure that 'their health projects were a real innovation, and not mere management reforms. Knowledge has been a bulwark [*rempart*] which has put us outside all social reality' (MLC 68–9). It suggested that doctors conduct such inquiries or investigations within a closed system of knowledge, 'the carceral space within which what we call "science" traps them' (MLC 71). In sum, they wanted 'to break down the "inquirer-inquiry [*enquêteur-enquête*]" distance that exists at the heart of the conventional doctor-ill person [*malade*] relation' (MLC 69).

> We want more than a medicine of profit, we want more than a medicine which objectifies man [*réifie l'homme*], we want more than a knowledge which is nothing more than a clever mask for oppression [*un masque habile de l'oppression*]. We know that medicine, precisely because it affects a fundamental human good, health, is among others a site of class struggle.
>
> We have chosen to participate in this struggle. (MLC 72)

Some of the work of the GIS was based on the example of the 'popular tribunal' held in Lens to inquire into the death of sixteen men in a mining accident there (MLC 71). At the tribunal Sartre had played the role of prosecutor, suggesting that the explosion had been caused by the company putting profit ahead of safety. Doctors had been called as expert witnesses, and as well as the accident had testified about conditions such as 'black lung'.[16] In a February 1972 interview, 'On Popular Justice', Foucault had rejected this model of inquiry – and he explicitly mentions the Lens case – as too close to the existing bourgeois system (i.e. DE#108 II, 340–1, 357, 367; P/K 1–2, 22–3, 34). He closed his discussion by saying that a people's justice needed to take a different form:

> This justice must therefore be the target of the ideological struggle of the proletariat, and of the non-proletarianized people [*plèbe*]: thus the forms of this justice must be treated with the very greatest suspicion by the new revolutionary state apparatus. There are two forms that must not under any circumstances be adopted by this revolutionary apparatus: bureaucracy and judicial apparatus. Just as there must be no bureaucracy in it, so there must be no court [*tribunal*] in it. The *tribunal* is the bureaucracy of justice. If you bureaucratize popular justice then you give it the form of a court. (DE#108 II, 361; P/K 27)

In this collective piece the line is more positive. The inquiry was a major focus of the group's work.[17]

In their 1974 report *La médecine désordonnée*, which summarizes and documents their work to date, the GIS reuse some text from the May 1972 manifesto for their general purpose, and then move to more specific issues.

> Improving health conditions to the GIS means improving living conditions in all respects – in the workplace, on public transport, in leisure time, and in private life: A life without freedom, initiative, and flourishing [*épanouissement*]; a life that is truncated and fragmented. What we call a struggle for 'improving living conditions [*conditions de vie*]' is in fact a struggle for life. It is also a struggle for health. (MD 7)

The GIS's most important campaign concerned abortion.[18] At the time, abortion was illegal in France, but a public campaign had begun with an open letter signed by 343 women, published in *Le nouvel observateur* on 5 April 1971.[19] The letter declared that while an estimated million women a year had abortions, they were forced to do so 'in dangerous conditions because they are forced to do it in secret, while this operation, performed under medical supervision, is simple'. In order to break the silence, the women declared: 'I am one of them. I state that I have aborted. Just as we demand free access to contraceptives, we demand free abortion'. Signatories included Colette Audry, Simone de Beauvoir (who probably wrote the letter), Catherine Deneuve, Marguerite Duras, Gisèle Halimi and Liane Mozère. *Charlie Hebdo* magazine described them as the 343 'salopes' – sluts or bitches.[20] One month later, 252 doctors signed a manifesto declaring abortion should be allowed.[21]

Abortion was more easily available for women with money to travel to countries with more liberal laws: a choice not available to all. The October 1972 Bobigny trial, when a girl who had been raped and her mother were prosecuted for abortion, had clearly shown the law's problems (see MD 20–1). Halimi defended the mother and daughter, and a media campaign led to the acquittal of the daughter but a second trial for the mother. In early 1973 the GIS coordinated a second open letter, this time by 331 doctors who declared that they had conducted abortions. While the 1971 doctors's manifesto had demanded a change, this one took things a stage further by admitting involvement. This letter, published on 5 February 1973, called for contraceptives to be available to all, including minors, reimbursed by social security, with widely available information; and that abortion be freely available on the same terms. This was a decision, it declared, which should be entirely up to the women concerned.[22] This was the letter to which Minister Foyer was reacting, in the remarks Foucault quotes in his lecture of 7 February 1973 (PS 115–17/112–13).

The GIS partnered this media campaign with an anonymous pamphlet, *Oui, nous avortons!* [Yes, we abort!], also in 1973. It comprised a mix of statements, testimonies, information, images, a photo-story and cartoons. No authors were named, and it was simply billed as 'a special bulletin' of the GIS. It began with noting the prohibitions against 'abortion, incitement to abortion, or propaganda in favour of this act' to be found in the penal code and the public health code. It detailed the implications for women or medical personnel, but noted that while travelling abroad to have an abortion was an offence, it was 90 per cent likely that no charges would be brought, thus underlining the right being effectively available for some, but by no means all women: a class issue (ONA 4). This pamphlet, then, was an intervention against a situation where women could die or suffer physical or mental problems as a result of the lack of available, safe treatment. Written in the voice of a group of women, one of the opening parts states that 'It is for us to decide to bring a child into the world or not. We are the first ones responsible for our bodies and our lives at all times' (ONA 5). It stressed three key aspects: the availability of advice, the safety of possible treatments, and the ability to pay for them. It explained how pregnancy could be tested and terminated in the very early stages; detailed the 'aspiration' technique both with text and diagrams, some hand-drawn and some with photographs of equipment such as the speculum. It explained likely side effects and the recovery period. It then went on to look at methods for more advanced pregnancies, to discuss contraceptive methods and their benefits and side effects. It provided names and addresses of overseas doctors and clinics, along with costs. Much of the second half was given over to women telling their stories. An annexe reprints the doctors' letter (ONA 65–6), and the statement read to a press conference just a few days later (ONA 69–73). It closes by saying that signatures and foreign addresses are not enough to resolve the problem, and that 'they will wait no more... the law must be abolished' (ONA 74).

Despite the doctors who had signed the open letter, and the name and address for contributions and donations being given in the pamphlet, the publication led to Foucault, Alain Landau and Jean-Yves Petit being given a court-summons as the presumed authors. The three men note in a defiant statement in *Le nouvel observateur* on 29 October 1973 that police spies monitored attendance at group meetings, and they had been seen there. This was 'serious circumstantial evidence' against them. The three affirmed they did belong to the GIS, wrote and distributed the pamphlet and supported the cause (DE#128 II, 445–7; EW III, 423–5). Landau and Petit were both medics, though only Landau signs with the title 'Dr'. How much they were genuinely responsible for its writing, and how much they were shielding others remains unclear. Much of the tone of the text is written as a collective of women, and Foucault's involvement in the actual writing, which is largely specialist and outside his expertise, is likely to be minimal. Mauriac even recounts a conversation with Defert where Foucault confessed to confusion between the illegality of abortion and the availability of contraception.[23] But the response is more characteristic of his involvement, and Defert reports that he wrote it alone.[24] It states that the pamphlet was

> aimed at creating a situation in which [abortion] can be talked about, and in which, once they have come out of the shameful secrecy where some people seek to keep them, women can finally have free access to information on abortion and contraception: a situation in which they are no longer at the mercy of greedy and hypocritical doctors or left to themselves, forced to resort to procedures that are dangerous for their lives. (DE#128 II, 446; EW III, 424)

The three men suggest that the kind of information in the pamphlet is precisely that which the government wants to keep from women.

> For, if women learn that it is possible to have an abortion in a simple and risk-free way (using the aspiration method under the best sterile conditions) and without charge; if they learn that it isn't necessary to do seven years of study in order to practise this method, they risk deserting the commercial circuits of abortion and denouncing the collusion of doctors, police, and the courts, which makes them pay dearly, in every sense of the term, for the liberty they take in refusing a pregnancy. (DE#128 II, 446; EW III, 424)

The reforms currently being discussed in France were not, they suggest adequate. They propose a certain number of 'strictly limited cases' where it might be allowed – 'rape, incest, a definite abnormality in the embryo, and when the birth would risk provoking "psychic disturbances" in the mother' – but then only on the say of two doctors. This would mean 'a strengthening of a medical power that is already great, too great, but that becomes intolerable when it is coupled with a "psychological" power that has earned a reputation for incompetence and abuse in its application to internments, medico-legal evaluations, "children at risk", and "pre-delinquent" young people' (DE#128 II, 446–7; EW III, 424–5). The hospital or private clinic settings would replicate, rather than improve, the current situation: 'two abortion circuits: one, a restrictive hospital experience for the poor; the other, private, liberal – and expensive'. The government was thus constructing a polarization between 'good doctors' to whom it would 'give complete power and every benefit', and those, like the GIS, 'who would establish abortion, contraception, and the free use of one's body, as rights' (DE#128 II, 447; EW III, 425).

Abortion and contraceptive rights were part of a wider concern with sexual morality. In early 1972 a medical doctor, Jean Carpentier, had been charged for circulating a text on sex education outside a school.[25] The text was entitled 'Apprenons à faire l'amour [Learn to make love]' and was signed by the 'Comité d'Action pour la Libération de la Sexualité'.[26] At a hearing of the Conseil de l'ordre des médecins on 14 June 1972 he was prohibited from practising medicine for a year. Responding, the journal *Psychiatrie aujourd'hui* first circulated an open letter as a supplement to issue 9, shortly after the case was examined, and then devoted the whole of issue 10 to the case.[27] It contained the text in question, a statement by Carpentier, the judgment of the Conseil, analyses by a number of people, including Foucault, letters about the case and appeals. Making a political point, the original text was then published in a much-expanded version by radical publisher François Maspero in 1973.[28] The expanded text discusses puberty, intercourse, masturbation, venereal disease, contraception, homosexuality and the menopause. While hardly unusual today, homosexuality, contraception and abortion were of course much more politically contested at the time. In June 1972 Foucault spoke at a press conference on Carpentier's behalf, when he argued that medicine often exceeded any narrow boundaries and had become a 'guardian of morality', 'not only defining what is normal or not normal, but ultimately what is legitimate [*licite*] or illegitimate, criminal or not criminal, what is debauchery or malpractice [*pratique maligne*]' (DE#110 II, 381). The use of psychiatric expertise in criminal matters had been discussed in Foucault's Paris seminars in the early 1970s, and in 1975 he suggested he would publish dossiers of material on this theme (DE#156 II, 746; P/K 45). Sexual questions including masturbation would take centre-stage in *The Abnormals* course in 1975. Here the relevance is that under the proposed reforms they would have a crucial role in decisions by abortion doctors. Carpentier went on to become an editor of the GIA's journal *Tankonala-santé*, writing several texts for it, including its opening editorial.[29]

Another censorship case concerned the twelfth issue of the journal *Recherches*, entitled 'Grande Encyclopédie des homosexualités: Trois milliards des pervers', published in March 1973.[30] *Recherches* was the house journal of the Centre d'Études, de Recherche et de Formation Institutionnelle (CERFI), a group founded in 1967 by Félix Guattari, as a formalization of the 1965 Fédération des Groupes d'Études de Recherches Institutionnelles (FGERI).[31] Guattari was prosecuted and in May 1974 was convicted. He was fined and issues of the journal were seized and destroyed.[32] In one of his first explicit engagements with gay politics, Foucault wrote a short piece for *Combat* highlighting the problems in the political and legal process, and raising the question of 'the relation between politics and sexuality', a theme which was beginning to play a crucial role in his own work (DE#138 II, 536). Foucault explicitly links the political question of 'male and female homosexuality' to the wider struggle for women's liberation, mentioning the Mouvement de libération des femmes (MLF) and abortion rights. He underlines that it is because of a wider struggle for the uses of the body, as more than just labour force, that sexuality emerges as a political problem (DE#138 II, 537). Foucault would also work with CERFI on collaborative research, a topic discussed later in this chapter. Other attempts to widen the abortion debate also met state opposition. There was also a film *Histoires d'A* [A's Story], directed by Charles Belmont and Marielle Issartel, in which the GIS doctors were involved, and for which the group provided screenings, which helped to raise awareness of the issue (MD 7).[33] The film was banned on 22 November 1973, and the ban lifted on 15 October 1974.

The campaigns met with wider success. In 1975 the 'Veil law', named after the Minister of Health, Simone Veil, allowed termination of pregnancy. Initially for a trial period, this provision became permanent law in 1979. Until 1982 abortion was not supported by social security, and only in 1992 was it no longer an offence under the law, rather than an exception. In this struggle the GIS's involvement was part of a wider network of movements, such as Mouvement pour la Liberté de l'Avortement et de la Contraception (MLAC) founded in 1973; *Choisir* [choose], founded by Halimi in 1971; along with the earlier MLF.[34] MLAC's work was regularly featured in the GIA's journal *Tankonalasanté*, alongside the work of the GIS.[35] One issue presented MLAC's position statement:

> I am not a politician [*homme politique*],
> I am not a doctor,
> I am not a lawyer,
> I am a woman,
> I demand the right to decide myself
> If I have to have an abortion.
> My body belongs to me and I do not recognize
> that politicians, doctors, lawyers,
> or society
> have the right to decide
> when I will have children.
> I demand the recognition of this right
> and serious and accurate information
> on the means of having children
> that I want, when I want them.
> I demand that contraception and abortion
> Are freely available for all women
> And reimbursed by Social Security.[36]

As Halimi notes, groups like *Choisir*, the GIS, the GIP and Association de Soutien aux Travailleurs Immigrés (ASTI – Association of Support for Immigrant Workers), were important because they were picking up issues neglected by mainstream politics: 'The value of these movements is that they rouse the torpid consciences of the well fed, and that they are like a shout in the silence'.[37] Yet while the GIS's concern was 'to reopen the question of liberal medicine',[38] *Choisir* pushed further. As Claire Duchen argues, the GIS's focus on 'the nature of medical practice' meant that it 'saw the issue of abortion in terms of what was wrong with medicine rather than in terms of women'.[39] This is certainly true, but due in large part to the GIS's wider concerns:

> Whether it is a question of asylums, prisons, social work, or the way that the sick are cared for in public hospitals and private clinics, over-worked city doctors, the profits and scandalous practices of pharma-ceutical companies, or also in the medicine which is practised in the workplace, in factories, information is truncated, one-sided, sometimes even dishonest, provided sometimes by unscrupulous journalists looking for scandal, sometimes by *specialists* who condescend to give up a part of their knowledge to 'mass education'.
>
> To inform is already subversive in itself: we have two examples with the GIS: the banning of the film 'Histoires d'A' and the judicial proce-dure initiated against the 'authors' of the 'Oui, nous avortons' pamphlet.
>
> Information is indeed never neutral; the person who informs [*l'informateur*], whether doctor or not, always has another goal besides the obvious one. They can want to cause their listener to reflect, to go deeper, to understand, then to participate and stand up for themselves, or they can comfort the listener with received ideas and put them to sleep ('medicine has made spectacular progress' or 'we are well looked after'). (MD 95)

In terms of reproduction health this is an examination of what might be called the biopolitics of birth.[40] Foucault would go on to do more work on health, but only rarely mentioned abortion after this time – once in 1975 and it is raised in a 1977 interview (DE#157 II, 755; P/K 56; DE#200 III, 260; PPC 114). The doctors that Foucault and Defert met at this time were later involved in another project with Defert after Foucault's death, the establishment of the *AIDES* group on HIV/AIDS.[41] Like the work of the GIP, the GIA and other groups such as Group d'Information des Travailleurs Sociaux (GITS) – a social work advocacy group – the GIS saw the labour as political, and information as itself a struggle. All had the goal of 'opening up [*débloquer*] information'.

Collaborative Research Work on the 'Equipments of Power'

Foucault's collaborative model of working was not confined to the streets, meeting halls or gatherings at his apartment for the GIS or GIP. As the discussion of the Pierre Rivière case in Chapter 4 showed, it also characterized work he conducted in the seminar room. While Foucault established some important practices in his Paris seminar, his collaborative work was not confined to it. In the early 1970s he also began working with the CERFI. The research with which Foucault was involved led to a series of projects undertaken with Gilles Deleuze, Guattari and François Fourquet into urban infrastructure, public utilities and related themes. Foucault's first direct involvement was a collaborative work by Lion Murard and Fourquet entitled *Les équipements du pouvoir*. This was part of a productive research process, which led to several reports, many of which were reissued as issues of *Recherches* or books in a related series. One exception was the report led by Foucault on hospitals, which when it appeared as a book was in a very different form.

The first outputs from the CERFI work, though with no obvious involvement of Foucault, included a study of new towns, and an initial statement of the work undertaken.[42] They were followed by a volume entitled *Les équipements du pouvoir*, envisioned as part of a wider 'Genealogy of Capital'.[43] In its published form, originally as an entire number of the CERFI journal *Recherches*, and then reprinted as a book, this deals with towns, territory and other collective means of social organization and infrastructure, and though Fourquet and Murard wrote the bulk of the material, Foucault, Deleuze and Guattari contribute in discussion sections. It makes use of many of Foucault's ideas and doubtless inspired others. A second volume – again originally a journal number, and then a reprinted book – contains an extended essay by Fourquet that was originally intended to serve as an appendix but was published separately due to its length.[44] This discusses broader themes that can be derived from the research.

The 'equipments' of power analysed in this book are the three items in the subtitle: towns, territories and 'utilities' – *équipements collectifs*. By these Fourquet and Murard mean something akin to public amenities or the infrastructure of society. These are tools that are utilized collectively – roads, transportation and communication networks, and the more static apparatus of towns. Circulation necessarily plays a crucial role, with the flux and flow of people, goods, and capital as money (EP 35). For Fourquet and Murard, these infrastructural elements are means of production, or perhaps more accurately the means by which production can be achieved (EP 32). The town is, in their terms, just such a 'collective equipment' or amenity, 'and the network [*réseau*] of towns distribute capital across the whole of the national territory' (EP 35). Foucault himself takes part in two dialogues in the book, originally conducted in May and

September 1972 (EP 47) after the outlining of various ideas by Four-quet and Murard. In the English translation of the dialogues the order is reversed, and the accompanying material left aside, which makes for a peculiarly decontextualized discussion.

Fourquet and Murard note that the three key terms that they are interested in thinking through are power, territory and production, particularly in their interrelation (EP 7). The stress on power and territory within a broadly Marxist analysis allows for a 'displacement' rather than a revision or critique (EP 8). This context is supplemented by an interest in Deleuze and Guattari's work *Anti-Oedipus*, and earlier texts which the authors received while working on this, together with an interest in Foucault's work on madness and the clinic (EP 10). The original title of the work, *Généalogie des équipements collectifs* (EP 9), shows this Foucauldian influence – a Foucault then engaging with Nietzsche's ideas in detail. Indeed in the extended introduction, Fourquet and Murard acknowledge the importance of Deleuze and Foucault's readings of Nietzsche, as well as the pioneering work of Bataille and Klossowski (EP 17). All sorts of Foucauldian themes are found in this work – the use of the Panopticon, relations of power and knowledge, surveillance, control of population and normalization of individuals and so on. The dating of the material to the early 1970s shows that this relation was not solely one-way. Murard and Fourquet utilize Foucault's research on madness, medicine and other issues, but the bulk of the material predates *Discipline and Punish*, although there is some editing between the 1973 journal issue and the 1976 book. Some of Foucault's ideas about the division of space in schools and the control of children's bodies and medical plans for towns are discussed in this work (see EP 197–8, 210, etc.). A range of other contemporary thinkers are utilized, including those of a more obviously Marxist perspective such as Henri Lefebvre (see EP 55–6) and Manuel Castells. The ideas of normalization are explicitly related to Canguilhem, just as Foucault does in his *The Abnormals* lectures (EP 155, see 157). But the other key role is played by *Annales* historian Fernand Braudel, who is mentioned in a number of places (EP 7, 10, etc).

The book is organized on the following plan:

1. *La ville-ordinateur* – the town-machine
2. *La ville-métaphore* – the town-metaphor
3. *Les territoires* – territories
4. *Formation des équipements collectifs* – formation of collective amenities or public utilities
5. *Le discours du plan* – planning discourse

6. *Économie politique sans famille* – political economy without the family

In the second dialogue Foucault takes the example of a road, and suggests that it plays three strategic functions: to produce production, to produce demand, and to normalize. While the first two are unsurprising from a Marxist perspective, the third is perhaps most interesting. Production requires transport, the movement of goods and labour, and the levies or tithes of state power and tax collector. The bandit is an 'antithetical person' in these relations. Demand requires 'the market, merchandise, buyers and sellers', it creates a whole system of coded places of business, regulates prices and goods sold. The inspector, controller or customs agent face to face with the smuggler of contraband, the peddler (EP 215–16; FL 106). Both production and demand are the subject of the procedure of normalization, in the adjusting and regulation of these two domains. Foucault talks about the *aménagement du territoire*, the control and planning of the land or territory of the state that the road allows. The role of engineers is important both as a product of normalizing power – their education and authentic knowledge – and as its privileged agent. In opposition to them are those who do not fit the allowed circuits, either because they move too much or too little – the vagabond or the sedentary: 'in both cases, abnormal' (EP 216; FL 107).

Foucault stresses that this is merely one example of the kind of collective equipment that Fourquet and Murard are analysing. He suggests that the chronology of the industrial and the disciplinary State – we should note that it is of the state not society that he is speaking – do not match up, although they are correlatives. '*Education* produces producers, it produces those who demand and at the same time, it normalizes, classes, divides, imposes rules and indicates the limit of the pathological' (EP 216–17; FL 107). Deleuze responds to this, suggesting that the three aspects are rather investment, treating someone as a producer in potential or actuality; control, treating someone as a consumer; the public service aspect, the citizen as a user. Utilizing concepts that he and Guattari would develop in their collaborative work, Deleuze argues 'the highway today is channelled nomadism, a partitioning into a grid, while public service implies a general nomadism' (EP 217–18; FL 107).

Foucault's point in response is that the state is tasked with the balancing of production (i.e. supply) with the production of demand. The state's role in other areas, such as the normalization undertaken by the police, hospitals, treatment of the insane is ambiguous: on the one hand the state's role expands, but on the other private corporations are part of a process of de-statization. Foucault's telling point is that the difference between socialist and capitalist utopias is that the latter worked. But now, instead of private ventures of this kind, there are 'housing projects' that the state must control, that 'depend on the State apparatus. The deck has been reshuffled' (EP 218–20; FL 108). Murard and Fourquet give their own examples, of hospitals that act as means of production in terms of producing the healthy workforce required by capital.

Foucault's examples of the road and the windmill demonstrate that he is both willing to consider issues outside his usual scope and that in 1972 his thinking is still rather inchoate. Three points emerge from this. The date is significant – conducted in mid-1972 this is the time between *Théories et institutions penales* and *The Punitive Society* and their more explicitly Marxist analysis. Here, especially as in the latter course, his analysis recognizes the state and production as a crucial background, the indispensable foundation of the types of analysis he is making. But rather than replicate the work done elsewhere, Foucault is interested in changing the angle, tightening the focus and concentrating on the small, the detail, the workings on the level of the everyday, the microphysics, here stressed as the third question of normalization. The contrast with Althusser's approach is becoming clearer. Second, Foucault is in a questioning mode here. His comments in the first dialogue are questions: what property relations are involved in collective equipment; how do they function; what type of production is involved; what relationship of power is at play; how do effects follow from this: 'the genealogical implication' (EP 45–7; FL 111–12). The stress on production, property and function is significant. Property relations have changed over time and 'the body of agricultural knowledge' in a medieval monastic library and a windmill, a bridge, and a road all play different roles. Third, in both Foucault's comments and those of his interlocutors, perhaps especially here Guattari, the question of territory or more broadly spatiality is important. Guattari discusses the way in which the city as a collective equipment radically alters the territorial issues of more primitive communities: 'the territoriality of the city becomes deterritorialization of fluxes'. But, and simplistic readings of Deleuze and Guattari on deterritorialization often miss this, 'Equipments as machines are reterritorialized at the same time. Deterritorialized fluxes constitute the city, material fluxes support deterritorialized fluxes, and the city reterritorializes the most deterritorialized fluxes of any given period' (EP 40–1; FL 109; see EP 173–4). On this point we can also look at his brief comments on the city as a spatial projection, 'a form of reterritorialization, of blockage', where the 'original despotic city is a military camp where soldiers are enclosed to prevent the flux of soldiers from spreading out' (EP 44; FL 110), which anticipates the analysis in *Discipline and Punish*.

Curing Machines and Habitat

This was far from the end of the project, and research continued over the next few years. The IMEC archives have papers outlining five interlinked projects, led by Fourquet, Deleuze, Guattari and Foucault. Funded by the Ministere de l'aménagement du territoire, de l'équipment, du logement et du tourisme, the five projects were as follows.[45]

1. Collective equipments and their social uses, looking especially at new towns such as Evry and Marne la vallée (Fourquet)
2. Two studies – mining towns and green spaces (Guattari)
3. The emergence of 'collective equipments' (Deleuze)
4. Urban 'equipments' in urban planning (Foucault)
5. A genealogy of 'equipments of normalization' – health and schools (Foucault)

In sum, over a million francs was projected for this work, worth about 840,000 euros today,[46] enough to support a fairly large team for a few years.[47]

The research conducted closely followed the themes noted above, though the publications only loosely deliver. The fourth theme on urban questions is the key absence from this work, at least as far as Foucault's role is concerned.[48] The fifth theme led to three volumes of reports under the general title *Généalogie des équipements collectifs*. These were published in 1975 and 1976. In the initial CERFI plan for the project it said that its concerns extended beyond the institutions of hospitals and schools to wider concerns with norms of health and hygiene in society as a whole, along with 'the power of the state in the determination of sanitary mechanisms'.[49] Foucault had little involvement in the work on the school, conducted by Anne Querrien, which led to the first volume; or in the third by Fourquet entitled *Histoire des services collectifs dans la comptabilité nationale*. Both these books were subsequently republished as issues of *Recherches* or as books by the associated press, Encres.[50]

The second volume was the one properly led by Foucault, entitled *Généalogie des équipements de normalisation: Les équipements sanitaires*, and was itself divided into three discrete parts. Only the first, entitled *L'institution hospitalière au XVIIIe siècle*, contains work by and directed by Foucault. The other parts are on psychiatry and mental health, but do not bear any trace of Foucault's involvement. The only text signed by Foucault is the essay 'The Politics of Health in the Eighteenth Century' (GEN 1–11).[51] This essay was reprinted in a later collective volume entitled *Les machines à guérir (aux origines de l'hôpital moderne)* in 1976 (MG1, 11–21), and then revised for a second edition of that text in 1979 (MG2, 7–18). Both versions were reprinted in *Dits et écrits* and are available in English translation.[52] As such, Foucault's involvement may seem to have been absorbed into the collected body of his work. But the major part of *L'institution hospitalière au XVIIIe siècle* is an unsigned text of three chapters and a conclusion on hospitals, illness, public health and the organization of urban space (GEN 13–79). This material has never been republished, and has not been translated into English. There are some clues that suggest that Foucault had a hand in its writing, and it certainly bears close thematic relation to his work on this topic, but other indications that he was not its principal author, such as the use of the first-person plural to describe the group under his direction, and the inaccurate references to Foucault's own work (GEN 49 n. 1, 65 n. 2).

The idea of a hospital as a *'machine à guérir*, a curing machine (GEN 20, 23), is developed in this report. This is the idea that the hospital itself, rather than just the practices that took place within it, could contribute to the medical process. The key to this is spatial organization. This research builds on work conducted in Foucault's 1973–4 Collège de France seminar, which studied 'the history of the institution and the architecture of the hospital in the eighteenth century' (PP 352/346).[53] Material for this seminar is archived at the BNF.[54] In this work Foucault and his colleagues show how the layout of rooms, the routes of passage, surveillance, circulation of air, water and other services, and cleaning and washing became issues of considerable concern (e.g. GEN 16, 17, 41, 73, 79). These architectural concerns would directly impact on the sick body (GEN 17); mirrored by the set of written records that also precisely located the sickness in the physical body of the sick (GEN 35). The location of the hospital within the urban environment was also important, as were wider issues of town planning in relation to health concerns. The report declares that 'the medicalization of urban space is based on a triple alliance: that of number, space and the town' (GEN 71). Number, or calculation, is there in the work of architects, but is also found in statistical measures of death, invalids, quantities of air, water and other services needed for the population and within hospitals (GEN 71).

Space is also there in the work of architects, but also in wider issues of town planning, which becomes 'an administrative colonization of the entire territory' for the purpose of improving and regulating health concerns (GEN 72). Between the individual body, the institution of the hospital and the urban environment we have a related set of spatial questions (GEN 45, 72). As well as the hygiene of the individual body there is a greater concern with issues of urban salubrity (GEN 45), a theme that relates to some of the claims he would make about the emergence of biopolitics as a study of the body in plural, the question of population. Salubrity is not a synonym for health, but rather its condition of possibility, at least its material and social basis. Some of the developments inside institutions and in the wider urban setting emerged from inquiries into conditions, either on behalf of the state and its agencies, or individuals such as John Howard's inquiries into prisons, hospitals and lazarettos (GEN 73). In the book there are indications that Foucault and his colleagues intended to develop this work in a broader study of the 'Architecture of Surveillance'. There they intend to study, under Foucault's direction, 'the regulatory and architectural *dispositifs* which create the hospital, prison and school between 1760–1820'. They note that the complexity of the questions have led them to concentrate in the present report just on the hospital (GEN 46).[55]

The book *Les machines à guérir* developed from this CERFI work, his 1973–4 seminar, and another research project under the leadership of Bruno Fortier entitled *La politique de l'espace parisien*.[56] The two editions of *Les machines à guérir* are substantially different: as well as Foucault's revised essay, the other chapters are revised and Fortier contributes an entirely different piece. In both editions, all the essays have named authors, and many of the themes of the earlier works are elaborated in detail. In particular, Blandine Barret-Kriegel's essay elaborates on the theme of the hospital as a 'curing machine', and the calculative mechanisms of the new medicine and public health.[57] Fortier's contribution to the first edition and François Beguin's chapter develop themes about the spatial organization of the hospital and urban structures more generally; Fortier is also looking at the medical inquiry into architectural conditions.[58] Anne Thalamy looks at the use of records, and analyses the military antecedents of the modern hospital; a theme that is elaborated in Fortier's contribution to the second edition, where he describes these institutions as 'inverse fortresses' with the protection, surveillance and security within instead of without.[59] The volume also includes an extensive dossier on the architecture, utilities, chronology and organization of the modern hospital (MG1 87–186; MG2 51–159), which includes substantial material on the inquiry (MG1 135–69; MG2 65–92). As Blandine-Kriegel notes, the inquiry is a 'tactical step' within a broader medicalization strategy, the ultimate goal of which is action (MG1 32; MG2 26).

A related report Foucault edited was entitled *Politiques de l'habitat (1800–1850)* from 1977, which has a brief unsigned foreword and then signed essays by Foucault's colleagues. While Foucault probably had at least a hand in the foreword, there is no essay by him in the collection. The volume contains discussion of public health initiatives, urban planning and management. The team analyse how the notion of habitat is 'constituted as an object of administrative and political intervention' (PH 3). Elements include 'medicine and hygiene, architecture, civil engineering, the social sciences and jurisdiction' (PH 3). There is again analysis of the use of statistics alongside material changes in the design and use of urban spaces, illustrated by rich empirical studies by Foucault's colleagues. The public health campaigns studied are both those for specific epidemics such as cholera in Blandine Barret-Kriegel's chapter,[60] or more general attempts to improve the condition of housing, especially for workers in the contribution by Danielle Rancière.[61] Opening up housing to the air and light is important, but there can be no simple architectural resolution to problems of 'social contagion' (PH 199). Workers' towns might be a more suitable project, but this is a much wider undertaking that requires town planning and spatial policy (PH 200). Anne Thalamy's study similarly discusses the 'economy of space, of architecture, materials and behaviour', the management of which produces and directs this notion of habitat (PH 42).[62] Habitat is therefore not just public space, but also private spaces and especially the intersection of public and private spaces, in places such as pavements, roads and crossroads.[63] François Béguin works on the town and house as means of social and spatial control.[64] Jean-Marie Alliaume analyses the discourses of reform.[65] There is a lot of detailed work in this study, which is conceived generally as 'a contribution to the history of architecture', both in terms of individual housing but also in the wider production of habitat or the urban environment (PH 4).[66]

Taken together, these collaborative projects show how Foucault's interest in medicine, already the focus of the 1963 book *Birth of the Clinic* was being extended beyond the institution of the hospital itself. *Birth of the Clinic* begins with the claim that 'this book is about space, about language, and about death; it is about the gaze [*le regard*]'.[67] In it, Foucault outlines what he calls three forms of spatialization. The first is the location of a disease in a family, nosology, the taxonomies of disease; the second is the location of disease in the patient's body, 'free of any group gaze and of hospital experience itself'; and finally the way diseases are located in a broader context: 'all the gestures by which, in a given society, a disease is circumscribed, medically invested, isolated, divided up into closed privileged regions, or distributed throughout cure centres, arranged in the most favourable way'. This is the space of 'heterogeneous institutions, time intervals [*décalages*], political struggles, demands and utopias, economic constraints, social confrontations'. Foucault claims that it is in the last of these that the changes that led to the most radical reformulation of medical knowledge occurred.[68] This is the space of scientific classifications, the space of corporeal physicality, and the space of social orderings.

Yet that book largely concentrates on the first and second of these, examining the form of medicine that emerges in the clinical hospital itself: clinical medicine. In this later work, initially collaborative projects in seminars and work with CERFI, Foucault is broadening the examination to encompass projects on urban hygiene, sanitation and public health.[69] His later collective volume on the 'politics of habitat' was an extension of that work. As Foucault later notes, the organization of space in architecture shifted in the eighteenth century from a simple display of royal or religious power to a concern with the 'problems of population, health and the town planning... it became a question of using the management of space for economic-political ends' (DE#195 III, 192; P/K 148).[70] All these concerns would prove important for his later development of work around the theme of governmentality. It would have a more immediate impact too.

The Rio Lectures on Social Medicine

As is clear from the preceding discussion, there is little Foucault included in these volumes on medicine and habitat. But he presented and developed many of these themes in some lectures given in October–November 1974 in Rio, shortly after completing the manuscript of *Discipline and Punish*. In these lectures Foucault links the development of hospital medicine to public health. Indeed, in *The Abnormals* lectures early the next year Foucault suggests that he may have been insufficiently clear in the *Psychiatric Power* course about the role of psychiatry in relation to medicine. He suggests that psychiatry in the eighteenth and nineteenth centuries was not really a branch of general medicine, but part of public hygiene. It is not insignificant, he notes, that some of the first works on psychiatry appeared in the *Annales d'hygiène publique* – the place he and his colleagues had found the case of Pierre Rivière (A 109/118).[71]

These 1974 Rio lectures were entitled 'Crisis of Medicine or Crisis of Anti-Medicine'; 'The Birth of Social Medicine'; and 'The Incorporation of the Hospital in Modern Technology'. These were published in 1976, 1977 and 1978, respectively, initially in Portuguese, then Spanish, and the versions in *Dits et écrits* are themselves translations back into French.[72] A French manuscript of part of the first is archived at the BNF;[73] the other materials may be lost or elsewhere in the archive. Unlike the 1973 Rio lectures, which drew extensively on previous Collège de France courses, these lectures are closer to a development of the research conducted that year in his Collège de France seminar. Defert suggests that Foucault actually gave two seminars and six talks on this trip to Brazil (C 45/56–7), for which limited archival traces are available, but even what we have provides a rich set of analyses.[74] Several important themes are anticipated in these lectures.

1. The relation between medicine and the social
2. Biohistory and biopolitics
3. The medicalization of sexuality
4. Health as an object of medical treatment
5. The relation of criminality and psychiatry
6. Mental illness, delinquency, dangerousness
7. The political economy of health

The first lecture looks at the relation between social welfare and medicine, with a particular focus on the Beveridge Plan in post-Second-World-War Britain. But part of Foucault's claim is that 'medicine has been a social activity since the eighteenth century...medicine has always been a social practice' (DE#170 II, 44; CMCA 8). These lectures are also important because they announce Foucault's interest in biopower. In a passage from the first lecture he outlines the shift from the individual to collective life:

> A new dimension of medical possibilities arises that I shall call bio-history. The doctor and the biologist are no longer working at the level of the individual and his descendants, but are beginning to work at the level of life itself and its fundamental events. This is a very important element in bio-history. (DE#170 II, 48; CMCA 11)

As he elaborates in the second lecture, 'capitalism...started by social-izing a first object, the body, as a factor of productive force, of labour power. Society's control over individuals was accomplished not only through consciousness or ideology but also in the body and with the body. For capitalist society, it was bio-politics, the biological, the somatic, the corporeal, which mattered more than anything else. The body is a bio-political reality; medicine is a bio-political strategy' (DE#196 II, 210; EW III, 137). The closing lines of the third lecture show how medicine plays a role he would later also attribute to sexuality: 'The medicine that is formed in the course of the eighteenth century is simultaneously a medicine of the individual and the population' (DE#229 II, 521; SKP 151).

They also begin to outline his thinking about the medicalization of sexuality, and government of populations:

> The objects that make up the area of medical treatment are not just restricted to diseases. I offer two examples. Since the beginning of the twentieth century, sexuality, sexual behaviour, sexual deviations or anomalies have been linked to medical treatment, without a doctor's saying, unless he is naive, that a sexual anomaly is a disease. The systematic treatment by medical therapists of homosexuals in Eastern European countries is characteristic of the 'medicalization' of something that is not a disease, either from the point of view of the person under treatment or the doctor.
>
> More generally, it might be argued that health has been transformed into an object of medical treatment. Everything that ensures the health of the individual; whether it be the purification of water, housing conditions or urban life styles, is today a field for medical intervention that is no longer linked exclusively to diseases. Actually, the authoritarian intervention of medicine in an ever-widening field of individual or collective existence is an absolutely characteristic fact. Today medicine is endowed with an authoritarian power with normalizing functions that go beyond the existence of diseases and the wishes of the patient. (DE#170 II, 49; CMCA 11–12)

In this lecture Foucault discusses the relation between state medicine and the emergence of police science directed towards health, and there is a discussion of the relation between criminality and psychiatry, looking at the relation between mental illness and delinquency, and the notion of 'dangerousness' (DE#170, II, 52; CMCA 15); and the political economy of medicine (DE#170 II, 53–8; CMCA 16–19). What is interesting about these lectures is that Foucault did not draw on previous Collège de France lecture material, with the exception of the relation between criminality and psychiatry. The material in these lectures is closer to work pursued in his seminars (see DE#196 III, 208; EW III, 135).

The Rio lectures also anticipate other future concerns. The notion of 'dangerousness', for example, was one of the themes of his 1976 Collège de France seminar (DE#187 III, 130; EW I, 64) and became a major theme in the 1977 lecture 'About the Concept of the "Dangerous Individual" in 19th Century Legal Psychiatry'; the work on police was developed in later seminars and in the 1977–8 and 1978–9 lecture courses on governmentality.[75] The third Rio lecture also relates to *Les machines à guérir* in its discussion of how maritime and military hospitals were transformed, not on the basis of developments in medicine, but in relation to the political technology of discipline (DE#229 II, 514; SKP 146). These texts provide Foucault's most detailed answer to a question he posed to the geographers of the French journal *Hérodote* in 1976: 'Do you think it is possible to undertake a geography – or taking into account scales, geographies – of medicine (not of illnesses, but of medical establishments [*implantations*] along with their zone of intervention and their modality of action?)' (DE#178 III, 95; SKP 20).

Foucault's themes in this research include such matters as the development of hospitalization, and in particular the spatial organization of its buildings, the mechanisms by which public health was carried out, and the study of environment and housing. This raises questions of waste collection, transport system and shared public infrastructures to allow the functioning of everyday life, particularly in the urban environment (DE#196 III, 208; EW III, 135; see PH). This should be revealing to us for the reason that Foucault argues that the themes that struck him in the literature on prisons had previously seemed important in his study of clinical medicine, particularly hospital architecture. Hospitals required knowledge of contacts, contagions, proximity and crowding, ventilation and air circulation: 'at the same time to divide space and keep it open, assuring a surveillance which is both global and individualizing, carefully separating apart the individuals to survey'. This comes in an interview published as the preface to the 1977 French edition of Jeremy Bentham's *Panopticon*, and indeed Foucault suggests the research on hospitals is where he first came across the Panopticon (DE#195 III, 190; P/K 146; see GEN 79).[76] What is of interest here is how Foucault's concerns with surveillance interrelate with concerns about society as a whole – not in the total institution of the prison, but in the realm of public health.

Foucault's principal claim is that one of the changes of the years 1720–1800 was the appearance of a collection of modes of intervention that were neither therapeutic nor even medical in the strict sense. Instead they were concerned with modes of life, food, dwelling and environment. In all of these areas, questions of spatiality and the surveillance of populations are important. During this time medicine becomes an essential element for the maintenance and development of collective life, for society. For the capitalist society, it is bio-politics above all which is important, that is the biological, the somatic, the bodily. As Foucault puts it, 'the body is a bio-political reality, medicine is a bio-political strategy' (DE#196 III, 210; EW III, 137). Biopolitics also first emerges as a topic in these 1974 lectures. The development of statistics, population profiles and monitoring and surveillance become important as there is a move to prevention and regulation – not only in sites of exclusion, but in the society more generally. This is an anticipation of the arguments he will make in the first volume of *History of Sexuality* and lecture courses from *'Society Must Be Defended'* to *The Birth of Biopolitics* that, in this period, governments deal not just with a territory and the individuals or a 'people' within, but with an 'economic and political problem' – population.[77] Before this time only exceptional circumstances – the regulations applied in times of epidemic, the measures used in plague-infected towns, the quarantines imposed in large ports, along with the more mundane assistance shown to paupers – showed the constitution of these kinds of authority-led medical interventions (DE#257 III, 727).

In the second of the Rio lectures we find the first presentation of the contrast between two methods of dealing with diseases: the treatment of leprosy and the plague. As Chapter 5 showed, this introduced the 'Panopticism' chapter of *Discipline and Punish*. There they are used to trace the emergence of the disciplinary society more generally; here Foucault is more interested in public health campaigns. He suggests that 'urban medicine, with its methods of surveillance, hospitalization, etc. is nothing other than the development...of the political-medical plan [*schéma*] of quarantine' (DE#196, III, 218–19; EW III, 146).

When Foucault discusses the different models of medicine in Germany, France and England, it is notable that the French model is of 'urban medicine' (compared to state medicine and medicine of the labour force). Foucault underlines three things that this particular version of medicine means. Urban medicine brings medical expertise close to sciences such as chemistry, which allows it to trade on a whole range of established scientific practices. Foucault also makes the point that 'urban medicine is not really a medicine of man, the body, and the organism but a medicine of things – air, water, decompositions, fermentations. It is a medicine of the living conditions of the milieu of existence' (DE#196, III 222; EW 150). But in a sense it is the third idea that is most important: the emergence of a concept of salubrity. Public hygiene emerges at the same time with the *Annales d'hygiène publique* first appearing in 1829 and becoming 'the organ of French social medicine' (DE#196, III 222–3; EW III 150–1).

Foucault suggests that social medicine is developed in France along with the expansion of urban politics, and organization of the town. The situation of cemeteries, on the edge of towns is one aspect analysed. He suggests that the shift from older style ossuaries is not due to a shift in Christian belief, but a more medical concern for contagion. Abattoirs are similarly shifted from the centre of Paris to the west, to Villette. The key concern however is with circulation, with movement and the control of flows of water and air. Air was associated with the transmission of miasmas, and there was a fixation about the temperature of air and its facilitation of disease. Proximity to swamps and marshes is linked to the spread of disease. In terms of water and drainage, Foucault examines the development of sewers, where the authorities control the subsoil, even when the space above was privately owned. This also allowed minerals to be mined and appropriated for the general good (DE#196 III, 219–21; EW III, 146–9; SMBD 218/245). Public hygiene is the political-scientific control of the environment. A large part of the scientific medicine of the nineteenth century – the birth of the clinic, in the dual sense of the hospital and clinical medicine – finds its origin in the lessons of the urban medicine developed at the end of the eighteenth century. The hospital is turned into a 'curing machine' (DE#257 III, 738).

In the family, the organization and distribution of space is also important. The space of the home needs to be 'purified, cleaned, aerated', and there is a medically optimal distribution of individuals, beds, and household objects (DE#257 III, 732). Such themes will be developed in *The Abnormals* course in relation to campaigns against childhood masturbation and incest. However it is urban space more generally which is the most dangerous location for the population as a whole. 'The situation of different quarters, their humidity, their orientation, the aeration of the entire town, the system of sewerage and disposal of waste water, the situation of cemeteries and abattoirs, and population density, all of these are the factors which play a decisive role in the mortality and morbidity of the inhabitants' (DE#257 III, 734). This requires the growth of medical interventions beyond the previously privileged places of illness – prisons, boats, ports, and hospitals. These interventions isolate and constitute the points of application of the much more intensified medical use of power.

As a general technique of health, medicine takes its place within the administrative structures and machinery of power (DE#257 III, 734–5). We therefore have this medicalization, part through surveillance and control, at a number of different levels or scales – the urban environment, the institution of the hospital, and the individual home. This is an administration of the polity, of the space of social order. And the political stakes are important – in an interview conducted on this trip he clarified his position:

> Q: In your work, the State seems to occupy a privileged place. And the State represents a privileged instance for understanding historical-cultural formations. Could you specify the conditions of possibility which underpin the State?
>
> A: It is true that the State interests me, but it only interests me differentially [*différentiellement*]. I do not believe that the entirety [*ensemble*] of the powers which are exercised in the interior of a society – and which assure in that society the hegemony of a class, an elite, or a caste – are entirely contained in the State system. The State, with its grand judicial, military and other apparatuses [*appareils*], only represents a guarantee, the reinforcement of a network of powers which come through different channels, different from these main routes. My problem is to attempt a differential analysis of the different levels of power in society. As a consequence, the State occupies an important place in this, but not a preeminent one. (DE#163 II, 812)

From all this a number of valuable insights can be gleaned. We can see clearly here that the models of the disciplinary society were never merely the prison – as a superficial reading of *Discipline and Punish* might suggest – but the army, religious institutions, and the hospital, both the psychiatric hospital and that concerned with general medicine. As Foucault suggested, the book was not an attempt at 'writing the history of the different disciplinary institutions, with all their individual differences, but only of mapping some of the essential techniques that most easily spread from one to another through a series of examples' (DP 163/139). The relations which run through these institutions are, crucially, linked to the transition from the inquiry to the examination:

> *Supplice* was the logical outcome of a procedure governed by the Inquisition. Putting under 'observation' is a natural extension of a justice imbued with disciplinary methods and the procedure of the examination. Is it surprising that the cellular prison, with its regular chronologies, forced labour, its authorities of surveillance and registration, its experts in normality, who continue and multiply the functions

of the judge, should have become the modern instrument of penality?
Is it surprising that prisons resemble factories, schools, barracks, hospitals, which all resemble prisons. (DP 264/227–8)

In addition as this Rio interview indicates, he was already beginning to search for a different way of formulating questions that
would decentre the state from his analysis, something that again
reaches fullest expression in the work on governmentality later in
the 1970s.

Conclusion: Towards Foucault's Last Decade

Towards the end of the *Psychiatric Power* course Foucault opens an extended parenthesis to discuss the history of truth in general (PP 235–47/235–47). On the one hand there is a common relation of scientific knowledge to a ground in truth, a truth that is absolute for all times and spaces. But there is another kind of truth, which has a geography and a calendar (or at least a chronology) (PP 236/236). It also has its privileged and exclusive operators, and this is what might be called a non-universal version of truth. In this sense it is truth not as a relation of knowledge [*connaissance*] but of domination and victory, of power (PP 237/237). Foucault is clearly more interested in the second series, which he says he has been tracing in his previous courses (PP 238/238). In all this his aim has been one of

> Showing that scientific demonstration is basically only a ritual, showing that the supposed universal subject of knowledge is in reality only a historically qualified individual according to a certain number of realities, showing that the discovery of truth is in reality a certain modality of the production of truth; putting what is given as the truth of observation [*constatation*] or as the truth of demonstration, back on the level of rituals, of the qualifications of the knowing subject, the system of truth-event, this is what I call the archaeology of knowledge. (PP 238/9)

He considers that his more recent work provides a sketch of the 'genealogy of knowledge [*connaissance*]', 'the indispensable historical other side [*envers*] to the archaeology of knowledge [*savoir*]'. There are three themes or 'dossiers' of this relation – judicial practice;

psychiatry; and pedagogy and childhood (PP 239/239). The first theme was treated in the opening salvo of courses at the *Collège – Lectures on the Will to Know, Théories et institutions pénales* and *The Punitive Society*; the second theme in *Psychiatric Power*; and the question of children will come to some degree in the following year's course, *The Abnormals*. Childhood was also the topic of an intended volume of the original plan for the *History of Sexuality*,[1] and he would return to this theme in the 1982 book *Le désordre des familles*. In all we can see the relation of power to knowledge, because the technology of truth is seen as akin to the event, the strategy, or even the hunt. It is for this reason that Foucault would pursue the thesis that knowledge as power functions as war, at least until he felt he could go no further (see DE#178 III, 94–5; SKP 19–20). More broadly we can see how the archaeological and genealogical approaches are different yet complementary formulations.

It is important to remember that between 1969 and 1974, Foucault only wrote one book: *Discipline and Punish*, which was published in February 1975. The published volumes of material that we now have from this period can give a misleading impression: most are transcripts of lectures, interviews, press conferences, discussions. Much of what he wrote was to be spoken, and many of the texts from this period are collaborative, anonymous, some seemingly peripheral. Research was conducted in his seminars that was then used in his lectures; the courses tried out ideas that would be re-elaborated in his books. He took interviews very seriously, in part for the spontaneous creation of ideas and connections, but the transcripts were often extensively edited before publication. When he wrote, rather than spoke, it was almost exclusively by hand, and the materiality of the texts that remain can be revealing.[2] In *Discipline and Punish* Foucault talks of a 'laboratory of power' (DP 238–9/204), and we can conceive of the different types of speaking and writing as developing, testing and deploying the fruits of this labour.[3] This book has tried to be respectful of the important differences in genre, and in tone, between these different sources of evidence. In addition, we now have access to some of Foucault's preparatory reading notes, which help to contextualize his remarks on a range of subjects. All this, perhaps, helps to explain his comments on the writing process in 1975:

> Basically, I do not like to write. This is a very difficult activity to overcome. Writing interests me only to the degree that it incorporates the reality of combat, as an instrument, a tactic, a spotlight. I would like

my books to be like a kind of scalpel, Molotov cocktails, or undermining tunnels [*galeries de mine*] and to be burned up after use like fireworks. (DE#152 II, 725)

Looking at the materal archived at the BNF is revealing, because this volume of notes and drafts can only be achieved by the daily discipline of application and formation. In 1969 Foucault spoke of 'a very strong obligation to write', and that 'we feel extremely anxious and tense when we haven't done our daily little page of writing'.[4] But the political activism of this period helps to explain his continual purpose. As he said in 1975:

The use of a book is directly linked to the pleasure it can give, but I do not conceive of what I have done as a work [*une œuvre*], and I'm shocked that one can call oneself a writer. I am an instrument dealer, a recipe maker, a guide to objectives, a cartographer, a plan maker, an armourer. (DE#152 II, 725)

As he declared in another interview conducted in 1975 around the time of *Discipline and Punish*, but only published in 2004, he developed this idea:

I am an artificer. I make something that ultimately serves a siege, a war, a destruction. I am not for destruction, but only so we can pass, so we can advance, so we can tear down the walls.

An artificer is primarily a geologist. They examine the layers of terrain, the folds, the faults. What is easy to dig? What will resist? They examine how fortresses are grounded. They examine the features [*reliefs*] that can be used to hide or to launch an assault.

While this is well mapped, it remains experimental, provisional. Reconnaissance is sent out, look-outs are posted, reports are sent back. These define the tactics that we will employ. Is it a trench [*la sape*]? A siege? Is it digging a mine, or a direct assault?...The method, ultimately, is nothing other than this strategy. (E 92)[5]

This is a telling self-description: Foucault as an artificer, a sapper, a technician or a mechanic, someone who conceives, develops or constructs, breaks things down or clears the way. This fits with his suggestion – borrowing a line first used by Deleuze in their 1972 interview (DE#106 II, 309; LCP 208) – that his books are like 'tool boxes' from which readers can take things to address problems (DE#151 II, 720; FL 149; E 73). In the early 1970s, the key tool developed was his theorization of power. This built on his work on knowledge, and supplemented the archaeological approach with the development of genealogy.

While the link between the work of the GIP and *Discipline and Punish* is well known, here the parallel work on asylums and health has been integrated into the analysis. In addition to collaborative activism, this book has sought to bring collaborative research into the account. The documentary traces for that activist and research work are largely unpublished, or in anonymous and uncollected pamphlets and reports, but viewing them in relation to the published works and lecture courses has been important in providing a rounded story.

Foucault would never again be as politically active as he was in the early 1970s. While in the later 1970s and 1980s he was involved in campaigns against the execution of militants in Franco's Spain,[6] in support of the Vietnamese boat people and Solidarity in Poland, met militant groups in Germany,[7] and wrote about the Iranian revolution,[8] he did not take on the facilitating and activist role he had served with the GIP. Defert notes that 'there is no politics without logistics', and that the practical work Foucault did was crucial,[9] though no doubt also exhausting. As Foucault remarked when asked to take a more active role with *Libération*, he had already done his 'two years' service.[10] Foucault would continue to sign petitions throughout this period, from ones against the US bombing of Vietnamese dykes and the country more generally in 1972,[11] to support for Palestinians in 1973;[12] to later concerns with imprisonment of left intellectuals in Italy,[13] the situation in Poland, the fate of refugees and French politics.[14] Yet he confessed his ambivalence to petitions in a 1979 interview: 'signing nothing or signing everything, either way, it amounts to the same'.[15]

Today the tools and concepts Foucault developed – genealogy, power-knowledge, biopolitics, governmentality and so on – are more utilized than his concrete analyses and campaigns. But as Keith Reader wrote in 1987, it is important to recognize that that 'his major impact on the French left since 1968 came through the areas he examined, rather than the concepts he deployed to examine them'. While recognizing that it is not possible 'entirely to disentangle' them, Reader stresses that 'Foucault's political significance lay in the attention he gave to areas often considered politically as well as socially marginal – madness, imprisonment, the medical clinic, the origins of our ideas of and on sexuality.[16]

A balance has been attempted here. The tools were developed and the concepts theorized in order to address those concrete concerns, and Foucault may seem to move away from them once they had served their purpose. Yet the specific topics remain crucial to understanding his significance. Foucault would go on to utilize genealogy and power in his last work, the long-promised sequel to the *History of Madness*, a *History of Sexuality*. That project, with all its many detours, would occupy the last decade of his life. Strikingly, new tools would be again developed as his work progressed, generating new means of approaching the questions. Chapter 5 of this book ended with the links between *Discipline and Punish* and the first volume of the *History of Sexuality*; Chapter 6 noted how Foucault was already indicating some of the themes he would explore in his later 1970s work on governmentality and bio-power.

The choice of 1974 as the break between the analysis of this book and that of *Foucault's Last Decade* is then, in part, one of convenience. The two books were certainly conceived to work together. But they deal with different questions: that one with the genesis, conception, abandonment, reconfiguration and near completion of a single, albeit wide-ranging project; this one with the interwoven relations between his lecture courses, political activism and the production of the book *Discipline and Punish*. Through the initial chapters on Measure, Inquiry and Examination, to their deployment in political and academic work on Madness, Discipline and Health, this book has sought to illuminate this crucial period in Foucault's work.

This story can be understood in greater detail today because of the new availability of material. In this study the published works have been situated alongside the lecture courses, archival traces of activism and collaborative research have been outlined and examined, and all these supplemented by his reading notes. These sources clearly show the importance for Foucault of working with others, both politically and in research teams; the interrelation of academic research and political activism; and the much broader research upon which his publications rested. We can now more closely trace the emergence and growth of his research interests and the tools for their analysis, especially highlighting the gradual development of themes and techniques. *Discipline and Punish* is the culmination of collaborative work in and beyond his seminars, of political activism, lectures, and extensive reading. Yet it transcends any of those individual sources when viewed as the single, integrated text that for so long was the only major published output of this tumultuous period.

Notes

Abbreviations

1 For a valuable discussion, see Jeroen Vandaele, 'What is an Author, Indeed: Michel Foucault in Translation', *Perspectives: Studies in Translatology*, 24 (1), 2016, pp. 76–92.
2 See Richard A. Lynch, 'Michel Foucault's Shorter Works in English', in Christopher Falzon, Timothy O'Leary and Jana Sawicki (eds.) *A Companion to Foucault*, Oxford: Blackwell, 2013, pp. 562–92.

Introduction: Out of the 1960s

1 See Jean-François Bert and Elisabetta Basso (eds.), *Foucault à Münsterlingen: À l'origine de l'*Histoire de la folie, Paris: EHESS, 2015.
2 While the translation, with a brief editorial note, was published as Immanuel Kant, *Anthropologie du point de vue pragmatique*, Paris: Vrin, 1964, the introduction only appeared posthumously. They are now collected as Immanuel Kant, *Anthropologie du point de vue pragmatique*, preceded by Michel Foucault, *Introduction à l'Anthropologie*, Paris: Vrin, 2009; while Foucault's text is translated by Roberto Nigro and Kate Briggs as *Introduction to Kant's Anthropology*, Los Angeles: Semiotext(e), 2008.
3 To date, only Jacques Lagrange's notes from this course are available in archives. They are preserved at IMEC FCL 3.8, 'Cours de Michel Foucault donnés à l'École Normale Supérieure (1953–5) (notes prises et mises en forme par Jacques Lagrange)'. 'Problèmes de l'Anthropologie, [ENS rue d']Ulm 1954–5' is in folder 4. There are plans to publish the course itself.

4   Stuart Elden, *Foucault's Last Decade*, Cambridge: Polity, 2016.
5   David Macey, *The Lives of Michel Foucault*, London: Hutchinson, 1993, p. 323.
6   See Gérard Petitjean, 'Les Grands Prêtres de l'université française', *Le nouvel observateur*, 7 April 1975, pp. 52–7 (the quote comes from p. 55); and *Foucault's Last Decade*, introduction.
7   Defert, LWK 276-7/269.
8   Ewald and Harcourt, TIP 246.
9   On 29 May 1973 Foucault gave a lecture in Bela Horizonte on the same trip. The entire lecture is unpublished, but fragments which discuss his thought in relation to Nietzsche, Heidegger and others; his take on dialectics; and his relation to literature can be found in DE#124 II, 423–5.
10 Gilles Deleuze, *Foucault*, Paris: Minuit, 1986, p. 122; trans. Séan Hand as *Foucault*, London: Athlone, 1988, p. 115 (hereafter French and English are cited separated by /).
11 Deleuze, *Foucault*, p. 32/24; see 'Le Pouvoir', lecture of 7 January 1986, https://www.cla.purdue.edu/research/Deleuze/Course%20Transcriptions.html
12 See *Foucault's Last Decade*, especially ch. 4 and pp. 200–1.
13 Interview with Defert, 12 April 2015; conversation with Henri-Paul Fruchaud, 18 November 2015.
14 One course is published in Arabic: Mohsen Sakhri (ed.), *Foucault: Qari'an le-Descartes* [*Foucault: Reading Descartes*], Tunis: Merkaz al-amna al-hadari, 1992. A summary is available as 'Plan détaillé du cours de Michel Foucault (1966–7 à la Faculté des Lettres et Sciences Humaines) sur Descartes', Appendix to Rachida Boubaker-Triki, 'Foucault en Tunisie', *Rue Descartes*, no. 61, 2008, pp. 112–13. On this period, see Didier Eribon, *Michel Foucault*, Paris: Flammarion, third edition, 2011, pp. 295–6; *Michel Foucault*, trans. Betsy Wing, London: Faber, 1991, pp. 188–9 (hereafter French and English are cited separated by /); Macey, *The Lives of Michel Foucault*, p. 189; Rachida Boubaker-Triki, 'Foucault en Tunisie', in Foucault, *La peinture de Manet*, pp. 51–63; Dominique Séglard, 'Foucault à Tunis: A propos de deux conferences', *Foucault Studies*, no. 4, 2007, pp. 7–18; and the special issue '*Michel Foucault en Tunisie (1966–8)*', *CELAAN* XII (1&2), 2015.
15 See Michel Foucault, *La peinture de Manet, suivi de Michel Foucault, un regard*, ed. Maryvonne Saison, Seuil, Paris, 2004; and the others in 'Foucault en Tunisie', *Les Cahiers de Tunisie* 149–50, 1989. On the planned Manet book, see Eribon, *Michel Foucault*, p. 298–9/190–1; Macey, *The Lives of Michel Foucault*, p. 189.
16 See Eribon, *Michel Foucault*, pp. 304–6/193–4; Macey, *The Lives of Michel Foucault*, 203–6; Dosse, *A History of Structuralism Volume 2*, pp. 120–1; and essays in the *CELAAN* theme issue. On the general context, see Keith A. Reader, *Intellectuals and the Left in France since 1968*, Houndmills: Macmillan, 1987; Keith A. Reader with Khursheed Wadia, *The May 1968 Events in France: Reproductions and*

Interpretations, New York: St Martin's Press, 1993; Kristin Ross, *May '68 and its Afterlives*, Chicago: University of Chicago Press, 2002.

17 It can be found in BNF NAF28284 (1). The opening pages are reproduced as 'Le livre et le sujet' in Philippe Artières, Jean-François Bert, Frédéric Gros and Judith Revel (eds.), *Cahier de L'Herne 95: Michel Foucault*, Paris: L'Herne, 2011, pp. 70–91. For a general discussion of the book and its drafting, see Martin Rueff, in Œ II, 1401–30.

18 Interview with Daniel Defert, 12 April 2015; see Daniel Defert, 'Je crois au temps…', *Review Recto/Verso*, no. 1, 2007, pp. 1–7.

19 BNF NAF28284 (1), p. 241a.

20 BNF NAF28284 (1), p. 335b. See also DE#47 I, 583. On the history of the present see DP 40/31 and ch. 5 below.

21 BNF NAF28730 (48). An excerpt has been published as ' "Introduction" à l'Archéologie du savoir', edited and introduced by Martin Rueff, *Les Études philosophiques*, no. 153, 2015, pp. 327–52. On pp. 349–51 Rueff provides a summary description of some of the contents of BNF NAF28730 (48), which indicate Foucault's detailed notes on J. L. Austin, W. V. Quine, Gilbert Ryle, Bertrand Russell and other Anglo-American philosophers. See also Rueff, in Œ II, 1428–9.

22 Sources for Foucault's time at Vincennes are limited. See Eribon, *Michel Foucault*, Part III, ch. 1/ch. 14; Macey, *The Lives of Michel Foucault*, ch. 9; Gérard Miller, 'Comment Michel Foucault devint un "camarade"!', in Jean-Michel Djian (ed.), *Vincennes: Une aventure de la pensée critique*, Paris: Flammarion, 2009, pp. 46–9; François Dosse, 'Vincennes (1969–74): entre science et utopies', in Philippe Artières and Michelle Zancarini-Fournel (eds.), *68: Une Histoire collective (1962–1981)*, Paris: La Découverte, 2008, pp. 505–13, which draws heavily on François Dosse, *A History of Structuralism Volume 2: The Sign Sets, 1967–Present*, trans. Deborah Glassman, Minneapolis: University of Minnesota Press, 1997, ch. 14; and Foucault's 1970 text 'Le piège de Vincennes', DE#78 II, 67–73. A more general account can be found in Bruno Tessarech, *Vincennes*, Paris: NiL, 2011.

23 Eribon, *Michel Foucault*, p. 324/207, suggests ' "The discourse of sexuality" and "the end of metaphysics" ' in 1969, and 'the epistemology of the sciences of life' and 'Nietzsche' in 1969–70.

24 IMEC, FCL 3.8 'Cours de Michel Foucault donnés à l'École Normale Supérieure'. The material on heredity is in folder 3.

25 *Maladie mentale et personnalité*, Paris: PUF, 1954; *Maladie mentale et psychologie*, Paris: PUF, 1962; trans. A.M. Sheridan-Smith as *Mental Illness and Psychology*, New York: Harper & Row, 1976.

26 Some notes on this are filed in BNF NAF28730 (12).

27 See C 34/41; Macey, *The Lives of Michel Foucault*, pp. 209–10, 219–20, 225–6; Élie Kagan, Alain Jaubert and Philippe Artières, *Michel Foucault, une journée particulière*, Paris: Ædelsa, 2004, pp. 56–7; see also a 1970 interview where he talks about the political situation in universities ('A conversation with Michel Foucault by John K. Simon', *Partisan Review* 38 (2), 1971, pp. 192–201; DE#89 II, 182–93).

28 For the documents on these two processes, see Eribon, *Michel Foucault*, Annex 3 and 4, pp. 557–77 (not in English translation).

29 Annex 3, in Eribon, *Michel Foucault*, pp. 566–7.

30 Annex 4, in Eribon, *Michel Foucault*, p. 570.

31 *Raymond Roussel*, Paris: Gallimard, 1963; trans. Charles Ruas as *Death and the Labyrinth: The World of Raymond Roussel*, London: Athlone, 1987.

32 *Ceci n'est pas une pipe*, Montpellier: Fata Morgana, 1973; trans. James Harkness as *This is Not a Pipe*, Berkeley: University of California Press, 1983. This is an expanded edition of a text reprinted as DE#53 I, 635–50; EW II, 187–203.

33 See Philippe Sabot, 'La littérature aux confins du savoir: sur quelques "dits et écrits" de Michel Foucault', in Pierre-François Moreau, *Lectures de Michel Foucault Volume 3: Sur les* Dits et écrits, Lyon: ENS Éditions, 2003, pp. 17–33. Some of these themes are discussed in Michel Foucault, *Le beau danger: Entretien avec Claude Bonnefoy*, ed. Philippe Artières, Paris: Éditions EHESS, 2011; *Speech Begins after Death*, trans. Robert Bonnano, Minneapolis: University of Minnesota Press, 2013.

34 The lectures on de Sade have been published in Michel Foucault, *La grande étrangère: À propos de literature*, eds. Philippe Artières, Jean-François Bert, Mathieu Potte-Bonneville and Judith Revel, Paris: Éditions EHESS, 2013; trans. Robert Bonnano as *Language, Madness, and Desire: On Literature*, Minneapolis: University of Minnesota Press, 2015. Foucault later suggests that there is a continuity between his treatment of Roussel and the work on Pierre Rivière (E 85), and presumably Herculin Barbin and the *lettres de cachet*.

35 Jacques le Goff, *Hérésies et sociétés dans l'Europe pré-industrielle, 11e-18e siècles*, Paris: Mouton & Co, 1968. Foucault's lecture and subsequent discussion is reprinted in DE#52 I, 624–35; and the lecture translated in *Religion and Culture*, ed. Jeremy R. Carrette, London: Routledge, 1999, pp. 50–6.

36 *Religion and Culture*, p. 56.

37 The English translation is of the original text. For the changes see François Delaporte's notes to the reedition in Œ I, 1528–52; and James Bernauer, *Michel Foucault's Force of Flight*, Humanities Press, New Jersey, 1992, pp. 188–92.

38 DE#16 I, 268–72; DE#25 I, 412–20 (reprinted in HM 575–82/541–9 in 1972); DE#44 I, 557–60; DE#62 I, 753–67.

39 Colin Gordon, 'History, madness and other errors: a response', *History of the Human Sciences*, 3 (3), pp. 381–96, p. 389; see 'History of Madness', in Christopher Falzon, Timothy O'Leary and Jana Sawicki (eds.) *A Companion to Foucault*, Oxford: Blackwell, 2013, pp. 84–103.

40 See also Vuillemin, Annex 4, in Eribon, *Michel Foucault*, pp. 575–6.

41 See in particular BNF NAF28730 (10), folder 4: Degenerescence.

42 On what limited publishing traces remain see Defert, Œ II, 1458–9.

43 Samuel Beckett, 'The Unnameable', in *The Beckett Trilogy: Molloy, Malone Dies, The Unnameable*, London: Picador, 1979 [1959], p. 382.

44 See Stuart Elden, *Mapping the Present: Heidegger, Foucault and the Project of a Spatial History*, London: Continuum, 2001, ch. 4.
45 Notes on this theme are filed in BNF NAF28730 (39), especially folder 1.
46 See François Jacob, *La logique du vivant: Une histoire de l'hérédité*, Paris: Gallimard, 1970; *The Logic of Life: A History of Heredity* and *The Possible and the Actual*, trans. Betty E. Spillmann, London: Penguin, 1989.
47 BNF NAF28730 (39), folder 3.

1 Measure: Greece, Nietzsche, Oedipus

1 Defert, LWK 276/278; see 'Translator's Note' in LWK – /xiv–xv.
2 Alan Sheridan, *Michel Foucault: The Will to Truth*, London: Tavistock, 1980; Hubert Dreyfus and Paul Rabinow, *Michel Foucault: Beyond Structuralism and Hermeneutics*, Brighton: Harvester, 1982.
3 See, for instance, James Bernauer and David Rasmussen (eds.), *The Final Foucault*, Cambridge, MA: The MIT Press, 1988 and Jeremy Moss (ed.), *The Later Foucault: Politics and Philosophy*, London: Sage, 1998.
4 As Defert notes, 'the inaugural lecture announces a genealogy of knowledge without the expression itself being used by Foucault. Nietzsche in a sense initiated a genealogy of *savoir* which dynamited all theories of *connaissance* as faculty, the traditional theory in philosophy' (LWK 259/264).
5 Defert, LWK 271/274. Defert continues to suggest that in the 'Nietzsche, Genealogy, History' essay, as in this course, 'Foucault proposes as genealogy what Deleuze presents as differential ontology' (LWK 271/274).
6 See Gilles Deleuze, 'Désir et plaisir', *Deux régimes de fous: Textes et entretiens 1975–1995*, ed. David Lapoujade, Paris: Minuit, 2003; 'Desire and Pleasure', in Arnold I. Davidson (ed.), *Foucault and his Interlocutors*, Chicago: University of Chicago Press, pp. 183–92, pp. 189–90.
7 Defert, LWK 262 n. 16/–notes that the distinction was already there in *Histoire de la folie* (HM 572–3/460–2), a fact unfortunately not adequately recognized in the English translation *History of Madness*. This part of Defert's note is missing from the English translation of the course.
8 The medieval period and the inquiry generally are discussed in ch. 2.
9 'City-state' is Foucault's translation (LWK 153/160).
10 See the editorial notes to this page (LWK 147–8/153–4), showing that the list changes from three to four elements, with 'nature' the addition. The delivered course did not include this, and all mentions of nature are of later addition in different ink.
11 This comes in notes written at a later date included in the manuscript Defert has appended to this lecture.

12 Burchell, LWK -/143 n. †.
13 This page of the manuscript is an addition from a lecture at SUNY, Buffalo in March 1972 (LWK 151 n. */158 n. *)
14 See LWK 28/28 n.; and Defert, LWK 276/279.
15 Defert, LWK 264/267–8.
16 BNF NAF28730 (33), boxes a and b, with the label of 'Reading Notes on German Philosophy from the 1950s'. But there are notes in these folders that undoubtedly date from a later period.
17 Defert, LWK 264/268. See Friedrich Nietzsche, *Sämtliche Werke: Kritische Studienausgabe*, eds. Giorgio Colli and Mazzino Montinari, Berlin and Munich: W. de Gruyter and Deutscher Taschenbuch Verlag, fifteen volumes, 1980, vol. I, p. 99; *The Birth of Tragedy* and *The Case of Wagner*, trans. Walter Kaufmann, New York: Vintage, 1967, §15, p. 96 – Kaufmann translates this as 'hunger for knowledge'. Defert references *Le livre du philosophe: Études théorétiques*, trans. Angèle Kremer-Marietti, Paris: Flammarion, 1969, pp. 52, 44, which equates to *Philosophy and Truth: Selections from Nietzsche's Notebooks of the Early 1870s*, edited and trans. Daniel Breazeale, Atlantic Highlands: Humanities Press, 1979, pp. 9 (§30), 16 (§46).
18 Defert, LWK 265/269.
19 Defert, LWK 263/267.
20 There are important developments particularly in 1976, see SMBD, and *Foucault's Last Decade*, ch. 2.
21 Defert, LWK 265/269. On that book, see *Foucault's Last Decade*, especially ch. 3.
22 Daniel Defert, 'The Emergence of Power in Michel Foucault's 1970–71 lectures', *The Foucault Effect 1991–2011*, Birkbeck, University of London, 3 June 2011.
23 Defert, LWK 30 n. 13/30 n. 13.
24 Nietzsche, *Sämtliche Werke*, vol. I, p. 875; *Writings from the Early Notebooks*, eds. Raymond Geuss and Alexander Nehamas, trans. Ladislaus Löb, Cambridge: Cambridge University Press, 2009, p. 253.
25 These remarks are reused in the 'Truth and Juridical Forms' lectures (DE#139 II, 544; EW III, 6).
26 Defert, LWK 274/277.
27 Back-cover text of the French edition; and see Defert, LWK 279/281, where he says that while Heidegger does not feature explicitly in the manuscript, the notes from the audience and the McGill lecture show he was mentioned.
28 Defert, LWK 96 n. 31/99 n. 32.
29 *Nietzsche*, Frankfurt am Main: Vittorio Klostermann, two volumes, 1996 [1961]; *Nietzsche*, trans. Pierre Klossowski, Paris: Gallimard, two volumes, 1971. The English version does not quite match the German. The courses and some of the essays can be found in *Nietzsche*, trans. David Farrell Krell, Frank Capuzzi and Joan Stambaugh, San Francisco: HarperCollins, 4 vols., 1991, and the remainder in *The End of Philosophy*, trans. Joan Stambaugh, London: Souvenir Press, 1975.

30 BNF NAF28730 (33), box a, folder 0, subfolder 1.
31 The first appears in *Vorträge und Aufsätze*, Pfullingen: Günther Neske, 1954 and is translated in *Nietzsche*; the second in *Holzwege* and is translated by Julian Young and Kenneth Haynes in *Off the Beaten Path*, Cambridge: Cambridge University Press, 2002.
32 This course was published as *Die Grundbegriffe der Metaphysik. Welt – Endlichkeit – Einsamkeit*, Frankfurt am Main: Vittorio Klostermann, 1992; trans. William McNeill and Nicholas Walker as *The Fundamental Concepts of Metaphysics: World, Finitude, Solitude*, Bloomington: Indiana University Press, 1995.
33 Defert, LWK 213n. 41/223 n. 41.
34 Defert, LWK 266/269–70. See Nietzsche, *Le livre du philosophe*; Gilles Deleuze, *Différence et Répétition*, Paris: PUF, 1968; trans. Paul Patton as *Difference and Repetition*, New York: Columbia University Press, 1994; Marcel Detienne, *Les maîtres de vérité dans la Grèce archaïque*, Paris: François Maspero, 1967; trans. Janet Lloyd as *The Masters of Truth in Archaic Greece*, New York: Zone Books, 1996.
35 Defert, LWK 19–20 n. 2/19 n. 2; 270/3. Eugen Fink, *Spiel als Weltsymbol*, Stuttgart: Kohlhammer, 1960; and see his *Nietzsches Philosophie*, Stuttgart: Kohlhammer, 1960; trans. Goetz Richter as *Nietzsche's Philosophy*, London: Continuum, 2003.
36 The only known reference is in the introduction to Ludwig Binswanger's *Dream and Existence* from the early 1950s (DE#1 I, 104); and a citation of a Nietzsche text from his work, likely around the same period, in BNF NAF28730 (33), box b, folder 5.
37 See BNF NAF28730 (33). Foucault sometimes abbreviates Jaspers to 'J' in these notes. See Karl Jaspers, *Nietzsche: Einführung in das Verständnis seines Philosophie*, Berlin: Walter de Gruyter, 1936; trans. Charles F. Wallraff and Frederick J. Schmitz as *Nietzsche: An Introduction to the Understanding of his Philosophical Activity*, Baltimore: Johns Hopkins University Press, 1997 [1965]. The only reference to Jaspers's reading of Nietzsche in published work is very brief (DE#41 I, 566). There are only a few other references to Jaspers, all in early work (DE#1 I, 79; DE#2 I, 127, 129; DE#8 I, 191); except for a brief mention in an interview in Japan in 1970 (DE#82 II, 107–8).
38 Defert, LWK 264/267–8; C 34/41. *Hommage à Jean Hyppolite*, Paris: PUF, 1971. Foucault's essay is reprinted in DE#84, II, 136–56; and translated in EW II and elsewhere. An earlier version in typescript exists at IMEC: 'La Généalogie Nietzschéene', FCL 15 (D218r). There are some minor changes, but also some rewriting and expansion of claims between the two versions. Only one change, noted below, is significant for the argument developed here.
39 'Avertissement', in *Hommage à Jean Hyppolite*, p. i. This brief text, while signed 'M.F.', does not appear in *Dits et écrits*.
40 'La Généalogie Nietzschéene', FCL 15 (D218r), p. 24.
41 Hermann Cohen, *Kants Theorie der Erfahrung*, Berlin: Dümmlers, 1871.

42 It is notable that after the 1973 Rio lectures Foucault does not discuss Nietzsche in detail. See his comments in 1975 (DE#156 II, 753; P/K 53–4).

43 Line references to Sophocles' play are to the version in *The Three Theban Plays*, trans. Robert Fagles, London: Penguin, 1984.

44 Defert, LWK 265–6/269.

45 See *Foucault's Last Decade*, ch. 5.

46 Defert, LWK 277/279–80.

47 Gilles Deleuze and Félix Guattari, *Anti-Oedipus: Capitalism and Schizophrenia*, trans. Robert Hurley, Mark Seem and Helen R. Lane, London: Athlone, 1984.

48 For an analysis, see John Marks, *Gilles Deleuze: Vitalism and Multiplicity*, London: Pluto, 1998, pp. 94.

49 Sophocles, *Oedipus Tyrannus*, 1201.

50 Sophocles, *Oedipus Tyrannus*, 1526.

51 Sophocles, *Oedipus Tyrannus*, 14.

52 Sophocles, *Oedipus Tyrannus*, 1379–81.

53 Judith Butler, *Antigone's Claim: Kinship between Life and Death*, Columbia University Press: New York, 2000, p. 62.

2 Inquiry: Revolt, Ordeal, Proof

1 Roland Mousnier, *Fureurs paysans: Les paysans dans les révoltes du XVIIe siècle (France, Russie, Chine)*, Paris: Calmann-Lévy, 1967, p. 105; trans. Brian Pearce as *Peasant Uprisings in Seventeenth-Century France, Russia, and China*, London: George Allen & Unwin, 1971, p. 97.

2 A. Floquet (ed.), *Diaire ou Journal du voyage du Chancelier Séguier en Normandie après la sedition des Nu-Pieds (1639–40) et documents relatifs à ce voyage et à la sedition*, Rouen: Édouard Frère, 1842; and Vte d'Estaintot (ed.), *Mémoires du président Bigot de Monville sur la sedition des Nu-Pieds et l'interdiction du Parlement de Normandie en 1639*, Rouen: Société de l'Histoire de Normandie, 1876.

3 Mousnier, *Fureurs paysans*, pp. 97–121; *Peasant Uprisings*, pp. 87–113.

4 Boris Porchnev, *Les soulèvements populaires en France de 1623 à 1648*, trans. Mme Ranieta and Robert Mandrou, SEVPEN, 1963; republished in abridged form as *Les Soulèvements populaires en France au XVIIe siècle*, Flammarion, Paris, 1972. The 1972 edition omits the part on the *Nu-Pieds*, so references below are to the 1963 edition, which was the one Foucault used. While 'Porchnev' is the French transliteration from the Cyrillic; 'Porshnev' is more common in English.

5 Porchnev, *Les soulèvements populaires*, p. 303.

6 Some documents appear as an appendix, Porchnev, *Les soulèvements populaires*, pp. 585–657.

7 Roland Mousnier, 'Recherches sur les soulèvements populaires en France avant la Fronde', *Revue d'histoire moderne et contemporaine*, 5 (2),

1958, pp. 81–113; reprinted in *La plume, la faucille et le marteau*, Paris: PUF, 1970, pp. 335–68. Mousnier based his review on the German translation. Foucault used the reprint of Mousnier's essay, which is the version referenced below.

8 Madeleine Foisil, *La révolte des Nu-Pieds et les révoltes normandes de 1639*, Paris: PUF, 1970.

9 These would include Yves-Marie Bercé; *Histoire des Croquants: Étude des soulèvements populaires au XVIIe siècle dans le sud-ouest de la France*, Geneva/Paris: Librarie Droz, 2 vols., 1974; *Croquants et Nu-pieds: les soulèvements paysans en France du XVII au XIXe siècle*, Paris: Gallimard, 1974.

10 Mousnier, *Fureurs paysans*, p. 97 n. 1; *Peasant Uprisings*, p. 87 n. 1.

11 Claude-Olivier Doron, 'Foucault et les historiens: Le débat sur les "soulèvements populaires" ', TIP 291–307 is an invaluable overview. Some of Porshnev's other works are available in English: *Social Psychology and History*, trans. Ivan Savin, Moscow: Progress Publishers, 1970 (which references Foucault's *Folie et déraison*, p. 8 n. 1); *Muscovy and Sweden in the Thirty Years' War, 1630–1635*, ed. Paul Dukes, trans. Brian Pearce, Cambridge: Cambridge University Press, 1995.

12 See Porchnev, *Les soulèvements populaires*, p. 392.

13 See, for example, Porchnev, *Les soulèvements populaires*, pp. 395–6.

14 See Doron, TIP 293–4.

15 Doron, TIP 295.

16 Doron's essay (TIP 293 n. 6) references two books and an article in French, but provides no bibliographical references. These include *Essai d'économie politique du féodalisme*, Paris: Éditions du Progrès, 1979, but the other titles appear to be translations of the Russian texts, taken from Igor Filippov, 'Boris Porchnev et l'économie politique du féodalisme', in Serge Aberdam and Alexandre Tchoudinov, *Ecrire l'histoire par temps de guerre froide: Soviétiques et Français autour de la crise de l'Ancien régime*, Paris: Société des études robespierristes, 2014, pp. 149–76, p. 150.

17 Mousnier, *La plume, la faucille et le marteau*, p. 337.

18 Mousnier, *La plume, la faucille et le marteau*, p. 339.

19 Mousnier, *La plume, la faucille et le marteau*, p. 345.

20 Mousnier, *La plume, la faucille et le marteau.*, p. 352.

21 Mousnier, *La plume, la faucille et le marteau*, p. 360.

22 Mousnier, *La plume, la faucille et le marteau*, p. 361.

23 For more on this reading, see Mousnier *Fureurs paysans*; *Peasant Uprisings*.

24 Mousnier, *Fureurs paysans*, p. 114; *Peasant Uprisings*, p. 106.

25 Mousnier, *Fureurs paysans*, p. 118; *Peasant Uprisings*, p. 110.

26 Mousnier, *La plume, la faucille et le marteau*, p. 367.

27 Mousnier, *La plume, la faucille et le marteau*, p. 367.

28 Doron, TIP 297–8.

29 Perry Anderson, *Lineages of the Absolutist State*, London: Verso, 2013 [1974], p. 37 n. 37.

30 BNF NAF28730 (2), folder 7, subfolder 2.
31 See Mousnier, *Fureurs paysans*, pp. 120–1; *Peasant Uprisings*, pp. 112–13; Porchnev, *Les soulèvements populaires*, pp. 475–92. See Doron, TIP 298, 296.
32 Foisil, *La révolte des Nu-Pieds*, Part III.
33 Richelieu, Armand Jean du Plessis, *The Political Testament of Cardinal Richelieu*, trans. Henry Bertram Hill, Madison: University of Wisconsin Press, 1964. On Richelieu, see Anthony Levi, *Cardinal Richelieu and the Making of France*, New York: Carroll & Graf, 2000.
34 Porchnev, *Les soulèvements populaires*, stresses Richelieu's role much more than Foucault does.
35 This chronology is indebted to Mousnier, *Fureurs paysans*, pp. 120–1; *Peasant Uprisings*, pp. 112–13; see Porchnev, *Les soulèvements populaires*, pp. 480–95; Foisil, *La révolte des Nu-Pieds*, pp. 163–71, 287–301; and Floquet (ed.), *Diaire ou Journal*, pp. 451–61. The editors of Foucault's course provide a summary based on Foisil and Floquet (TIP 15 n. 10).
36 See also Harcourt, PS 95–6 n. 2/93 n. 2; 305/292; and ch. 3 below.
37 Harcourt, TIP 53–5 n. 16; see also SP 95–6 n. 2/93–4 n. 2.
38 Harcourt, TIP 54 n. 16.
39 Doron, TIP 299.
40 Doron., TIP 300.
41 'Cérémonie, théâtre et politique au XVIIe siècle', lecture in Minnesota, 7 April 1972, English summary by Stephen Davidson in *Acts (Proceedings of the Fourth Annual Conference on XVIIth Century French Literature)*, Graduate School of the University of Minnesota, vol. I, pp. 22–3; translated back into French in TIP 235–41. The lecture summary, not being by Foucault's own hand, did not appear in DE in 1994, but is here given semi-canonical status.
42 Claude de Seyssel, *La Monarchie de France*, Book I, ch. VIII, in *La Monarchie de France et deux autres fragments politiques*, ed. Jacques Poujol, Paris: Librarie d'Argences, 1961, p. 115; *The Monarchy of France*, trans. J. H. Hexter, ed. Donald R. Kelley, Yale University Press, 1981, p. 51. For a discussion, see William Farr Church, *Constitutional Thought in Sixteenth-Century France: A Study in the Evolution of Ideas*, Cambridge: Harvard University Press, 1941, pp. 24–30. Foucault has detailed notes on Church's work in BNF NAF28730 (18), folder 8.
43 The word 'apparatus' is a translation of *appareil*: the term *dispositif*, which is sometimes translated that way, does not appear in this course.
44 Ernst H. Kantorowicz, *The King's Two Bodies: A Study in Medieval Political Theology*, Princeton: Princeton University Press, 1957; and *Laudes Regiae: A Study in Liturgical Acclamations and Mediaeval Ruler Worship*, Berkeley: University of California Press, 1946.
45 As Doron, TIP 293–4, notes, Porshnev does not consider, unlike Foucault, that there is a fundamental difference or contradiction between rent and tax.

46   This course page is missing from the manuscript, but has been filled in on the basis of a photocopy and verified by Defert's notes (see Harcourt, TIP 24 n.a).

47   J. J. Thonissen, *L'organisation judiciaire, le droit pénal et la procedure pénale de la loi saliques*, 1881, pp. 164–5 (2nd edn, Paris: Maresq, 1882, pp. 244–5). See TIP 124 n. 27; BNF NAF28730 (1), folder 2, subfolder 3.

48   This is based on a claim by E. Perrot, *Les cas royaux: origine et développement de la théorie aux XIII et XIVe siècles*, Paris: Arthur Rousseau, 1910, p. 35. As the edition notes (TIP 124 n. 29), Perrot dates this to the fourteenth century. Foucault's notes on this book and theme are in BNF NAF28730 (1), folder 2, subfolder 1.

49   See Foisil, *La Révolte des Nu-Pieds*, pp. 117–31.

50   This summary is preserved in two versions (TIP 138–9; 139–40).

51   Harcourt, TIP 180 n. 19.

52   The question of confession is a major theme of *Foucault's Last Decade*, especially chs. 3 and 5.

53   Ewald and Harcourt, TIP 279.

54   Ewald and Harcourt, TIP 272–3.

55   BNF NAF28730 (32).

56   BNF NAF28730 (33a-b).

57   Michael Walzer, *The Revolution of the Saints: A Study in the Origins of Radical Politics*, London: Weidenfeld & Nicolson, 1965; Robert K. Merton *Science, Technology and Society in Seventeenth Century England*, New York: Howard Fertig, 1970 [1938]; Richard Foster Jones, *Ancients and Moderns: A Study of the Rise of the Scientific Movement in Seventeenth-Century England*, St Louis: Washington University Studies, 1961 [1936].

58   George Sarton, *The Study of the History of Mathematics* and *The Study of the History of Science*, New York: Dover, 1957 [1936]; *The Life of Science: Essays in the History of Civilization*, New York: Henry Schuman, 1948.

59   Sarton, *The Life of Science*, pp. 61–4; quoted in BNF NAF28730 (32), folder 2.

60   Christopher Hill, *Intellectual Origins of the English Revolution*, London: Panther, 1972 [1965]. See, for example, the notes on p. 3 in BNF NAF28730 (32), folder 2. 'Ideas do not advance merely by their own logic ... Ideas were all-important for the individuals whom they impelled into action; but the historian must attach equal importance to the circumstances that gave their ideas their chance ... the thinkers were not isolated from their societies'.

61   E. G. R. Taylor, *Tudor Geography 1485–1583*, New York: Octagon Books, 1968 [1930]; *The Mathematical Practitioners of Tudor and Stuart England*, Cambridge: Cambridge University Press, 1954; *The Haven-Finding Art: A History of Navigation from Odysseus to Captain Cook*, London: Hollis & Carter, 1956; 'The Surveyor', *Economic History Review* 17 (2), 1947, pp. 121–33.

62 Ernest Faligan, *Histoire de la légende de Faust*, Paris, Hachette, 1888; BNF NAF28730 (32), folder 2.

63 Honoré de Balzac, *La Peau de Chagrin*, in Paris: H. Delloye and Victor Licou, 1838, pp. 48–9; *The Wild Ass's Skin*, trans. Herbert J. Hunt, London: Penguin, 1977, p. 52. (Damiens the regicide's quartering is also mentioned in this book, pp. 101/89–90.)

64 BNF NAF28730 (1–5).

65 Georges Duby, *L'économie rurale et la vie des campagnes dans l'occident mediéval (France, Angleterre, Empire, IXe-XVe siècles*, Paris: Éditions Montaigne, 2 vols., 1962. Foucault takes detailed notes from pp. 449–61 and 462–500 in BNF NAF28730 (1), folder 1.

66 BNF NAF28730 (1), folder 1. See TIP 179–80 n. 16.

67 BNF NAF28730 (2), folder 7, subfolder 1 on popular revolts, and subfolder 2 on the 'Nu-Pieds'.

68 BNF NAF28730 (1), folder 2.

69 BNF NAF28730 (1), folder 3.

70 The first two are cited in TIP 218 n. 7. See A. Esmein, *A History of Continental Criminal Procedure: With Special Reference to France*, trans. John Simpson, Boston: Little, Brown, 1913; P. Guilhiermoz, *Enquêtes et Procès: Étude sur la procédure et le fonctionnement du Parlement au XIVe siècle*, Paris: A Picard, 1892; Adolphe Tardif, *La procédure civile et criminelle au XIII–XIVe siècle*, Paris: Alphonse Picard, 1885 and *Histoire des sources du droit français, origines romaines*, Paris: Alphonse Picard, 1890; and Alec Mellor, *La torture: Son histoire – son abolition – sa réapparition au XXème siècle*, Les Horizons Littéraires, 1949.

71 BNF NAF28730 (1), folder 3.

72 BNF NAF28730(2), (3) and (4).

73 Ewald and Harcourt, TIP 261.

74 See *Naissance de la biopolitique: Cours au Collège de France (1978–9)*, ed. Michel Senellart, Paris: Seuil/Gallimard, 2004, p. 79; trans. Graham Burchell as *The Birth of Biopolitics: Lectures at the Collège de France 1978–9*, London: Palgrave, 2008, p. 77; discussed in *Foucault's Last Decade*, ch. 4.

75 Ewald and Harcourt, TIP 259. On this relation, see especially Jacques Bidet, *Foucault avec Marx*, Paris: La Fabrique, 2014.

76 Etienne Balibar, email to Harcourt, TIP 286–7.

77 See Stuart Elden, *The Birth of Territory*, Chicago: University of Chicago Press, 2013.

3 Examination: Punishment, War, Economy

1 The first appears as an appendix to LWK, and is discussed in ch. 1.

2 For a fuller discussion see ch. 5; see Harcourt, PS 273–4/265–6.

3 On the reconciliation with Sartre, see Claude Mauriac, *Et comme l'espérance est violente: Le temps immobile 3*, Paris: Grasset, 1976, pp. 311–13.

4 Michael Scott Christofferson, *French Intellectuals Against the Left: The Antitotalitarian Moment of the 1970s*, New York: Berghahn, 2004, p. 72.

5 Manifesto of *Libération*, reprinted in F.M. Samuelson, *Il était une fois Libération: Reportage historique*, Paris: Seuil, 1979 pp. 140–5, p. 140.

6 *I, Pierre Rivière* is discussed in ch. 6; *Herculine Barbin* and 'Lives of Infamous Men' in *Foucault's Last Decade*, ch. 3.

7 Mauriac, *Et comme l'espérance est violente*, p. 454 (and generally pp. 447–56). I have used the translation in Macey, *The Lives of Michel Foucault*, p. 316.

8 A second brief interview – perhaps another part of the same interview – was published in *Libération* a couple of months later (DE#123 II, 421–3). It discusses the relation of the intellectual to workers.

9 Harcourt, PS 273/265.

10 See Harcourt, PS 204 n. 21/199 n. 21.

11 Throughout this section there is a discussion of Claude Lévi-Strauss especially *Tristes tropiques* (Paris: Plon, 1955), on cannibalism, though he is quite critical of some of its analyses (PS 3–7/2–6).

12 See Harcourt, PS 21 n. 18/19. Giorgio Agamben, *Homo Sacer: Il potere sovrano e la nuda vita*, Torino: Einaudi, 1995; *Homo Sacer: Sovereign Power and Bare Life*, trans. Daniel Heller-Roazen, Stanford: Stanford University Press, 1998.

13 See Mark Neocleous, *Administering Civil Society*, London: Macmillan, 1996, p. 61. There detailed notes on the army in BNF NAF28730 (5), folder 9, only some of which are used in publications.

14 For a full discussion of those courses, see *Foucault's Last Decade*, ch. 2 and 4.

15 Some additional manuscript pages relate this to argument in sociology, especially functionalism (PS 15–16 n. a/14 n. *)

16 See Harcourt, PS 40–41 n. 4/38 n. 4.

17 On the first of these, his reference is to E.P. Thompson, 'The Moral Economy of the English Crowd in the Eighteenth Century', *Past and Present* 50, 76–136 (PS 42 n. 20/40 n. 20; citing typescript p. 290; on the second, see TIP and ch. 2 above; and his source for the third is likely to be Thompson's *The Making of the English Working Class*, London: Victor Gollancz, 1963 (PS 43 n. 24/40 n. 24). Thompson is only named by Foucault in his preparatory manuscript, but is brought much more to the fore in Harcourt's exemplary notes and 'Course Context' (PS 287–92). Foucault's notes on the essay can be found in BNF NAF28730 (8), folder 3 and NAF28730 (11), folder 3, subfolder 17.

18 Henri Lefebvre *De l'État*, Paris: UGE, 1976–8, 4 vols., vol. I, pp. 162–3.

19 Harcourt, PS 312/298.

20 On SMBD, see *Foucault's Last Decade*, ch. 2.

21 Karl Marx, 'Proceedings of the Sixth Rhine Province Assembly. Third Article: Debates on the Law of the Theft of Wood', in Karl Marx and Friedrich Engels: *Collected Works*, Volume I, New York: International

Publishers, 1975 [1842]. Harcourt notes E.P. Thompson had also discussed this theme (PS 76 n. 5/75 n. 5). On this theme, see also DP 101/85.

22 Alain-René Le Sage, *Histoire de Gil Blas de Santillane*, Paris: Gallimard Folio, 1999 [1715–35].

23 Ann Radcliffe, *Les visions du château des Pyrénées*, trans. Germain Garnier and Mme Zimmermann, Paris, Lecointe et Durey, 4 vols., 1821; new edition trans. Yves Tessier, Paris: Éditions, BIEN, 1946. See also the discussion in the 'Eye of Power' interview (DE#190 III, 196–7; P/K 153–4). On the relation between Bentham and Radcliffe, see Claire Wrobel, 'Gothique, réforme et Panoptique', *Revue d'études benthamiennes*, no. 7, 2010, http://etudes-benthamiennes.revues.org/214 and her thesis 'Gothique et panoptique', 2009, http://bdr.u-paris10.fr/theses/internet/2009PA100110.pdf (see Harcourt, PS 60 n. 20).

24 There are detailed notes on Radcliffe in BNF NAF28730 (39), folder 4.

25 Edmund Burke, 'Thoughts and Details on Scarcity', *The Portable Edmund Burke*, ed. Isaac Kramnick, New York: Penguin, 1999, pp. 194–212, p. 196; quoted in PS 109/106.

26 Harcourt, PS 122 n. 17/119–20 n. 17.

27 Burke, 'Thoughts and Details on Scarcity', p. 196.

28 The passage in parentheses is found only in the manuscript (PS 111 n. */108 n. *).

29 Detailed notes on this work, using the French translation, are in BNF NAF28730 (6), folder 8.

30 Harcourt, PS 230 n. a./226 n. †.

31 Notes on Bentham and the Panopticon can be found in BNF NAF28730 (3), folder 9, but these notes are undated. A folder of images, including those used in *Surveiller et punir*, but also others, can be found in BNF NAF28730 (17).

32 Arlette Farge and Michel Foucault, *Le désordre des familles: Lettres de cachet des Archives de la Bastille au XVIIIe siècle*, Paris: Julliard/Galliamard, 1982. For a discussion, see *Foucault's Last Decade*, ch. 8; and Stuart Elden, 'Home, Street, City: Farge, Foucault and the Spaces of the *Lettres du cachet*', in Nancy Luxon (ed.), *Archives of Infamy*, Minnesota: University of Minnesota Press, 2017.

33 Foucault's dossier of material on hermaphrodites, discussed in *Foucault's Last Decade*, pp. 65–6, is now available as BNF NAF28730 (15), folder 1.

34 See also DE#107 II, 331 on the dual sense of correct: to punish and teach.

35 See Harcourt, PS 308/295.

36 As well as the references to Thompson, see for example, Harcourt, PS 248 n. 21, picking up on what may have been an oblique reference to Georg Rusche and Otto Kirchheimer. *Punishment and Social Structure*, New York: Columbia University Press, 1939, discussed in DP 32–3/24–5.

37 Harcourt, PS 290/279.

38 Harcourt, PS 290/279.
39 Harcourt, PS 299–300/287.
40 On the relation to Althusser, see Harcourt, PS 272–3.
41 Harcourt notes that the term 'mob' is also criticized by E.P. Thompson, PS 155 n. 2/152 n. 2.
42 Paul Bois, *Paysans de l'Ouest: Des structures économiques et sociales aux options politiques depuis l'époque révolutionnaire dans la Sarthe*, Le Mans: Mouton, 1960.
43 On this theme, see DE#127 II, 435–45.
44 Foucault took part in a roundtable debate in 1972, published in *Esprit*, in which the relation between the working class and the dangerous class, both born with capitalism, is suggested by Jacques Julliard (DE#107 II, 322).
45 Alphonse Grün, *De la moralisation des classes laborieuses*, Paris: Guillaumin, 1851. Foucault's most detailed notes on Grün are in BNF NAF28730 (11), folder 22, on the theme of 'moralization'.
46 The passage in parentheses is from the manuscript: PS 251 n. 28/247 n. 28.
47 Note that Foucault distinguishes seclusion [*réclusion*] from sequestration [*séquestration*], the former excluding 'marginal individuals', and the latter aimed at 'inclusion and normalization' [DE#139 II, 614; EW III, 78–9). However this text is a translation back into French from a Portuguese edition, and it is not clear which French words were originally used. The Portuguese has '*reclusão*' and '*sequestro*': *A verdade e as formas jurídicas*, Rio de Janeiro: Nau Editora, 3rd edn, 2002, p. 114.
48 The second sentence is from the manuscript: PS 201 n. a/196 n. *
49 The phrases in parentheses comes from the manuscript: PS 104 n. b/101 n. *
50 Hysteria becomes a major theme in *Psychiatric Power*, and was an intended topic of a volume of the originally planned *History of Sexuality*. See *Foucault's Last Decade*, chs. 1 and 3; and BNF NAF28730 (14).
51 BNF NAF28730 (5), folder 1.
52 The content of the New York lectures is unspecified. The Montreal lecture was on madness and antipsychiatry and is discussed in ch. 4.

4 Madness: Power, Psychiatry and the Asylum

1 Jean-Pierre Peter, 'Entendre Pierre Rivière', *Le Débat*, no. 66, 1991, pp. 110–18, pp. 111–12. Substantial parts of this article are reproduced in an untitled preface to later French (but not the English) editions of PR.
2 A detailed typed contents list of this journal, presumably prepared for this seminar, can be found in BNF NAF28730 (13), folder 1; photocopies of several articles are in BNF NAF28730 (17bis).
3 'Condamnation à mort d'un aliéné homicide', *Annales d'hygiène publique et de médecine légale*, Série 1, no. 15, 1836, pp. 128–205.

4 'Débat avec Michel Foucault au centre culturel de L'Athénée français (Tokyo, 21 April 1978)', IMEC F2.13, p. 3.

5 Macey, *The Lives of Michel Foucault*, pp. 248–9.

6 See 'Débat avec Michel Foucault', IMEC F2.13, pp. 5–6.

7 David Macey, *Michel Foucault*, London: Reaktion, 2004, p. 107.

8 Peter, 'Entendre Pierre Rivière', p. 114.

9 Pierre-François Lacenaire, *Mémoires*, ed. Monique Lebailly, Paris: L'instant, 1988 [1836].

10 Peter, 'Entendre Pierre Rivière', p. 114.

11 See for example the comment in PR 247 n. 1/180 n. 8 about the lack of time for archival research.

12 See the discussion in ch. 3 above, and *Foucault's Last Decade*, ch. 3.

13 Jean-Pierre Peter, 'Le corps du délit', *Nouvelle revue de psychoanalyse*, 3, 1971, pp. 71–108; 'Ogres d'archives: Textes présentes par Jean-Pierre Peter', *Nouvelle revue de psychoanalyse*, 6, 1972, pp. 249–67. See also Peter and Favret, PR 249–50/182–3.

14 For a fuller discussion of those texts see *Foucault's Last Decade*, chs. 1 and 3. See also Macey, *Michel Foucault*, p. 106; *The Lives of Michel Foucault*, p. 249. The interview was conducted on 8 October 1976 for Radio-France and is transcribed as 'L'Expertise médico-légale', IMEC FCL M D3r.

15 *Moi, Pierre Rivière, ayant égorgé ma mère, ma soeur et mon frère...* directed by René Allio, 1976. Another film by Christine Lipinska, entitled *Je suis Pierre Rivière*, had appeared in 1975; and Foucault mentions three theatrical productions in a Japanese discussion of the film and case. See 'Débat avec Michel Foucault', IMEC FCL 2.13, p. 14.

16 BNF NAF28730 (26). The press book is the first item in the box; the second folder contains the correspondence. Defert says that the deal required Foucault to sign an exclusive five-year contract in 1975 with Gallimard to fund the film (C 50/61), but there is no mention or trace of this in the file.

17 BNF NAF28730 (26), folder 3.

18 For a discussion of those late concerns, see *Foucault's Last Decade*, especially chs. 6–8.

19 For a longer reading of *History of Madness*, see my *Mapping the Present*, ch. 5.

20 The English translation HM includes all these texts; the 1961 preface in French can be found as DE#4 I, 159–67. There is a brief exchange on this between Foucault and Mauriac in *Et comme l'espérance est violente*, pp. 403–4. For the critique of the reading of Descartes, see Jacques Derrida, *L'Écriture et la différence*, Paris: Seuil, 1967, pp. 61–97; 'Cogito and the History of Madness', in *Writing and Difference*, London: Routledge, 1978, pp. 36–76. Foucault's reply (HM 583–603/550–74; DE#102 II, 245–68) is a developed and expanded version of a critique first published in Japan in 1970 (DE#104 II, 281–95; HM –/575–90). For a brief discussion and references, see *Mapping the Present*, pp. 189–90 n. 17.

21   See Gilles Deleuze, 'Qu'est-ce qu'un dispositif', in François Ewald (ed.), *Michel Foucault philosophe*, Paris: Seuil, 1989, pp. 185–95; Giorgio Agamben, *What is an Apparatus? And Other Essays*, trans. David Kishik and Stefan Pedatella, Stanford: Stanford University Press, 2009; and *Mapping the Present*, pp. 110–11.

22   Now available in the volume of Althusser's work from this time: *Sur la reproduction*, Paris: PUF, 1995; trans. G.M. Goshgarian, *On the Reproduction of Capitalism: Ideology and Ideological State Apparatuses*, London: Verso, 2014.

23   Cited in Jacques Lagrange, 'Versions de la psychiatrie dans les travaux de Michel Foucault', in Philippe Artières and Emmanuel da Silva (eds.), *Michel Foucault et la médecine: Lectures et usages*, Paris: Éditions Kimé, 2001, pp. 119–42, p. 139.

24   Philippe Pinel, *Traité médico-philosophique sur l'aliénation mentale, ou la manie*, Paris: Richard, Caille et Ravier, 1801, p. 192; *A Treatise on Insanity*, trans. D.D. Davis, New York: Hafner, 1962, p. 188.

25   J. M. A. Servan, *Discours sur l'administration de la justice criminelle*, Geneva, 1767, p. 35.

26   There are notes on monasteries, including from Cuthbert Butler, *Benedictine Monachism: Studies in Benedictine Life and Rule*, London: Longmans & Co, second edition, 1924, which are likely from this time period, in BNF NAF28730 (5), folder 4.

27   On the distinction between these words, see ch. 2.

28   'Dialogue on Power', in Simeon Wade (ed.) *Chez Foucault*, Los Angeles: Circabook, 1978, p. 12; DE#221 III, 470.

29   This claim is treated in detail in my *Mapping the Present*, chs. 4 and 5; and the essays and references in SKP.

30   Sometimes called the Groupe d'Information sur les Asiles.

31   Macey, *The Lives of Michel Foucault*, p. 290. The quote from Castel comes from an interview with Macey. Castel went on to have an important role in the wider movement. See Collectif International, *Réseau-Alternative à la psychiatrie*, ed. Mony Elkaïm, Paris, Union Générale d'Éditions, 1977; and Robert Castel, *La gestion des risques: De l'anti-psychiatrie à l'après-psychanalyse*, Paris: Minuit, 1981.

32   GIA, 'Non, l'asile n'est pas fait pour soigner' in *Psychiatrie et univers pénitentiaire*, special issue of *Psychiatrie aujourd'hui*, 7 (1) 1972, pp. 106–7.

33   All issues of the journal can be found at http://archivesautonomies.org/ spip.php?article877 For the compilation see *Tankonalsanté*, Paris: François Maspero, 1975. Some other documents can be found in Partisans, *Garde-fous arrêtez de vous serrer les coudes*, Paris: François Maspero, 1975, pp. 168–80.

34   The first issue (February–April 1975) can be found online: http:// www.groupeinfoasiles.org/allfiles/documents/000075Psychiatrises_en _lutte_1.pdf

35   'La ligne du journal?...' *Tankonalasanté*, no. 8, 1974, p. 1.

36   Macey, *The Lives of Michel Foucault*, p. 290.

37 On the book's reception, see Philippe Artières et al. *Histoire de la folie à l'âge classique de Michel Foucault: Regards critiques 1961–2011*, Caen: IMEC/Presses Universitaires de Caen, 2011 and Philippe Artières and Jean-François Bert, *Un succès philosophique: L'Histoire de la folie à l'âge classique de Michel Foucault*, Caen: IMEC/Presses Universitaires de Caen, 2011.

38 IMEC GIP 6.19 [GIP2 Di-20].

39 Groupe Information Asiles, *Psychiatrie: La peur change de camp*, Paris: GIA, 1973, p. 13.

40 Groupe Information Asiles, *Psychiatrie*, p. 18. See also Giovanni Jervis, *Psychiatrie et lutte des classes*, Front Politique de lutte ideologique de Strasbourg, supplement to *Cinéthique* no. 15, 1972.

41 See Jean-Jacques Brochier, 'Antipsychiatrie, antipsychanalyse: Entretien avec Félix Guattari', *Magazine littéraire*, no. 112–13, 1976, pp. 28–30.

42 BNF NAF28730 (7), folder 2 includes a newspaper clipping on this theme: Francis Cornu, 'La peur du fou', *Le Monde*, 17–18 June 1973, p. 18. The piece asks the question:'the life of the mentally ill in secure hospitals: patients or prisoners'. See also the theme issue on 'La médecine en milieu pénitentiare', *Cahiers Laënnec*, 31 (2), June 1971.

43 Charte des internés, supplement to *Psychiatrisés en lutte*, no. 3–4, 1976; reprinted in *Garde-fous*, no. 11–12, 1978, pp. 29–30.

44 Subsequent issues contained updates on the campaign. See also GIA, *La psychiatrie devant les tribunaux*, supplement to *Psychiatrisés en lutte*, no. 7–8, 1976. Foucault discusses the 1838 law in a few places, including DE#142 II, 664–75; FL 287–91.

45 GIA, *La psychiatrie devant les tribunaux*, p. 2.

46 Des Internés de Ste Anne et le Groupe Information Asiles, 'Un tract du GIA: Hôpital Psychiatrique Sortons en attaquant', *Garde-fous*, no. 11–12, 1978, p. 31.

47 See Artières and Bert, *Un succès philosophique*, p. 234.

5 Discipline: Surveillance, Punishment and the Prison

1 The literature on the group is extensive. As well as the almost comprehensive documentary work in AL and IN, see Daniel Defert and Jacques Donzelot, 'La charnière des prisons', *Le Magazine Littéraire*, 112–13, May 1976, pp. 33–5; Paul Rabinow and Keith Gandal, 'Foucault and the Prison: An Interview with Gilles Deleuze', *History of the Present*, no. 2, 1986, pp. 1–2, 20–21; and the retrospective discussion in DE#273 III, 806–18. For commentaries, see Keith Gandal, 'Intellectual Work and Politics', *Telos*, no. 67, 1986, pp. 121–34; Philippe Artières, 'L'ombre des prisonniers sur le toit: Les heritages du GIP' in Didier Eribon (ed.), *L'infréquentable Michel Foucault: Renouveaux de la pensée critique*, Paris: EPEL, 2001, pp. 101–11; Julian Bourg, *From Revolution to Ethics: May 1968 and Contemporary French Thought*, Montreal: McGill-Queen's University Press, 2007,

ch. 6; Marcelo Hoffman, *Foucault and Power: The Influence of Political Engagement on Theories of Power*, London: Bloomsbury, 2014, ch. 2; Perry Zurn and Andrew Dilts (eds.), *Active Intolerance: Michel Foucault, The Prisons Information Group, and the Future of Abolition*, London: Palgrave, 2015.

2   Defert, AL 317; Daniel Defert, *Une vie politique: Entretiens avec Philippe Artières et Éric Favereau*, Paris: Seuil, 2014, p. 55. See Mads Peter Karsen and Kaspar Villadsen, 'Foucault, Maoism, Genealogy Genealogy: The Influence of Political Militancy in Michel Foucault's Thought', *New Political Science*, 37 (1), 2015, pp. 91–117 and Thanasis Lagios, 'Foucauldian Genealogy and Maoism', http://www.fsw.uzh.ch/foucaultblog/featured/130/foucauldian-genealogy-and-maoism#ref1

3   See Defert, *Une vie politique*, p. 41, and that chapter generally.

4   'Freedom and Knowledge', in Fons Elders, *Freedom and Knowledge*, trans. Lionel Claris, Amsterdam: Elders Special Productions, 2012, pp. 40–1. There is unfortunately no published version of the French text of this interview.

5   See 'Redonner la parole aux détenus', *Tribune socialiste*, no. 522, 20 January 20 1972, p. 10. On the hunger strikes, see Les prisonniers politiques, *Le combat des détenus politiques: Grève de la faim, procès des diffuseurs de 'La cause du peuple'*, Paris: François Maspero, 1970; AL 31–3.

6   Artières et al., AL 28, 30.

7   *Quadrillage* is a grid-like systematic division and control of an area.

8   Macey, *The Lives of Michel Foucault*, p. 515 n. 1, notes that *Garde à vue* 'refers to the common police practice of holding people without charge for a period of up to twenty-four hours'. In the 1970s the British army imprisoned Northern Irish Catholics without trial in a policy known as 'internment'. However neither detention nor internment capture the visual sense of the French term. I am grateful to Graham Burchell for a discussion on this point.

9   *J'accuse*, no. 2, 1971, pp. 14–15; *La cause du peuple* no. 35, 17 February 1971; *L'esprit*, no. 401, March 1971, pp. 531–2.

10   Mitchell Abidor, 'La gauche prolétarienne', http://www.marxists.org/history/france/post-1968/gauche-proletarienne/introduction.htm   This tactic of protection through association was later used by Foucault, who leant his name to the journal *Zone des tempêtes* in 1973. This was not a new journal, but a new title for the journal *Nouvel Africasia*. Foucault signed an editorial, but either edited an existing text or simply agreed for his name to be used. The true editor was Ahmed Baba Miské (C 43/53). See 'Un nouveau journal?' *La parole aux peuples: Zone des tempêtes*, no. 2, 1973, p. 3; reprinted as DE#121 II, 419–20.

11   A text by Foucault written to accompany the questionnaire is reproduced in AL 50–1; a translation is in Macey, *The Lives of Michel Foucault*, pp. 261–2.

12   '*Investigation in 20 Prisons* by the Information Group on Prisons', trans. Marcelo Hoffman, in Hoffman, *Foucault and Power*, pp. 155–204.

13 See C 38–43/46–53; Defert in AL 324–6

14 IN 192–204; Michel Foucault, Catharine von Bülow, Daniel Defert, 'The Masked Assassination of George Jackson', in Joy James (eds.), *Warfare in the American Homeland: Policing and Prison in a Penal Democracy*, Durham: Duke University Press, 2007, pp. 140–58. See Edmund White, *Genet*, London: Picador, 1993, pp. 652–4, 794 n. 43. For discussion see Michelle Koerner, 'Line of Escape: Gilles Deleuze's Encounter with George Jackson', *Genre*, 44 (2), 2011, pp. 157–80; Kevin Thompson, 'The Final Word on Power: Foucault and Deleuze on Resistance', forthcoming.

15 On this pamphlet see Kevin Thompson, 'Problematization and the Production of New Statements: Foucault and Deleuze on Le Groupe d'Information sur les prisons', *The Carceral Notebooks*, forthcoming.

16 Christine Martineau and Jean-Pierre Carasso, *Le travail dans les prisons*, Paris: Champ Libre, 1972.

17 Robert Badinter, *L'exécution*, Paris: Bernard Grasset, 1973.

18 See AL 144; Comité Vérité Toul, *La Révolte de la centrale Ney 5/13 décembre 1971*, Paris: Gallimard, 1973, pp. 181–3; Macey, *The Lives of Michel Foucault*, pp. 272–3.

19 On these, see Foucault in AL 151–5; 'La Révolte de la prison de Toul: déliquance sociale et justice gauchiste', *Négation*, avant-premier numéro, 1971; Katia D. Kaupp and Franz-Olivier Giesbert, 'Les prisons de Pleven', *Le nouvel observateur*, 17 January 1972, pp. 24–6; Comité Vérité Toul, *La Révolte de la centrale Ney*; Marc Kunstlé and Claude Vincent, *Le Crépuscule des prisons*, Paris: Julliard, 1972; Philippe Artières, 'La prison en procès: Les mutins de Nancy (1972)', *Vingtième Siècle: Revue d'histoire*, no. 70, 2001, pp. 57–70; Anne Guérin, *Prisonniers en révolte: Quotidien carcéral, mutineries et politique pénitentiaire en France (1970–1980)*, Marseille: Agone, 2013; *La Révolte de la prison de Nancy, 15 janvier 1972*, Cherbourg-Octeville: Le Point du jour, 2013; and the recent film *Sur les toits* [On the roofs], directed by Nicolas Drolc, 2014. *La Révolte de la prison de Nancy* contains the GIP's dossier on the revolt (pp. 114–21), as well as other documents.

20 'Hier, les prisonniers de Fleury-Merogis se sont révoltés', n.d. [January 1972], IMEC G.1.5a (14) [GIP2. Ad-13].

21 See Cecile Brich, 'The Groupe d'information sur les prisons: The voice of prisoners? Or Foucault's?' *Foucault Studies*, no. 5, 2008, pp. 26–47; Hoffmann, *Foucault and Power*, pp. 20–21.

22 *Les prisons aussi*, 1972, directed by René Lefort and Hélène Châtelain, available at https://vimeo.com/120066997

23 Bruce Jackson (ed.), *In the Life: Versions of the Criminal Experience*, New York: Rinehart & Winston, 1972; translated as *Leurs prisons: Autobiographies de prisonniers et ex-détenus américains*, Paris: Plon, 1975. Foucault's preface is on pp. i–vi; reprinted as DE#144 II, 687–91.

24 For a visual and texual documentary of that day, see Kagan et al., *Michel Foucault*. Jaubert was a journalist who had been beaten by the police in May 1971. An independent commission, including Foucault,

Deleuze, Mauriac and Denis Langlois was set up to examine the case. See DE#92 II, 198–9; DE#93 II 199–203; see Mauriac, *Et comme l'espérance est violente*, pp. 357–63.

25 Philippe Artières, 'Archives of a Collective Action', in Kagan et al., *Michel Foucault*, p. 49. Speeches by Foucault and Sartre, and the prisoners' statement, can be found in *Bulletin quotidien de l'Agence de presse 'Libération'*, no. 16, 18 January 1972, reproduced in *La Révolte de la prison de Nancy*, pp. 79–87.

26 'M. Chazelle (socialiste) demande la création d'une commission d'enquête sur les prisons', *Le Monde*, 19 January 1972, p. 28.

27 'Freedom and Knowledge', p. 41.

28 Bourg, *From Revolution to Ethics*, p. 48.

29 '*Investigation in 20 Prisons*', p. 158. A brochure entitled 'Contre le casier judiciaire' was promised as forthcoming (IN 84), but this was never published. A one-page statement on this topic, probably from June 1971, signed by Domenach, Foucault, and Vidal-Nacquet can be found as IMEC GIP Aa-04 [GIP 1.4]. It became a concern of the CAP in late 1972, see *CAP: Journal des prisonniers*, no. 2, 1973, p. 8. On the difference between the French and British system, see Macey, *The Lives of Michel Foucault*, p. 270.

30 The statement is reprinted in IN 250–60; and the edited version from *La Cause du peuple-J'accuse*, no. 15, 18 December 1971 reproduced in AL 164–6. See also Edith Rose, 'Je puis affirmer', *Le nouvel observateur*, no. 372, 27 décembre 1971–2 January 1972, p. 15. The same page includes the text by Foucault, 'Le discours de Toul', reprinted as DE#99 II, 236–8. See Thompson, 'Problematization and the Production of New Statements'.

31 Charles Dayant with Arnaud Still, *J'étais médecin à La Santé*, Paris: Presses de la Cité, 1972. See also his *Plaidoyer pour une anti-médecine: L'art et la manière d'être malade*, Paris: Presses de la Cité, 1974.

32 Michèle Manceaux, 'L'école des "matons"', *Le nouvel observateur*, 3 May 1971, pp. 69–82; parts are reproduced in Comité Vérité Toul, *La Révolte de la centrale Ney*, pp. 23–7.

33 Défense Collective, *Manuel de l'arrêté*, Paris: Liberté de Presse, 1972.

34 Défense Collective, *Manuel de l'arrêté*, p. 6.

35 Défense Collective, *Manuel de l'arrêté*, p. 7.

36 Denis Langlois, *Guide du militant*, Paris: Éditions du Seuil, 1972. He was previously the author of *Les dossiers noirs de la police francaise*, Paris: Seuil, 1971, an exposé of police malpractice; he would go on to produce *Les dossiers noirs de la justice francaise*, Paris: Seuil, 1974 on miscarriages of justice.

37 Macey, *The Lives of Michel Foucault*, p. 282.

38 Defert and Ewald, DE#137 II, 529 n. * See 'Jean Genet chez les "Panthères Noires"', interview with Michèle Manceaux, *Le nouvel observateur*, 25 May 1970, pp. 38–41; and Genet's'Introduction' to *Soledad Brother: The Prison Letters of George Jackson*, New York: Coward-McCann, Inc., 1970, n.p.; AL 117–22. See Philip S. Foner (ed.), *The*

Black Panthers Speak, Philadelphia: J. B. Lippincott Company, 1970; and for discussions, see Brady Thomas Heiner, 'Foucault and the Black Panthers', *City* 11 (3), 2007, pp. 313–56; Jason Demers, 'Prison Liberation by Association: Michel Foucault and the George Jackson Atlantic', *Atlantic Studies*, 2015, 13 (2), 2016, pp. 165–86. Heiner rather overstates the case; Demers is a more balanced assessment.

39 See Jonathan Simon, *Mass Incarceration on Trial: A Remarkable Court Decision and the Future of Prisons in America*, New York: The New Press, 2014, especially ch. 1.

40 *CAP: Journal des prisonniers* (often called *CAP*), 1972–81. Foucault, along with Defert and Serge Livrozet, is listed as one of the editors of the first issue from 11 December 1972, and then as one of the team that worked with the editor, Annie Livrozet, for the next two issues from January and February 1972. Then his name no longer appears.

41 Serge Livrozet, *De la prison à la révolte: Essai-témoinage*, Paris: Mercure de France, 1973. Foucault's preface is on pp. 7–14, and reprinted as DE#116 II, 394–9.

42 See 'La deuxième generation du GIP', *Le Monde*, 6 December 1972, p. 20; Marc Krevetz, 'Qu'est ce que le GIP?' *Magazine littéraire*, no. 101, 1975, p. 13; Mauriac, *Et comme l'espérance est violente*, pp. 490–1, 496–7; Macey, *The Lives of Michel Foucault*, p. 288. Foucault did co-sign one ADDD document. See 'L'Association de Défense des Droits des Détenus demande au gouvernement "La discussion en plein jour du système pénitentiaire" ', *Le Monde*, 28–9 July 1974, p. 8.

43 The CAP and the GIP, 'Pourquoi?' *CAP: Journal des prisonniers*, no. 1, 1972, pp. 1, 7.

44 Audrey Kiefer, 'Foucault et les prisons: une pratique philosophique', https:// detentions.files.wordpress.com/2009/12/seminaire-pvt.pdf, p. 49.

45 Defert and Ewald, DE#86 II, 174; see Brich 'The Groupe d'information sur les prisons', p. 29; Michael Welch, 'Counterveillance: How Foucault and the Groupe d'Information sur les Prisons Reversed the Optics', *Theoretical Criminology* 15 (3), 2011, pp. 301–13, p. 305.

46 Bouchard, LCP 124–5 n. 20.

47 For a reading of different aspects, see *Mapping the Present*, ch. 5.

48 'Entretien inédit entre Michel Foucault et quatre militants de la LCR membres de la rubrique culturelle du journal quotidien Rouge (July 1977)', http://questionmarx.typepad.fr/files/entretien-avec-michel -foucault-1.pdf, p. 19.

49 Notes on colonies and deportation are found in BNF NAF28730 (4), folder 5, subfolder 5.

50 See also the contrast on DP 299/257, or 308/264, etc.

51 See *The Birth of Territory*, especially chs. 4, 5 and 6.

52 On the political technology of the body, see also DP 34/26.

53 See *Foucault's Last Decade*, ch. 5.

54 Rusche and Kirchheimer, *Punishment and Social Structure*.

55 Marx, *Capital: A Critique of Political Economy Volume One*, trans. Ben Fowkes, London: Penguin/New Left Review, 1976, ch. XIII – a

chapter entitled 'Co-operation'. François Guéry and Didier Deleule, *Le corps productif*, Paris: Editions Mâme, 1972; *The Productive Body*, trans. Philip Barnard and Stephen Shapiro, Winchester: Zer0 books, 2014. Barnard and Shapiro's excellent introduction helps to situate this book in relation to Foucault and Marx.

56 Julien Offray de la Mettrie, *Man a Machine*, French–English edition, La Salle: Open Court, 1912.

57 For a more detailed reading of this, see *Mapping the Present*, pp. 139–41.

58 Marx, *Capital*, vol. I, p. 449.

59 See *Mapping the Present*, pp. 144–7.

60 While 'diagram' is an important theme in Deleuze's book on Foucault the word there is *diagramme*, which can be found in this text – i.e. the description of the military camp as 'the diagram of a power that acts by means of general visibility' (DP 202/171).

61 See Farge and Foucault, *Le désordre des familles*; *Foucault's Last Decade*, ch. 8.

62 See *Foucault's Last Decade*, ch. 5.

63 Raymond Bellour, 'Foucault et les historiens: Entretien avec Jacques Revel', reprinted in Philippe Artières et al. (eds) *Surveiller et punir de Michel Foucault: Regards critiques 1975–1979*, Caen: IMEC/Presses universitaires de Caen, 2010, p. 92.

64 Interview with Arlette Farge, June 1985, reported in Gandal, 'Intellectual Work and Politics', p. 133 n. 30.

65 This reference is to an interview not in DE. See Bernard Pivot (ed.), *Ecrire, lire, et en parler: Dix années de littérature mondiale en 55 interviews publiées dans LIRE*, Paris: Robert Laffont, 1985, p. 359. On the more academic reception, see Michelle Perrot (ed.), *L'impossible prison: Recherches sur le système pénitentiaire au XIXe siècle: Débat avec Michel Foucault*, Paris: Éditions du Seuil, 1980 and Artières et al. (eds) *Surveiller et punir de Michel Foucault*.

66 See also the comment in 1975: 'I believe, following Nietzsche, that truth is to be understood in terms of war' (E 135).

67 Sheridan omits 'the right of the sword [*droit de glaive*]' from his translation. Foucault's reference is to Muyart de Vouglans, *Les lois criminelles de France, dans leur ordre naturel*, Paris: Merigot, Crapart and Benoît Morin, 1780, p. xxxiv.

68 Interview with Daniel Defert, 25 March 1990, cited in James Miller, *The Passion of Michel Foucault*, London: HarperCollins, 1993, pp. 240–1.

6 Illness: Medicine, Disease and Health

1 Quoted in Pol Echevin and Jean-V. Manevy, 'Les hors-la-loi de l'avortement', *L'Express*, 12–18 February 1973, p. 42. See Harcourt, PS 124 n. 37/121 n. 37.

2   'Des médecins "s'accusent"': Manifeste des 331', *Le nouvel observateur*, no. 430, 5 February 1973, pp. 4–5, 55.
3   It is sometimes called Groupe d'Information sur la Santé, even by the group themselves (e.g. DE#128 II, 445; EW III, 423) but Groupe Information Santé is how they describe themselves in publications.
4   GIS, text dated 14.5.72, IMEC GIP 6.15 [GIP 2.Di-15].
5   See Comité d'action santé, *Médecine: Ce texte n'est qu'un début* (*Cahiers Libres* 138), Paris: François Maspero, 1968, especially pp. 40, 75. For a later text by the Comité, see Partisans, *Gardez-fous arrêtez*, p. 164. On the GIS, I learned much from my interview with Defert, 12 April 2015.
6   Centre National des jeunes médecins, 'Médecine et repression', [1968], IMEC GIP 6.8 [GIP 2.Di-08], p. 2.
7   Comité d'action santé, *Médecine*, p. 53.
8   The archives of the group are deposited at the Centre des Archives du Féminisme at the Université Angers. This archive is catalogued by Lucy Halliday, 'Fonds GIS (Groupe Information Santé); Fonds Sylvie Rosenberg-Reiner', http://bu.univ-angers.fr/sites/default/files/repert ._numer_det._gis.pdf Several key documents are filed at IMEC in the GIP collection.
9   Halliday, 'Fonds GIS (Groupe Information Santé)', p. 6.
10 See their brochure *Le contrôle patronal sur les ouvriers malades*, Paris: Liaisons directes, 1975. They also worked with trade unions on specific issues, such as with the PTT. See Fédération unifiée des PTT et des telecommunications, *Travailler dans les égouts en 1976*, Paris: Les imprimeurs libres, 1976, especially p. 28 which notes the support of the GIS.
11 Penarroya is regularly spelt as Pennaroya, but this seems to be a mistake.
12 See Serge Karsenty, 'La médecine en question', *Le Magazine Littéraire*, no. 112–13, May 1976, pp. 38–41; Macey, *The Lives of Michel Foucault*, pp. 290–1.
13 See, for example, 'Fiche practique du G.I.S.', *Tankonalasanté*, no. 4, 1973, p. 11.
14 *Tankonalasanté*, no. 5–6, 1973–4, pp. 5–11.
15 See Philippe Artières, '1972: naissance de l'intellectuel spécifique', *Plein Droit*, no. 53–4, 2002, pp. 37–8.
16 See Bourg, *From Revolution to Ethics*, pp. 72–3, 100; Macey, *The Lives of Michel Foucault*, pp. 297–8.
17 On the wider context of inquiries post May 1968, see 'Le role politique de l'enquête', *Cahiers de mai*, no. 22, 1970, pp. 13–16. For an illuminating discussion, see Marcelo Hoffman, '*Enquêtes* in Foucault's Theory and Practice', forthcoming; and Ross, *May '68 and its Afterlives*, pp. 110–2.
18 The bulk of MD is devoted to documentary evidence of the campaign, including newspaper reports.
19 'Un appel de 343 femmes', *Le nouvel observateur*, no. 334, 5 April 1971, p. 5; available at http://tempsreel.nouvelobs.com/societe/20071127

.OBS7018/le-manifeste-des-343-salopes-paru-dans-le-nouvel-obs-en
-1971.html; see MD 18–19.

20 From the front cover of *Charlie Hebdo*, 12 April 1971. http://
www.lejdd.fr/Medias/Presse-ecrite/Quand-Charlie-Hebdo-inventait-le-
manifeste-des-343-salopes-sur-l-avortement-713140 The caption reads:
'Who knocked up the 343 sluts of the manifesto for abortion?' Gaullist
politician and former Prime Minister Michel Debré replies, 'It was for
France!'

21 '252 médecins: "L'avortement doit être libre!" ', *Le nouvel observateur*,
3 May 1971, pp. 48–9.

22 'Des médecins "s'accusent" '; see MD 23. See Hervé Chabalier, 'L'acte
des médecins', *Le nouvel observateur*, no. 430, 5 February 1973, p. 55.

23 Mauriac, *Et comme l'espérance est violente*, pp. 532–3.

24 See Defert, 'Je crois au temps…'.

25 This case is briefly discussed in Macey, *The Lives of Michel Foucault*,
pp. 320–1; and MD 97.

26 'Apprenons à faire l'amour', in Jean Carpentier, *Textes Libres*, Paris:
L'impensé radical, 1972, pp. 81–4.

27 *La faute du docteur Carpentier: Faute professionnelle ou délit d'opinion*,
special issue of *Psychiatrie aujourd'hui*, no. 10, 1972.

28 *Apprenons à faire l'amour*, Paris: François Maspero, 1973.

29 *Tankonalasanté*, no. 1, 1973, p. 1.

30 Original copies of the issue are hard to find, but a reproduction was
recently published, *Trois milliards de pervers: Grande encyclopédie des
homosexualités – Réédition de l'édition de 1973*, preface by J.-J. Lebel
et J.-P. Duteuil, Les Lilas: Acratie, 2015.

31 See Liane Mozère, 'Foucault et le CERFI: Instantanés et actualité', *Le
Portique*, 13–14, 2004, http://leportique.revues.org/index642.html

32 For Guattari's notes for his defence, see 'Trois milliards de pervers
à la barre', *La révolution moléculaire*, Fontenay-sous-Bois: Encres,
1977, pp. 110–19; 'Three Billion Perverts on the Stand', trans. Sophie
Thomas, *The Guattari Reader*, ed. Gary Genosko, Oxford: Blackwell,
1996, pp. 185–92.

33 See Romain Lecler, 'Le succès d'Histoires d'A, "film sur l'avortement":
Une mobilisation croisée de ressources cinématographiques et militantes
(enquête)', *Terrains and travaux*, 2 (13), 2007, pp. 51–72; Halliday,
'Fonds GIS', p. 6.

34 The best overall account of this period is in Jean-Yves Le Naour and
Catherine Valenti, *Histoire de l'avortement: XIXe–XXe siècle*, Paris:
Seuil, 2003, chs. 6 and 7. On the involvement of doctors, see Sandrine
Garcia, 'Expertise scientifique et capital militant', *Actes de la Recherche
en Sciences Sociales* 158 (3), 2005, pp. 96–115. On MLAC, see Michelle
Zancarini-Fournel, 'Histoire(s) du MLAC (1973–5)', *Clio: Femmes,
Genre, Histoire*, 18, 2003, pp. 241–52; Maud Gelly, 'Le MLAC et la
lutte pour le droit à l'avortement', *Fondation Copernic*, 2005, http://
www.fondation-copernic.org/spip.php?article75; Bibia Pavard, 'Genre
et militantisme dans le Mouvement pour la liberté de l'avortement et

de la contraception. Pratique des avortements (1973–9)', *Clio: Femmes, Genre, Histoire* 29, 2009, pp. 79–96. For a more general history, see Mouvement francais pour le planning familial, *Liberté, sexualités, feminisme: 50 ans de combat du planning pour les droits des femmes*, Paris: Le découverte, 2006; and Pavard Bibia, 'Quand la pratique fait mouvement. La méthode Karman dans les mobilisations pour l'avortement libre et gratuit (1972–1975)', *Sociétés contemporaines*, no. 85, 2012, pp. 43–63.

35   See, in particular, the section on 'L'avortement' in *Tankonalasanté*, pp. 85–101, which collects material from a range of issues. The key issue was no. 3, 1973, which included the charter of MLAC and articles on free clinics in the USA and the struggle in France.

36   MLAC, 'Prise de position', *Tankonalasanté*, no. 9, 1974, p. 16.

37   Gisèle Halimi, *La cause des femmes*, Paris: Bernard Grasset, 1973, p. 88; *The Right to Choose*, trans. Rosemary Morgan, St. Lucia: University of Queensland Press, 1977, p. 50.

38   Halimi, *La cause des femmes*, p. 85; *The Right to Choose*, p. 48.

39   Claire Duchen, *Feminism in France: From May '68 to Mitterrand*, Abingdon: Routledge, 1986, p. 53.

40   On this theme, but not using documentary sources to develop the argument, and mainly on Agamben, see Penelope Deutscher, 'The Inversion of Exceptionality: Foucault, Agamben, and "Reproductive Rights" ', *South Atlantic Quarterly* 107 (1), 2008, pp. 55–70. Deutscher also discusses Michèle Le Doeuff, *Hipparchia's Choice: An Essay Concerning Women, Philosophy, Etc.*, trans. Trista Selous, Oxford: Blackwell, 1991.

41   Interview with Defert, 12 April 2015. On *AIDES* see Defert, *Une vie politique*.

42   *La programmation des équipements collectifs dans les villes nouvelles (Les équipements d'Hygiene mentale)*, Fontenay-sous-Bois: CERFI, 1972; François Fourquet, Christian Hennion, Hervé Maury, Liane Mozère, Anne Querrien, Lion Murart [sic], *Généalogie des équipements collectifs: première synthèse*, Fontenay-sous-Bois: CERFI, 1973.

43   'Généalogie du capital 1: Les équipements du pouvoir villes, territoires et équipements collectifs', *Recherches*, no. 13, December 1973; reprinted as EP (all references are to that edition).

44   'Généalogie du capital 2: L'idéal historique', *Recherches*, 14, January 1974, reprinted as François Fourquet, *L'idéal historique*, Paris: Union Générales d'Éditions 10/18, 1976.

45   Taken from the files on each project and the letter from M. H. Conan to Guattari, 26 June 1973, IMEC D.2.3/FCL2.A04–04.

46   Conversion for 1973 francs taken from http://www.insee.fr/en/indicateur/achatfranc.htm

47   On CERFI, see François Fourquet, 'L'accumulation du pouvoir, ou le désir d'État: Synthèse des recherches du CERFI de 1970 à 1981', *Recherches*, no. 46, 1982; the special issue of *Site*, no. 2, 2002, http://www.sitemagazine.net/issues/2_2002; Mozère, 'Foucault et le CERFI'; and François Dosse, *Gilles Deleuze and Félix Guatarri: Intersecting*

Lives, trans. Deborah Glassman, New York: Columbia University Press, 2010, ch. 15.

48 The closest related project is Bruno Fortier (ed.) *La politique de l'espace parisien (à la fin de l'Ancien Régime)*, Paris: CORDA, 1975.

49 IMEC D.2.3/FCL2.A04–04.

50 Anne Querrien, *Généalogie des équipements collectifs: L'école primaire*, Fontenay-sous-Bois: CERFI, 1975; 'L'enseignement 1. L'école primaire', *Recherches*, no 23, 1976. François Fourquet, *Généalogie des équipements collectifs: Histoire des services collectifs dans la comptabilité nationale*, Fontenay-sous-Bois: CERFI, 1976; *Les Comptes de la puissance: histoire de la comptabilité nationale et du plan*, Paris: Recherches, 1980.

51 The original manuscript, and then a typescript, both missing the final paragraph, can be found in BNF NAF28730 (8), folder 2, subfolder 3.

52 DE#168 III, 132–7; P/K 166–82 (and multiple reprints); and DE#257 III, 725–42; trans. Richard A. Lynch, *Foucault Studies*, no. 18, 2014, pp. 113–27.

53 See Macey, *The Lives of Michel Foucault*, pp. 324–6; Macey, *Michel Foucault*, pp. 108–9.

54 BNF NAF28730 (25), folder 1.

55 Various document in the archive indicate this project was planned from 1975. See IMEC D.2.2.a/FCL2.A04–02.01; IMEC D.2.2.b/FCL2 .A04–02.02.

56 Fortier (ed.), *La politique de l'espace parisien*. The first edition was little-noticed. One rare review was by Georges Canguilhem, *Le Monde*, 6 April 1977, p. 16.

57 Blandine Barret-Kriegel, 'L'hôpital comme équipement', MG1 23–42; MG2 19–30.

58 Bruno Fortier, 'Architecture de l'hôpital', MG1 71–86; François Beguin, 'La machine à guérir', MG1 55–69; MG2 39–43.

59 Anne Thalamy, 'La médicalisation de l'hôpital', MG1 43–53; MG2 31–8; Bruno Fortier, 'Le camp et la forteresse inversée', MG2, 45–50. Macey notes that Thalamy was Foucault's niece: *The Lives of Michel Foucault*, pp. 324–5.

60 Blandine Barret-Kriegel, 'Les demeures de la misère. Le cholera-morbus et l'"émergence de l'Habitat"', PH 73–143.

61 Danielle Rancière, '"La loi du 13 juillet 1850 sur les logements insalubres". Les philanthropes et le problème insoluble de l'Habitat du pauvre', PH 185–209.

62 Anne Thalamy, 'Réflexions sur la notion d'habitat aux XVIIIe et XIXe siècles', PH 5–71.

63 IMEC D.2.2.c/FCL2.A04–02.03, p. 2.

64 François Béguin, 'Savoirs de la ville et de la maison au débat du XIXe siècle', PH 211–324.

65 Jean-Marie Alliaume, 'Anatomie des discours de réforme', PH 145–84.

66 *Les machines à guérir* and *Politiques de l'habitat* are also discussed in *Foucault's Last Decade*, ch. 4.

67 *Naissance de la clinique: Une archéologie du regard médical*, Paris: PUF, ninth edition, 2015, p. 5; trans. Alan Sheridan as *The Birth of the Clinic: An Archaeology of Medical Perception*, London: Routledge, 1973, p. ix.
68 *Naissance de la clinique*, pp. 26–7; *The Birth of the Clinic*, pp. 15–16.
69 Foucault's thematic filing of notes can make it hard to tell dates of materials, but BNF NAF28730 (6), the first of several boxes filled with materials for courses and research c. 1974–5, in folder 2 contains many notes which appear to date from the early 1960s at the time of *Birth of the Clinic*. Some other examples can be found in BNF NAF28730 (7). It is possible that Foucault returned to some of his previously gathered material with this new focus.
70 Originally published in Jeremy Bentham, *Le panoptique*, Paris: Pierre Belfont, 1977, pp. 9–31. This edition also includes an important post-face by Michelle Perrot, 'L'inspecteur Bentham', pp. 169–219.
71 These courses are more fully discussed in *Foucault's Last Decade*, ch. 1.
72 DE#170, III, 40–58; CMCA; DE#196, III, 207–28; EW III, 134–58; DE#229, III, 508–21; SKP 141–52.
73 BNF NAF28730 (8), folder 1.
74 There is a twenty-page manuscript of what appears to be a lecture entitled 'Hôpital' in BNF NAF28730 (8), folder 2. See also the interview 'Asiles, Sexualité, Prisons', conducted on this trip (DE#160, II, 771–82).
75 For a longer discussion of the work on danger, see *Foucault's Last Decade*, ch. 3; and on governmentality, ch. 4.
76 A photocopy of a detailed analysis in Italian, Robert Evans, 'Panopticon', *Controspazio*, October 1970, pp. 4–18, can be found in the GIP archive (IMEC GIP Df-02 [GIP4.12]). It is not clear who made this copy, or whether Foucault saw the material at this time, or did indeed discover it later. The archive also contains a copy of a thesis directed by Paul Virilio which uses Foucault's *History of Madness* to think about incarceration: André Cartoux, *Le lieu de détention*, 1972, GIP DF-01 (GIP 4.15). Again it is not clear if Foucault himself saw this.
77 See, for example *Histoire de la sexualité I: La Volonté de savoir*, Paris: Gallimard, 1976, pp. 35–6; trans. Robert Hurley as *The History of Sexuality I: The Will to Knowledge*, London: Penguin, 1978, p. 25; and SMBD, 214–20/241–7.

Conclusion: Towards Foucault's Last Decade

1 There are detailed notes in BNF NAF28730 (15).
2 For a discussion, see *Foucault's Last Decade*, pp. 206–8.
3 I am grateful to Eduardo Mendieta for a discussion on this point. See his 'Philosophy's Paralipomena: Diaries, Notebooks, and Letters' in *Journal of Speculative Philosophy*, 28 (4), 2014, pp. 413–21.
4 *Le beau danger*, p. 55; *Speech Begins after Death*, p. 64.

5   This, among other indications, confirms Deleuze's view that 'Archaeology, genealogy is also of course a geology'. Gilles Deleuze, *Pourparlers 1972–1990*, Paris: Les Éditions de Minuit, 1986, p. 131.

6   See Costa-Gavras, Régis Debray, Michel Foucault, Jean Lacouture, R.-P. Laudouze, Claude Mauriac and Yves Montand, 'L'appel des Sept,' *Le nouvel observateur*, no. 568, 29 September 1975, p. 41; Eribon, *Michel Foucault*, p. 417–22/263–6; Macey, *The Lives of Michel Foucault*, pp. 341–51.

7   See Matthew Hannah, 'Foucault's"German Moment"': Genealogy of a Disjuncture', *Foucault Studies*, no. 13, 2012, pp. 116–37.

8   See Janet Afary and Kevin B. Anderson, *Foucault and the Iranian Revolution: Gender and the Seductions of Islamism*, Chicago: University of Chicago Press, 2005; Hoffman, *Foucault and Power*, ch. 4.

9   Defert, *Une vie politique*, p. 39.

10   Reported in Mauriac, *Et comme l'espérance est violente*, p. 454. For a brief discussion of what he did do, see ch. 3.

11   'Appel contre les bombardements des digues du Vietnam par l'aviation U.S.', *Le Monde*, 9–10 July 1972, p. 5; 'Une série d'appels lances en France', *Le Monde*, 23 December 1972, p. 3.

12   'Appel pour les Palestiniens', *Le Monde*, 14–15 January 1973.

13   'The Appeal by J. P. Sartre', in *Italy, 1977–8: 'Living with an Earthquake'*, London: Red Notes, 1978, pp. 36–7.

14   Many of the later texts are listed in Stuart Elden, 'The Uncollected Foucault', *Foucault Studies*, no. 20, 2015, pp. 340–53.

15   Quoted in Pierre Assouline, 'Mais à quoi servent les pétitions', *Les nouvelles littéraires*, no. 2672, 1–8 February 1979, p. 4

16   Reader, *Intellectuals and the Left*, p. 81.

Index